Streetfighter in the Courtroom

Charles Garry
and Art Goldberg

Streetfighter in the Courtroom

The People's Advocate

FOREWORD BY JESSICA MITFORD

E.P. DUTTON | NEW YORK

Library of Congress Cataloging in Publication Data
Garry, Charles R 1909–
  Streetfighter in the courtroom.
  1. Garry, Charles R., 1909– 2. Lawyers—United
States—Biography. I. Goldberg, Art, joint author.
II. Title
KF373.G33A35 345′.73′00924 [B] 77–2319
ISBN: 0–525–21110–1

Published simultaneously in Canada by Clarke, Irwin & Company Limited, Toronto and Vancouver

10 9 8 7 6 5 4 3 2 1

First Edition

THIS BOOK IS DEDICATED TO ALL THOSE
INVOLVED IN THE STRUGGLE FOR HUMAN RIGHTS
AND HUMAN DIGNITY.

Contents

Foreword
by Jessica Mitford

Whenever two or three are gathered together who know Charles Garry—and to know him is to love him—the conversation turns to "Garryisms," examples of his endearing inability as a self-taught man to cope with the English language: the time he wrote "Hap Hazard" on a courtroom blackboard; his question to a witness: "Did you by chance or otherwise shoot and kill Officer Frey?"; and his classic, "And then the client proceeded to die."

Streetfighter in the Courtroom, an inspired title that exactly describes the author, traces the development of this phenomenal personality from a poverty-stricken childhood to his position as folk hero of the New Left and partner in one of the most militant and effective radical law firms in the country: Garry, Dreyfus, McTernan, Brotsky, Herndon & Pesonen.

As a devoted Garry-watcher of some three decades, I have long known that his unique courtroom style derives from his radical outlook, from his belief that "the system is rotten, the special task of the 'movement' lawyer is to expose the system and tie it up." The thread that runs through this book is Garry's use of the courtroom as a platform from which to attack the status quo.

To illustrate from my own observation: In 1968, at the height of the Vietnam war, I attended the trial of Dr. Spock and four others for the purpose of writing a book about their case. A few months later I had the chance to watch Charlie in action at the Oakland Seven trial (described in Chapter 6). The two cases presented almost identical issues: defendants charged with conspiracy to disrupt the draft. But the defense strategies afforded a fascinating study in contrasts: the traditional-legalistic versus the radical approach.

Thus James D. St. Clair, representing the Reverend Mr. William Sloane Coffin, Jr., one of Spock's co-defendants, set out to convince the jury that his client had never intended to impede the draft—on the contrary, by turning in draft cards he had actually expedited the induction process! "How did you believe it speeded up a man's induction?" asked St. Clair, to which Coffin replied: "I knew a man that lost his 2-S deferment and became a 1-A delinquent. . . . " (To those of us who heard this incredibly shabby bit of legal chicanery, it came as no surprise when some years later St. Clair was retained as counsel by the greatest trickster of them all.)

Charlie, on the other hand, faced (as were the Spock defenders) with a middle-aged, middle-class jury, headed straight into the eye of the hurricane. Far from trying to hoodwink or placate the Oakland Seven jury by presenting a cleaned-up version of his youthful clients' activities, he emphasized and painstakingly explained their radical politics, building his case around the rightness of their cause. He called forty-seven witnesses, primarily young—ranging from supporters of Eugene McCarthy to Crazies—with a scattering of older respectables thrown in for good measure. As Frank Bardacke, one of the Seven, wrote later: "He turned our trial into a teach-in on free speech, police brutality, and the war in Vietnam—just as he turned the Huey Newton trial into a teach-in on racism and self-defense." (The footnote, of course, is history: Coffin was found guilty while the Oakland Seven were all acquitted.)

Is there, despite Garry's avowed Marxist views, a touch of the occult in his method? Late one evening, after the Oakland Seven jury had been out for three solid days, my husband Bob Treuhaft (whose law partner was one of the defense team) and I restlessly wandered down to the courthouse to find out what was going on. The place was a shambles: defendants were variously playing softball in the corridors, lying full-length on the counsel tables, strumming revolutionary songs on guitars. Garry, white with fatigue, sat stoically on a spectator's bench. "Oh, Charlie, you look *so* tired," I said. "Do I? Well I haven't done my yoga excercises lately." Whereupon he stalked off to the witness box, methodically removed jacket and shoes, and proceeded (as he would say) to stand on his head, a position he maintained for a full five minutes. As he lowered himself down, the bailiff was heard shouting for order in the court: the jury had arrived at a verdict. Softball players, sleepers, guitarists now rushed to their appointed seats to hear the golden words, "Not guilty on all counts." Two years later, we saw in the morning paper a photo of Garry standing on his head in front of the New Haven courthouse where he was defending two Panthers, Bobby Seale and Ericka Huggins. We, of course, knew then what the outcome of *that* case would be.

A final Garryism illustrates Charlie's total, single-minded dedication to the practice of law. He lives for the courtroom, and would never pass a general knowledge test on the trivia that titillate the rest of us: while we are watching the Oscar awards on TV, Charlie is poring over the legal Advance Sheets. Once Vanessa Redgrave telephoned to me from Hollywood. She would be in the U.S. only for a few days, she said; the only person in all America whom she craved to meet was Charles Garry. She would fly up immediately if I could arrange this. I called Charlie and relayed the message. There was a long silence. Finally: "But who is she?" he asked.

Streetfighter in the Courtroom

1.

"That Goddamned Armenian"

I learned to use my fists in grammar school. Ours was the only Armenian family living near Selma, California, in those World War I days, and the kids soon found that calling me a "goddamned Armenian" could throw me into a rage.

Though my family was religious—my father read to us from the Bible every night—I was not one to turn the other cheek. When I heard those hated words I invariably charged directly at whoever uttered them, and hit him as hard as I could.

As I fought my way through the schoolboy population with my fists, my situation gradually improved, but whenever a new kid came on the scene the others would urge him to "go call Charles a 'goddamned Armenian.'" Though I realized the newcomer had been innocently involved, those words always made me see red.

Sometimes an older boy would knock me down, but I never accepted defeat. If I couldn't beat him with my fists, I'd go after him with a stick. If there was no stick handy, I'd kick him in the balls. Once I was challenged to knock a wood chip off another boy's shoulder. Instead of reaching for the wood, I punched him right in the nose.

At twelve I got a good scare—I attacked a much bigger boy of about seventeen and knocked him unconscious, a condition in which he remained for several hours. Nevertheless, I continued to use my fists whenever it seemed necessary, while working in canneries all over Northern California and later, in the 1930s, while helping to organize the Cleaners & Dyers Union in San Francisco. In those days union organizing was a rugged job and the organizers were often attacked by goons or the rival Teamsters Union.

1

A combative nature is helpful to a trial lawyer, especially one dedicated to helping the poor and the minorities, though he learns to use powers of persuasion rather than raw physical power. All trials in the United States are "adversary proceedings." The prosecution tries to present a compelling case for conviction and the defense seeks to challenge and discredit the prosecution's evidence while at the same time presenting its own case for acquittal. A jury, or sometimes a judge alone, then decides "guilty" or "not guilty." In theory the trial judge mediates between the two battling adversaries, deciding on the legal and procedural questions, but in practice judges often work hand in glove with the prosecution, seeking conviction. Unfortunately, many judges are themselves former prosecutors with a tendency to pre-judge the defendant. Judges can also, by unsubtle as well as subtle means, tilt the advantage toward the prosecutor. A good defense lawyer is prepared for this and must sometimes do battle against both the prosecutor and the judge!

Although by law the defendant is presumed innocent until proved guilty, many if not most jurors seem to think that the defendant wouldn't be there in the first place if he had not done something wrong. Overcoming what amounts to a basic prejudice becomes a major job of the defense in every criminal case.

If the trial has been well-publicized, as have many of mine—Huey Newton, Bobby Seale, Inez Garcia, the Oakland Seven Anti-Draft organizers—then the defense attorney must also fight the negative image of his clients projected by the media, which has usually been created by information released by the police and the district attorney's office prior to the lawyer's entry into the case. Another skirmish takes place over access to information possessed by the prosecutor, information to which counsel has a legal right but which some prosecutors are extremely reluctant to divulge. The trial lawyer has to be a strong person, individualistic and self-confident, to walk into a courtroom and daily do battle for five or six hours. Win or lose, point by point, day by day, the defense lawyer must take temporary setbacks on the chin and come back the next day prepared to fight some more, a little bit harder, watching out for those unconstitutional or prejudicial "shortcuts" which, in the name of a speedy trial, prosecutors love and judges tend to ratify. But a speedy trial does the defendant no good—if he winds up in jail.

The defense lawyer must be a master strategist—one who can plot a clear path through a maze of often contradictory evidence. Equally important, he must be a psychologist, able to win the trust of his client. Most people charged with crimes intrinsically distrust lawyers, seeing them merely as an extension of the whole criminal justice system, a system which is known to send petty criminals to jail for years but one which also allows corporate and government officials convicted of crime to get off with a tap on the wrist.

The defendant who lies to his attorney is his own worst enemy, which is why I have a little sign on my desk that reads: THE ONLY CLIENTS OF MINE WHO GO TO SAN QUENTIN ARE THE ONES WHO LIE TO ME. Once I defended a postal employee accused of stealing from the post office. I sensed that there was something funny about his story and I told him, "If you tell that story on the witness stand you're going to be convicted."

"Oh, no," he protested, "that's the way it happened."

At the trial, as I rose to call him to the witness stand, I looked him squarely in the eye. He started forward, hesitated, then walked back and asked to speak to me privately. I asked for a short recess. In the seclusion of the toilet he then told me that he had been in the area of the theft, at about the time it took place, as part of his job routine. He hadn't noticed anything unusual, but he had obviously been afraid to tell me the truth for fear of prejudicing me. However, his story was bolstered by the truth and he was acquitted in less than an hour. The lie would probably have sent him to prison.

My political clients do not present this difficulty. They have all been honest with me from the start. Perhaps this is because they have chosen me to defend them knowing that I agreed with them politically, feeling that we were all on the same wavelength. This works to their advantage because when a lawyer and a client don't get along the result can be disastrous. Therefore, I take the trouble to get to know my clients before the trial begins, as an important part of pre-trial preparation and because, these days, I only take cases of people I like personally or who are involved in political or social causes I believe in.

It doesn't matter to me whether the defendant seems guilty or innocent; that's for the jury to determine, not the attorney. The defense lawyer must do the best possible job of representing his client even if he can't stand his views. Once I did some legal work for a group of American Nazis because I felt that the FBI had violated their constitutional rights. But when they asked me to represent them at their trial I refused because I found their viewpoint repellent. Finally, the American Civil Liberties Union defended them, but had there been no other lawyers in the area I would have had to take the case or be in violation of the canon of judicial ethics.

More recently I turned down Eldridge Cleaver after he returned from exile. I like Cleaver personally and had represented him before he left the country, but he had been in open conflict with the Black Panther party and I was the Panthers' chief counsel. The party charged Cleaver with being a government informer and held him responsible for the deaths of several party members. Though I have no idea if the charges are true or false, had I tried to represent both this clearly would have been conflict of interest. I remain chief counsel to the Black Panther party, a position I have held since 1968.

I have also represented nearly a hundred police officers. For the most part, they've been decent cops who have gotten a bad deal from their departments. Though I have a reputation for being tough on cops while they're on the witness stand, that's only if I have an indication they are covering something up or not telling the truth. On one occasion I pressed a policeman on cross-examination so hard that he completely lost his composure and pulled out his gun, pointing it directly at me! Now I ask the judge to direct police witnesses to leave their guns outside the courtroom.

Cross-examination is one of my strong points, and I make the best of it. It is essential to know when to cross-examine and how far to push it. Sometimes, the best cross-examination is no cross-examination. There is a story lawyers have heard many times about a man charged with biting off his neighbor's ear. The sole eyewitness was asked if he saw the man bite off the ear. He answered no. The district attorney said, "You didn't see him do anything to the ear?" The witness replied, "I didn't see him bite anything at all." Turning to the judge, the prosecutor said, "Well, I guess I have no case, your honor." The defense counsel, a pompous ass, chose to cross-examine instead of asking for dismissal. "Sir, if you didn't see this happen, why have you had the gall to come into this court and testify against my client?" The witness responded, "Well, I didn't see him bite off the ear, but I did see him spit it out."

A wise lawyer does his fishing before the trial starts not during cross-examination. Sometimes prosecutors also don't know enough to quit when ahead.

During an actual trial in San Francisco, a man charged with forcible rape produced a local priest as a character witness. The woman who brought the charge had been the prosecutor's chief witness. Knowing that the same priest had interviewed the woman right after the alleged incident, the prosecutor brought out on cross-examination that she had told exactly the same story to the priest as on the witness stand. Not satisfied with corroboration by a defense witness, he then asked, "And when she told you that story you believed her to be sincere, did you not?" The priest answered, "I believe her to be a liar and a common prostitute." The man was acquitted.

In some ways the trial lawyer is like the director of a play, studying the evidence as if it were a script to determine what the opposition witnesses might say. He should know his defense in advance and the points he wants to bring out on cross-examination, managing the trial so that the jury fully understands both his client and what has happened. It is the client not the lawyer who must be the star of the courtroom drama, with whom the jury must sympathetically identify. Too often, when involved in courtroom antics, lawyers forget this—and the defendant, forgotten by the jury, is then usually convicted. The criminal defense lawyer must be a special type—combative, competitive, willing to confront all sorts of people, a hard worker who hates to lose. These qualities, not surprisingly, produce people with colossal egos, mine being one of them. For this reason I find it very difficult to attend meetings of lawyers—so many inflated egos together in one room is simply overpowering. Of course, it is nice to have one of those monumental egos congratulate you on winning a case.

Though courtroom showmanship is often a characteristic of the trial lawyer, it isn't flamboyance that wins cases. It is ability. The lawyer must be able to persuade the jury that his case makes more sense than the opponent's. That means intensive, detailed investigation and preparation. The lawyer who has not done his homework usually loses. That's why preparation is always my top priority.

Being thoroughly prepared does not, of course, prevent me from jumping up to object to the prosecutor's questioning, and I have been known to stand directly in front of the district attorney when cross-examining his witness, to prevent him giving aid. Most of the time the jury does not realize I am doing this deliberately, and I do it for good reason, not to amuse the jurors.

In 1971, while waiting for the outcome of the Bobby Seale-Ericka Huggins trial, I was accused by the prosecutor of grandstanding. I stand on my head every morning as part of yoga exercises and, as the jury deliberations dragged on, my tension rose; so I went out on the New Haven Green and, directly in front of the courthouse, stood on my head to relax. An enterprising photographer snapped me in this position and the next day the photo was in newspapers all over Connecticut. The judge, perplexed by the prosecutor's charge, asked him, "What do you want me to do, Mr. Markle? Issue a court order forbidding Mr. Garry to stand on his head?"

Another characteristic of mine is a fondness for what friends call rather flashy clothes. I like red sports coats, canary-yellow pants, colored shirts, and I have a green suit or two in my closet. As a teenager back home in Selma I was something of a fashion trendsetter. Once I bought new brown shoes and painted them bright red. A few days later half the kids in town were wearing red-painted shoes. Even today I take a ribbing when I wear my blue boots to court —I painted them to match my favorite trousers. It's a shame so few people share my taste. Even my more conservative outfits, like a checkered sports coat with a black shirt and a silver tie, call forth snide comments such as "mafioso." But I don't try to please anyone but myself.

A reputation as a tough courtroom lawyer who attracts a lot of media attention has its drawbacks, but there are advantages, too. For example, in the late 1960s I was representing Frank Bardacke, a Berkeley student leader, on a misdemeanor charge in Berkeley Municipal Court. When Bardacke's case was called, I stood up in the very crowded room and announced, "Ready for the defense, your honor." Somewhat taken aback by my presence, the judge replied, "Oh, Mr. Garry, are you representing Mr. Bardacke?" I replied in the affirmative, saying we were ready to go to trial. At this the judge asked the prosecutor to come to the bench and confer. I couldn't make out the mumblings, but in a moment the young assistant district attorney returned to his place and startled me by moving to dismiss the case.

"Motion granted," the judge said quickly and it was all over. Knowing something strange had happened, because the district attorney's office had been out to get Bardacke for years, I then collared the prosecutor in the hall. "What the hell went on up there?" I demanded. He answered with a smile, "The judge said to me, 'Look, I'm not feeling too well, and I just can't take Garry this morning. Would you mind dismissing the case?' "

Sometimes from what they have read and heard about me judges assume I'm a troublemaker. I do stretch the rules when I legally can, but I have never been held in contempt of court or disciplined for misconduct in almost forty years of practice. One judge observed, with real surprise, "You're actually something of a gentleman here in court, Mr. Garry. It's only on the outside that you're a loudmouth."

Perhaps that judge had read one of my speeches. I go all over the country speaking to legal groups and law schools, and I've said more than once that two-thirds of all judges are senile or incompetent and that most are unnecessarily arbitrary. I've even said this to groups of judges. Even though I am not one to disguise my displeasure when an important ruling goes against me, and, at times, use a legal sledge-hammer to get my way, I get along fine with judges who know the law and let me try my cases fairly.

I'm not as smooth or as slick as most lawyers, and those who know me have often marveled at the ways I can mix metaphors, make up verbs, and generally mangle the English language. Around our office, these unusual turns of phrase are known as "Garryisms." (I once told a reporter that a client of mine was arrested "in the dead of late evening.") During a highly publicized murder trial, I so bungled a question I was attempting to ask a witness that my co-counsel called out in a stage whisper, "Try asking it in Armenian, Charlie," cracking up the courtroom. My partner, Barney Dreyfus, is the opposite. Cool, calm, reasonable, dignified—he is the perfect gentleman in court. Judges like him. But I'm still a streetfighter. Even in the courtroom.

FROM THE BEGINNING

I was born Garabed Hagop Robutlay Garabedian, on St. Patrick's Day, 1909, in Bridgewater, Massachusetts. My Armenian parents had come to the United States to escape the Turkish massacres that ex-tended from 1894–1914. During one slaughter, known as the "Forty Days of Musa Dagh," two million Armenians were killed by the Turks.

At eighteen, in 1896, my father left Turkey for Boston. Other immigrants worked long hard hours for little pay without complaint, just glad to be in a safe country, but my father was a natural rebel. At first he was employed by his older brother who ran a wood and coke factory. One day the factory employees went out on strike. My uncle asked to negotiate with the strike leader and my father was pointed out to him. He exploded with rage and kicked my father out.

So Hagop Robutlay Garabedian went to work in a shoe factory and hated every minute of it. He dreamed of being an independent farmer. In 1907 he married my mother, Varthouie Bananian, another Armenian immigrant to the United States. She had had a hard early life; her mother died young and she ran the household for her father and brothers. At school she was taunted for being a foreigner. Still, she developed an almost spiritual view of the world. She was religious and never spoke ill of anyone. She was beautiful, too— auburn hair, deep blue eyes, fair complexion. Unfortunately, I inherited neither her good looks nor her spiritual nature, but I always had a big mouth.

By 1914 my father had saved seven hundred dollars and, longing to escape the shoe factory, he bought ten acres of peach orchard in Selma, California. The fast-talking countryman who sold him the land neglected to inform my parents that the trees would take three years to bear fruit. There was neither house nor water well on the land.

Nonetheless, the family—now enlarged by my sister Louise—embarked by train from Massachusetts to California, a trip of nearly a week. Selma, not far from Fresno, in California's San Joaquin Valley was known as the "Home of the Peach." In addition to the hot, dry climate, it was characterized by bigotry and discrimination. The mostly Japanese and Mexican workers used to harvest crops were called "yellow bellies" and "greasers." Though California law of the time forbade Japanese to own property, they regularly produced more crops on rented land than did the native farmers. During my fifteen years there I saw only one black man, the porter in the barber shop, who lived in Fowler, an adjoining township. Fowler was the home of William Saroyan, another Armenian-American, Pulitzer Prize-winning playwright.

From the moment we arrived in California we were in financial straits. We managed to build a tiny boxlike house, but it was weeks before we had a regular water supply. The water table was much lower than anyone suspected and several wellshafts collapsed in the sandy soil. On Christmas Eve, 1914, we were so poor we had no food. We went to bed hungry. My father, knowing nothing about farming, went to work doing odd jobs on neighboring farms to learn as well as earn. He got fifty cents for a twelve-hour day.

Another addition to the family, Avedis, called Harvey, arrived that fall. Though all of us were given Armenian names, we were always called by our American ones. For a long time I didn't even know that my given name was Garabed; I had always been called Charles. We spoke Armenian at home and it was not until I started school at the age of seven that I began to speak English.

When I was eleven and twelve my mother and I both worked in a cannery forty miles from Selma while my father tended the farm. I managed to pass myself off as an adult and hung out with a group of semi-pro boxers who fought weekly in a nearby town, after they had put in a long day at the cannery. After a time of accompanying them to the fights I was allowed to fight in the curtain-raisers. These slugfests were usually called a draw. I may never have won one, but I never lost one either. I got ten dollars per fight.

EDUCATION

My father, an avid student of the Bible, used to say there were only two great books, the Holy Bible and *Les Miserables.* As a consequence, I had read Victor Hugo's classic three times before I entered high school. Jean Valjean was my father's hero and he also became mine. On the point of starvation Valjean was convicted of stealing a loaf of bread and then hounded for life by the authorities. I saw that many people in prison were simply the victims of unfortunate circumstances, mainly poverty, and I developed the notion that all people should be provided with the basic necessities of life—food, clothing, shelter, medical care—that no one should have to steal or beg to live decently.

Within three years of coming to Selma my parents had saved enough money to buy a forty-acre ranch. Another brother, Haig, was born there. When I began school at the Selma Union High School I worked in a grocery store before and after school. Jobs were scarce then and I was the only kid with a job. An ardent churchgoer, I also taught Sunday school at the Selma Presbyterian Church.

The early years in California were tough, but the 1920s were a disaster. The financial conditions preceding the crash of the stock market led the private fruit packers to pit the small farmers one against the other to drive prices down, and many farmers had to sell their crops for less than it cost to harvest them. The farmers tried a co-op, the Sun-Maid Growers Association, but it never was able to solve their problems. Many mortgages were foreclosed and some farmers left their crops rotting in the fields, like my father who declared bankruptcy.

In the middle of these financial difficulties, tragedy struck my family. During the summer of 1925, at the age of thirteen, my sister Louise died of cancer. Her death devastated my parents, especially my mother who never fully recovered from the shock. Afterwards, leaving my father behind to wind up the bankruptcy, we moved back East to Amesbury, Massachusetts, living with my mother's brother. My mother, who never once complained about our financial hardships, went to work in the Hudson automobile factory. I got a job cutting ice on the Merrimac River and did odd jobs until finally I found steady employment as a sheet-metal worker in the auto plant. Soon I developed lead poisoning and so I went to work for a tailor at the age of sixteen. My mother and I were supporting the entire family. My father rejoined us at the end of 1925, but he could not find work because the auto plant had laid off its male workers, bringing in 10,000 French-Canadian women to whom they paid one-third of the male wage.

After that, we moved several times more. My father opened a shoe-repair shop in Waverly, Massachusetts, where I worked at The Golden Bell Cleaning Plant. In the spring of 1927 I decided to return to California on my own; the Eastern winters disagreed with me. As the train pulled into Chicago I was out of money. I got off with a young woman I had met on the train to look for work. We found a room together and I got a job pressing pants. After a few weeks I had enough money to continue on but when I told her I was leaving she pulled out a pistol and fired at me. The bullet whizzed past my ear and sunk into the wall behind me. I dug it out with my knife as a reminder—and I carried it around for years. I am still a little gun-shy.

Back in Selma I got a job in the Libby, McNeil, Libby cannery. I had been there a couple of days, working as a dock-loader at forty cents an hour when a fellow I'll call Jones, who had the can-stacking contract, started cursing a couple of Armenian workers. The men were both wrestlers and could have beaten him up easily, but, with families to support and with jobs being scarce, they chose to hold their peace. But I punched Jones out. A few hours later he offered me a job. So I went to work as a can-stacker, making nine times as much as before.

A can-stacker puts the cans into long rows, thirty-two cans high, for easy removal and labeling. Soon I was so good at this I was making, on a piece-work basis, between three and four dollars an hour—not a bad wage for 1927! Shortly, I had enough money to send for the rest of the family. Late in 1927 they came back and my father opened another shoe-repair shop in Selma. My brothers were sent to school and I worked at the cannery for forty cents an hour, now that canning season was over.

Jones was a bit of a mystery. He wanted to be my friend, wanted me to go out drinking with him. He called me "Garry," his shorthand for Garabedian. He liked to go drinking in the Mexican quarter and invariably after a few drinks he became abusive toward the Mexicans. And I'd punch him out. A couple of weeks later he'd again invite me to go drinking. I would warn him, "If you start calling people names, I'll belt you," and I did, but he always came back. I've often wondered just what motivated him.

At one point I left the cannery and went to San Francisco to work in a tailor shop for Terence and Frances Baxter, returning to Selma to graduate from high school in 1929. That summer I got the can-stacking contract at the cannery instead of Jones. As the contractor gets an override on the other can-stackers in addition to his own work, and as I was already known around the plant as the "fastest can-stacker in the West," I made an incredible amount of money in just seven weeks—nearly $9,000. Most of this I gave to my parents, but I bought some clothes and a new car and went back to San Francisco to see the Baxters, who had become close friends. After high school I had taken the Stanford entrance examinations and passed, but the term did not begin until mid-October. It was August when I arrived in San Francisco, with $3,500 cold cash in my pocket. I got a job distributing telephone books on contract and increased this by nearly a thousand dollars in just two weeks. At twenty, I had all of this money and time to kill before school started. Like many people in the 1920s, Terence Baxter was playing the stock market. Following his example, I invested all I had in Anaconda Copper. Within a few weeks I was completely wiped out by the 1929 crash of the stock market. Instead of going to college, I went back to work, this time at the Owens-Illinois Glass Plant, packing hot-water bottles. That winter I worked the different shifts but lost the job when I asked for a raise. The boss was incredulous, "At your age I was only making nine dollars a week," he said. "Maybe that's all you were worth," said I, leaving his office with the pink slip of dismissal in my hand.

It was back to the Baxter's tailor shop until the summer of 1930 when a friend got me a job, again as a can-stacker, at a cannery in Berkeley. Once again I was making good money, four to five dollars an hour, in the middle of the Depression years.

By this time I was Charles Garry, having learned that *Garabedian* singled me out for second-class treatment. On many occasions I'd been on the verge of getting a job, I'd been interviewed, stated my qualifications, and was about to be hired, when I'd be asked my name. Suddenly the job would disappear, "filled" or "unavailable right now." I desperately wanted to be treated as a fellow human being, judged on the basis of my competence and what I could produce, not on my name.

So, as ethnically neutral Charles Garry I moved ahead quickly in the Berkeley plant. I became an assistant superintendent and there was talk of making me superintendent of the Hawaii plant. Though I was making money and was on the verge of promotion, the miserable wages of the plant workers nagged at my conscience. I went to the Central Labor Council in San Francisco; they referred me to the American Federation of Labor (AFL). There I reported my own position and prospects and talked of the poor wage being paid the other workers. I suggested that the union come in and organize, saying I would use what influence I could to get the workers to join. A day or two later I received a phone call from the main office instructing me to put in an appearance. I figured the Hawaii job had come through. But I was greeted with, "What in fucking hell's the matter with you, Garry? What do you mean going down to the AFL and telling them to organize the plant? Have you lost your mind?"

I pretended innocence, that I hadn't done it, but that didn't work and I was fired. It was only years later that it came out how corporations had infiltrated the labor movement. Robert LaFollette, the senator from Wisconsin, revealed this in a series of investigations into the labor spy racket, but my experience had already taught me this lesson and I never forgot it, especially when I became an activist in the labor movement.

After I lost my job I again returned to working for a dry cleaner. And in May 1932 I met Louise Evelyn Edgar from Hood River, Oregon, at a party in San Francisco. It was love at first sight and we saw each other every day from then on. We married on November 9, 1932. In January 1933, the height of the Depression, I lost my job at the cleaning plant. They had wanted me to take a pay cut from six to five dollars a day and I refused, so they fired me. I still owned a car; I took out a loan of $100 on it and rented a store in Richmond District, a middle-class, white-collar area near the Golden Gate Park. I paid a month's rent of twenty-five dollars, hired a sign painter to letter GARRY'S CLEANING AND TAILORING SHOP across the front window, and bought a second-hand sewing machine and some lumber to build a partition across the back of the store. Louise and I planned to live in the tiny partitioned-off room and cook on a hot plate.

But by the time we got the store open President Roosevelt had ordered the banks closed. It wasn't long before the seemingly secure district began to feel the aftereffects; the cleaning and tailoring business hardly prospered. Several months passed and suddenly I became severely ill. I was rushed to the county hospital with a ruptured appendix and peritonitis. The day of the operation I weighed 220 pounds; three months later I weighed little more than 100 pounds. While recovering, I made up my mind to go to law school. I had always wanted to be a doctor or a lawyer, but medical school required a college degree whereas law school did not. There was no time for college. My early experiences and feelings against the death penalty decided me: I would dedicate myself to ending capital punishment.

The hospital stay of three months gave me time to think about a lot of other things, too. In a country with abundant natural resources some people were starving while others were dumping food to keep prices up. Thousands were poorly housed, millions out of work—but those who spoke up against such conditions were labeled Communists or anarchists. My character had been forged by the reading of *Les Miserables* and by first-hand experiences of poverty and discrimination. From then on I worked for social change.

Upton Sinclair, whom I had met late in 1933, announced in 1934 that he would run for governor on an End Poverty in California (EPIC) platform. Having read nearly all of his books and being impressed with his exposition of the social evils of the time, I volunteered to work in his campaign. Despite a totally hostile press and threats by industry to move out of the state if he was elected, Sinclair lost by only a small margin to Frank ("Marbletop") Merriam, who went on to become one of California's worst governors.

In addition to the cleaning establishment and the election campaign, I became involved in the labor movement. At this time the old craft unionism of the AFL was being challenged by the new industrial unions of the CIO. Nationally, John L. Lewis of the United Mine Workers was the leader, but on the West Coast Harry Bridges, head of the International Longshoremen's and Warehousemen's Union (ILWU), was the central figure. I joined the CIO to help organize the cleaning and dyeing industry, eventually serving as a union delegate to the San Francisco Central Labor Council.

Finally, in the fall of 1934, I began attending night classes at San Francisco Law School. By day I worked in the cleaning store; by night I went to school. Whenever I could I studied, spending almost every Sunday at the law library; my wife became a law school widow. In 1936 came the Spanish Civil War. I wanted to go fight with the Loyalist forces against Franco, but friends persuaded me that getting my law degree was ultimately more important. While studying I continued my union activities, primarily as part of the leadership of the Cleaners and Dyers Union. In the middle of my fourth year of law school, I was threatened with expulsion because of my union work. I told the school that if they expelled me I would immediately sue. They allowed me to continue and I graduated in June of 1938, taking the bar examination a few months later, being admitted to practice on November 1, 1938.

LABOR AND THE LAW: EARLY CASES

All through law school I had been fascinated by cases involving unions and union rights. By the time I became a full-fledged lawyer I was already something of a labor law expert. In those years labor law was in a transitional phase: CIO affiliated unions were looked upon with disfavor by both the courts and the press. But those locals affiliated with the AFL weren't getting the help they needed from it and many decided to disaffiliate and join the more militant CIO.

This change of status was not a simple process, often involving long court proceedings; naturally the AFL did not relish losing dues-paying members and it fought back. I began representing the dissident locals, although once they were firmly established in the CIO, its lawyers took over. But, during the difficult period of transition from AFL to CIO, I represented them. This involved not only labor law but criminal law as well—since whenever these unions went on strike there were usually a number of arrests. Eventually I was representing sixteen different unions, hired on retainer to handle all of their legal problems from labor contracts to the divorce cases of the individual members. In addition, I handled a great number of criminal cases not related to labor relations. I needed the experience, but, as my ultimate goal was to do something about capital punishment, I wanted to develop competence in all phases of criminal law; there is no better place to do this than in the courtroom. I even regularly defended prostitutes, charging them $2.50 to $7.50 for a jury trial. Although I told the juries that the judge would instruct them that they must convict if they believed the defendant had committed an act of prostitution, I also told them that as jurors and citizens, the conscience of their community, they had to be fair. I argued that the only way to fairly try a prostitute was to bring the men who were her clients to trial as well. With that argument, I never lost.

At that time no case was too small for me to accept. Most of the time I could afford to represent poor people free of charge because I was making a good living from the union retainers. I practiced alone, and I fought each case as if my client's life depended on it. Evenings I spent researching the law, often sleeping in my office. Also I handled a number of civil cases, mostly personal injury claims. To better understand these cases I took courses in anatomy and studied brain and spinal injuries. Of the hundreds of claims I handled, I took thirty or forty to court each year.

Of course many cases were settled out of court without trial. After I tried and won a difficult case, one no insurance company believed a lawyer would spend time on, it was fairly easy to settle out of court those cases awaiting trial. However, in one instance in which everyone knew that the liability of the person being sued was questionable, the insurance company wanted to settle the case based on its nuisance rather than its real value. At the settlement conference the judge suggested $750. After consultation with my client, I agreed. Then the insurance company balked and said they would pay only $725. I refused, not because of the amount but because of the pettiness of the company. At a second settlement conference the judge said, "Garry and the company are only $25 apart; why don't we take up a collection so we don't tie up the court with a trial?" I would not accept the difference that way either; I took the case to trial. We won and collected $11,000.

On another occasion, I was offered a $15,000 settlement which I thought fair and advised my client to accept. But he would not, insisting we go to trial. I warned him of the pitfalls, but he still insisted. The jury brought back a verdict of only $3,500 and my client came away convinced that the opponent had bought off judge, jury, and his lawyer all together.

Melvin Belli pioneered the presentation of personal injury cases, and he has been called the "King of Torts" because of his great contribution to this field. Tort is the legal term for negligence law. Belli introduced the concept of demonstrative evidence—the use of a diagram, a model, or some other visual means to illustrate key points. This technique is based upon the realization that the average human mind can only grasp about 20 percent of what it hears. Without some visual backup, understanding is usually incomplete. Recognizing the value of Belli's concept, I adopted it and used it in my own work. I would bring a small skeleton into the courtroom, for example, for a doctor-witness to manipulate and graphically explain the injury to the jurors. Now I regularly use demonstrative evidence in my criminal cases too.

THE WAR YEARS

The National Lawyers Guild, founded in 1936, is an organization committed to social change and the defense of human rights. Prior to its existence, the only association for lawyers was the establishment-oriented American Bar Association. On the day I was admitted to the bar, I met Benjamin ("Barney") Dreyfus; we both joined the Guild that day and we became good friends, although nineteen years were to pass before we became partners together with Frank McTernan and Julius Keller.

In those early years of practice I shared an office with Milton Shapiro. We were not partners, but shared a reception room and the services of a secretary and kept our practices separate. It was an odd relationship. Shapiro was a Republican, a former state commander of the American Legion, his political views the antithesis of mine. Nevertheless we became friends; Shapiro later became a superior court judge. I was allied with the left-wing of the Democratic party and for a time I worked closely with Edmund G. ("Pat") Brown, who later became district attorney of San Francisco and then Attorney-General and governor of California. Pat Brown is the father of the current governor, Jerry Brown. Brown and I drifted apart because I was too far to the left of him politically, but after World War II he asked me to be his chief deputy; I refused as I could never be a prosecutor.

In 1939, soon after the Hitler-Stalin pact was signed, the California legislature passed a bill outlawing the Communist party. I headed a delegation that went to Sacramento to urge Governor Culbert Olsen, who had been elected as a New Deal candidate in 1938 with the help of a lot of leftists both within and outside of the Democratic party, to veto the bill. We had supported him because he seemed to agree with the ideas of Franklin Delano Roosevelt's administration and we expected his support in return, but he signed the bill. A few years later the Supreme Court ruled it unconstitutional, as I had told him it would.

Soon after December 7, 1941, the date of the Japanese attack on Pearl Harbor, President Roosevelt issued an executive order ordering all Japanese-Americans into detention camps on the grounds that they could not be trusted. A right-wing organization, the Native Sons of the Golden West, sought further restrictions of the Japanese: it brought suit in San Francisco Federal Court to enjoin the registrar of voters from sending absentee ballots to the people in the detention camps, thus depriving them of their right to vote. The San Francisco chapter of the National Lawyers Guild entered the case *amicus curiae,* or friend-of-the-court. The Guild designated Harold Sawyer, a well-known trial lawyer, and myself to argue the case. Opposing us was U. S. Webb, former Attorney-General of California for thirty-six years. He argued that since the United States Constitution recognized only whites as citizens only they could receive the full benefits of citizenship. The argument was clearly preposterous and Judge St. Sure threw the Native Sons' suit out of court. The Japanese–Americans got their ballots a short time later.

When the United States declared war I had tried to enlist in the Marine Corps but had been disqualified because of having an overbite. I asked—not thinking we were going to bite the enemy—why that should eliminate me and was told that I might have difficulty pulling the pin out of a hand grenade!

So, somewhat bewildered by it all, I enrolled in a military law course at the University of San Francisco. There, the instructor, an Army colonel, told the class that it was very important that the accused get a fair trial before being convicted. The class laughed, but later I found out that military justice worked just that way.

In the meantime I was appointed to a case that made me wonder if the federal courts also worked that way. Samuel White, a black man from Tennessee, had been indicted and convicted on charges of defrauding the government and was now in Alcatraz. While in the Memphis jail he had been given two WPA checks for $14.61 each, and had cashed them—White had previously been employed by the Works Projects Administration. The United States attorney contended that the checks were meant for another Samuel White, that White knew this and had cashed them anyway. As White could neither read nor write, he had no idea of the seriousness of the charge against him, and there was no lawyer to represent him nor did anyone explain the charge to him. Thinking he was charged with just one more disorderly conduct, which might get him thirty days, he pleaded guilty and was appalled to find himself being shipped to Alcatraz—the toughest of the federal prisons, several thousand miles from his Memphis home. He had been sentenced to serve seven years and to pay a fine of one thousand dollars; further, he was to remain in prison until the fine was paid. As he had no income nor any way of earning money, the situation was clearly ridiculous. In a writ of habeas corpus I argued that White had not known he was pleading guilty to a serious charge, that the Sixth Amendment requires persons charged with felonies to have the advice of counsel or to knowingly waive that right. To determine if White had indeed waived his right to counsel, we would have to interrogate the Memphis judge who had heard his case. I submitted a series of questions by mail and here, in part, is his reply:

> The general tone of these cross-interrogatories and certain specific questions is highly insulting and unwarranted, and in my judgment, the dignity of the United States courts will be lowered when district judges condescend to be cross-examined in any such insulting manner by criminal lawyers.

While denying prejudice against blacks, he refused to take an oath or to subject himself to the rules of perjury, as must any witness. Thus it was that Samuel White, who had cashed two checks totaling $29.22, became a maximum security prisoner. I brought his case to the attention of Judge Michael Roche in San Francisco Federal Court, pointing out that even if he was guilty it hardly called for such harsh treatment. "Have you ever lived in the South?" was his answer to me. Though he claimed sympathy for White's plight, he did nothing. He didn't want to rock the boat of "justice." This was my first taste of the racial injustice inherent in the judicial system. When I left San Francisco for the Army in 1943, two years later, White was still in prison.

Many years later, another biased judge was trying to do everything in his power to have my client convicted. During recess I went to his chambers, but he was barely civil and dismissed my complaints as unimportant. I was enraged, but I said quietly, "You know, Judge, I used to be in the dry cleaning business in the Richmond District and I delivered an awful lot of clothing to a couple of whorehouses in the neighborhood." His eyes widened in interest for the first time and I continued. "A lot of people would be very surprised to learn that you owned those whorehouses." Leaving him with a stunned look on his face, I turned and marched out. I hadn't really meant to say it, but his arrogance had pushed me into it. There was nothing he could do, because what I had said was true, but I was very careful with him after that. He had been sufficiently shaken up so that he presided over the remainder of the trial in a fair way and my client was acquitted.

In 1943, finding my overbite no hindrance to an infantryman, the Army drafted me. I needed a birth certificate and sent off to Massachusetts for it. When it came, I stared at my full name—Garabed Hagop Robutlay Garabedian—with amazement. I had not used it in years. I was, and had been for a long time, Charles R. Garry, so I dictated a petition to have my name changed legally. Not wanting to act as my own attorney, I asked Milton Shapiro to sign it.

"Who the hell is this person?" he asked, and I suggested that he read the whole petition. He did, and just shook his head. But he represented me and in March 1943 I legally became Charles R. Garry.

As a practicing attorney, I could have had a commission in the Army to the Judge Advocate General Corps, but I wanted to be an enlisted man, not an officer, and I wanted to be in combat in the fight against fascism. I received basic training at Camp Fannin, Texas. After the seventeen weeks of training, I was chosen to be sergeant-major of the cadre school, to help train the corporals and sergeants, even though I was still only a buck private. That assignment didn't last long. Having applied for the Counter-Intelligence Corps, I came under investigation. I was questioned thoroughly about, among other things, my friendship with Harry Bridges, my trip to Governor Olsen to ask him to veto the bill outlawing the Communist party, and about my objection to derogatory statements about blacks on barracks bulletin boards. At that time black and white soldiers were not allowed in the same units, and the two investigating officers, both Southerners, interrogated me about my views on "racial mixing." Their investigation resulted in my being removed from the cadre school; I was transferred from one camp to another with a note in my personal file that said I was not to be left in one location for too long, for, with my strong leadership qualities, I might prove to be an undesirable influence on other soldiers.

Persistent efforts finally landed me in Italy as a combat infantryman. Later, I came into contact with the Italian and Yugoslav partisans and served as liaison between them and local Army headquarters. When the fighting ended in Italy I was assigned to Fifth Army Headquarters in Lago di Guardia where I held the top security assignment in the whole place. It was my job to waken General Mark Clark each morning. While carrying out this vital mission I learned that a group of partisans had broken into a jail in Venice and rounded up several fascists and shot them. They were charged with murder and I petitioned the judge advocate's office to let me defend them, but the request was denied on the grounds that I was too valuable to be spared. Later on when my company asked for volunteers to go to Switzerland for a week as guests of the Swiss government, I applied and was accepted. My value to the war effort had obviously diminished quite rapidly.

From the outset I had been determined to go through the war as a buck private. There was nothing political in this: I simply did not want any rank. I had therefore refused all promotions, but when I was about to be discharged I saw that my papers listed me as a private first class. I protested and learned that Army regulations required that any soldier who had served overseas for more than a year and who had been given a Good Conduct Medal had to be discharged as a private first class. The only way I could leave the service as a buck private was to be reduced in rank by an infraction of the rules. As my military record was unblemished, I had to accept the discharge as a Pfc, but I have never cashed my final army paycheck—for the sum of five cents. It hangs on my office wall.

RUNNING FOR OFFICE

Back home in November 1945 I found that I did not have an office anymore. The government had requisitioned all available space. Other lawyers faced a similar situation, and several of us called a meeting of returning lawyer veterans. We chose a three-man committee to tackle the problem, one member being myself. Hundreds of lawyer veterans were being prevented from earning a living. We brought this to the attention of the state legislature and the state bar association and we urged the San Francisco Board of Supervisors to help, to no avail. Finally we threatened to erect a tent in Union Square, across from the fashionable St. Francis Hotel, and practice law from the tent under a banner reading: THIS IS WHAT THE GOVERNMENT HAS DONE FOR SERVICEMEN.

We contacted the press, who did a good job of presenting our situation to the public. Our committee surveyed the office space requisitioned, but no longer used, by the government and this resulted in its relinquishing the space not needed. Several months later a suite of offices on Post Street became available and Julius Keller and I rented it. It wasn't long afterwards that Keller and I formed the American Veterans Committee. We wanted to make sure there would never be another war. We were determined to support the fledgling United Nations, not allowing it to fall apart as had the League of Nations. Keller, an ex-Air Force captain, was our first chairman. At first our organization opposed the Cold War but, as time passed and circumstances changed, the veterans of World War II became less and less fervent in their dedication to ending all wars. I left the group in disgust.

Meanwhile I had resumed the practice of law, continuing to represent labor unions, trying personal injury cases, and defending poor people. More and more I was gaining courtroom experience and looking forward to the time when I could make a strong contribution to the fight against capital punishment.

Then in 1948 I was approached by members of both the Democratic party and the newly formed Progressive party and asked to run for Congress. At first I refused, but after thinking about the possibility of helping to prevent World War III and of fighting against the recently enacted Taft-Hartley Law—a real blow to the trade unions—I agreed to run in the Democratic primary against Richard Welch who had done an abysmal job of representing the Fifth District in Congress for nearly twenty years.

We had little campaign money but we had a lot of energy. Once, when I attempted to speak to longshoremen on the waterfront, police refused to grant me a permit to use sound equipment. I spoke anyway and when I finished speaking I was arrested. The following morning a small army of lawyers appeared in court ready to argue that the ordinance that required the permit was unconstitutional. The judge refused to hear the legal arguments and dismissed the charges, thereby making it unnecessary for him to rule on the law itself. Several years later the ordinance was declared unconstitutional, an unreasonable infringement of the right of free speech.

Interesting as the campaign was, we lost. Welch went on to win with ease in the general election in the strongly Democratic district. He died soon afterward. A special election was scheduled for the spring of 1949. The Republican candidate was Lloyd J. Cosgrove, a hardcore conservative; the Democratic contender was John J. Shelley, state senator. Personally, I liked Shelley, and I had worked with him when we were both delegates to the Central Labor Council. But I thought him gutless. He talked like a liberal but when it came time to act he backed down.

So, again I ran for the congressional seat, this time as the candidate for the Progressive party. As the Democrats were faced with the prospect of losing liberal votes, all three candidates stood an equal chance. In fact, I had turned in twice as many signatures as Shelley on my nominating petitions.

Shelley campaigned cleverly—in areas where I wasn't known, he'd denounce me as a Communist or a fellow traveler. But when he spoke to crowds who knew me he'd say ingenuously, "Why if I thought Charlie Garry could get elected I'd withdraw and support him myself. But if you vote for Garry you are really voting for Cosgrove," he would warn. It worked. He even scared my best friends. The *Sun-Reporter,* a black community newspaper whose publisher, Dr. Carleton Goodlett, was then and is now my good friend, ran an editorial urging its readers to vote for Shelley, who won the election and thereafter served several undistinguished terms in Congress before being elected mayor of San Francisco.

That was the last time I ran for political office. The campaigns were not only expensive but also extremely time-consuming. I felt that both time and money could be better spent elsewhere and I decided to fight for what I believed in through my legal work.

Though many lawyers profess to believe America has the most equitable judicial system in the world, I have no illusions about it. My experience has taught me, as will be demonstrated in the pages to follow, how difficult it is for the poor and the minorities to obtain justice here.

"I hate justice," said Oliver Wendell Holmes, Jr., for thirty years an associate justice of the United States Supreme Court. What Holmes meant by hating justice is illustrated by an anecdote told by one of his friends who, leaving Holmes at the Capitol, called as he walked off, "Do justice!" Holmes's sharp reply was, "That is not my job. My job is to play the game according to the rules."

On another occasion, before he left Boston in 1902 to take his seat in the Supreme Court, someone called out to him at a banquet, "Now justice will be done in Washington." To which Holmes replied, "Don't be too sure. I am going there to administer *the law.*"*

*Based on Charles McCabe, "The Fearless Spectator," *San Francisco Chronicle,* May 29, 1972.

2.

Fighting the Death Penalty

As a boy, while reading Dickens's and Dumas's descriptions of public executions, I began to develop a deep-seated revulsion toward capital punishment. The execution of Sacco and Vanzetti—poor immigrants like my parents—in 1927 when I was eighteen and living in Massachusetts—upset me greatly. My gut reaction to this event impelled me to study the law. Later on, while in school, I became aware of the ramifications of the death penalty: most often it was the poor, members of ethnic and racial minorities, who were sentenced to die. Those able to afford expensive defense lawyers almost always received lesser punishment.

It is my opinion that most people who commit violent crimes are mentally ill; they need psychological and medical treatment. And, as they frequently reveal their intentions far in advance, many criminal acts could be prevented—if only more people knew how to read the warning signs! Also, it has been definitely proved that capital punishment is no deterrent to crime. Therefore, I can see no justification for the legal murder of anyone.

Imagine, then, my sense of utter despair when I read the following, from the warden of San Quentin prison:

> Friday, May 27, 1949, at 10:00 A.M., is the date set for the execution of Wesley Robert Wells, condemned inmate of this institution.
>
> In conformity with the law, I am sending you this notification. If you desire to be a witness, present this letter at the prison gate, not later than 9:00 A.M., on that date.

Only six months previously I had become Wells's attorney, through the offices of Cecil Poole, a young black lawyer about to join the district attorney's staff in San Francisco. Poole told me there was a black inmate at San Quentin who was scheduled to be executed and badly needed a lawyer. It was my first capital case.

BOB WELLS—THE FIRST "BLACK PANTHER"

Born the same year as I, 1909, in Fort Worth, Texas, Wells's mother had died when he was a child. He and his two younger sisters had been raised by an impoverished aunt in Los Angeles who had three children of her own. As a youngster, Wells sold newspapers to buy shoes and clothing for himself and his sisters; when he didn't have enough money, he stole.

He often went to school hungry and his aunt frequently admonished him for eating too much at the dinner table. At fifteen he was working full time, but he lost several jobs because he was not as servile as some whites thought a black should be. While still a teenager, he fell in with a group of youths who worked at odd jobs and stole food and clothing to supplement their meager incomes. The police soon caught up with them, finding a suit valued at $26 in Wells's room. He was charged with possession of stolen property, tried, convicted, sentenced to from one to five years in prison, and sent to San Quentin, four hundred miles from family and friends.

He told us, "I was scared when I got to Quentin in 1928. I was only nineteen and I'd heard about how bad those convicts were. I wanted to get out of prison and I figured the way to do it was to act like the next guy. Talk tough. Be tough."

One day on the handball court a white prisoner told Wells to leave.

"Come on, black boy, get off the court and let me play."

"Don't talk to me that way," Wells replied.

"Why, you nigger, you ain't gonna do nothin'."

A fight ensued. When Wells was brought to the captain of the guards he explained that he had been called nigger.

"So what? That's what you are."

For ten days Wells was incarcerated in the "hole," a tiny, windowless cell with no toilet, no mattress, no light, and no means of communication with the outside. The food ration was one loaf of bread with water daily.

"They call it 'wrassling with the bear,' " he told us. "I almost went crazy in those ten days. The boredom of sitting there alone, talking to no one, my mind going back and forth from one wall to the other with nothing to do, nothing to see, nothing to listen to, and just one hot meal every three days."

After that, Wells was constantly in trouble for fighting at San Quentin because he refused to be degraded.

"There was a lot of racist stuff in Quentin in those days, just like there is now. Then you were continuously addressed as nigger, you got the worst jobs, and if you objected you were a marked number.

"I was young and I held my head up. I didn't take anything from prisoner, stoolie, or guard. As a result, I got it bad. I got the strap, the rubber hose, the club, the curses. In the three years I was there I spent 335 days in solitary or the hole, sometimes months at a stretch."

Wells was transferred to Folsom, a maximum security prison, in 1931, at the age of twenty-two, having been convicted only of possessing stolen property. He was greeted by Warden Larkin who told him:

"I see by your record that you're a tough nigger. Well, I'll have you eating out of my hand pretty soon."

"I address you civilly, Warden. Please do the same to me."

"I'll talk to you as I please, you black skunk," came the reply as the warden smacked Wells across the shins with a cane.

In a year Wells would have been eligible for parole, but several months after he came to Folsom there was a fight between a black gang and a white gang; a black inmate was knifed and died. Of all the prisoners who took part in the fight, only Wells was prosecuted. He was convicted of manslaughter and sentenced to an additional ten years in prison.

He was singled out for abuse by the guards. There were beatings, hosings, solitary, and the hole. Several times Warden Larkin and a deputy beat him unmercifully with a baseball bat. Once, he spent four straight months in the hole. He only survived because Larkin was replaced. The new warden took a liking to him and recommended his release. Returning to Los Angeles, he went to live with his younger sister. After thirteen years in prison, from 1928 to 1941, he found the world had changed a great deal.

For months he looked for work, but he had no trade, no experience. He swore he'd do anything but shine shoes, wash dishes, or sweep floors. Trying to get her employers to hire him lost his sister two jobs. In desperation, with her short of the rent money, he went out and tried to steal a car battery. He was arrested almost immediately, tried, convicted, and returned to Folsom.

Then, in 1944, shortly before he was again eligible for parole, he was warned that another inmate was going to knife him in the mess hall. He armed himself with a knife, but when the man came at him he managed to flick the knife out of his hand with his jacket, thus avoiding the confrontation. Nonetheless he was now prosecuted and convicted for illegal possession of a knife, his plea of self-defense going unheeded, and he was sentenced to from five years to life, although the other man was not prosecuted and was sent to San Quentin, considered, in prison terms, a promotion.

The prosecutor on Wells's case, a vindictive man named Albert Mundt, wrote a letter to the California Adult Authority recommending that Wells's term never be fixed, so that, technically, he could be considered a life-termer and thus could be executed under Section 4500 the next time an opportunity arose.

Section 4500 of the California penal code provides that a life-termer found guilty of assault while in prison can be put to death if the state can prove that the assault was premeditated and with malice aforethought. The assault need not even cause serious injury for the death penalty to be inflicted!

When a judge hands down an indeterminate sentence, as the law often requires, it is the Adult Authority which decides how much time is to be served. The Adult Authority has total power to determine and re-evaluate the length of sentences. Its decisions are virtually unchallengeable. It has more power than any judicial body in the United States. It is empowered to act without notice, without hearings, upon any or no evidence, to alone decide to act or not to act in any particular case. At parole hearings it does not allow the prisoners to be represented by counsel nor anyone to speak on their behalf. After a defendant has been sentenced, it permits the trial judge and the prosecutor to make observations and recommendations, but the defendant's attorney is not given the same right.

The Adult Authority followed Mundt's recommendation and declined to fix Wells's term.

Wells had heard of Mundt's letter through the prison grapevine; he knew the authorities were just waiting for the chance to execute him.

"Two years went by," he told me. "Two years of hell. I couldn't raise my hands without thinking: *This is what they're waiting for. This is how they'll kill me.*"

. Then one night in 1947, at bedcheck, a guard, Noble Brown, shined his flashlight directly into Wells's face instead of at his feet as the regulations specified. When Wells protested this violation of the rules he was put in solitary and scheduled for a disciplinary hearing before the warden. From previous experience Wells knew that his chances of again winding up in the hole were great. He felt he might go mad if placed in the modern dungeon once more. While he was in solitary, the prison's chief medical officer, Dr. Richard Day, noticed his mentally overwrought condition and sent him to the prison hospital for psychiatric help. Besides the mental harassment and physical beatings, Wells was prevented from learning a trade. Some trades, like welding, were restricted to whites, and none of the other prison shops would take Wells. On top of all this, prison officals had forced him to stop playing in the band for "colored" inmates.

Dr. Day and the prison psychiatrist, Dr. Burt Howard, both made written recommendations for treatment to combat his mentally unstrung condition. But two days passed and he received no treatment. His condition worsened. The day of the hearing arrived. Brown completely distorted the flashlight incident, but when Wells protested he was told to wait outside in the corridor. Moments later Brown emerged with a self-satisfied smirk on his face, swaggering toward him. Though there were guards all around, Wells grabbed a spittoon off the floor and hurled it at Brown, breaking his jaw. He was clubbed unconscious by the guards. Although Dr. Day's examination of Wells after he recovered consciousness showed him to be in the same paranoid state as before the incident, he was prosecuted under Section 4500.

Though defended by two able men, C. K. Curtright and Phillip C. Wilkins, who fought gallantly in his behalf, Wells was convicted. This in spite of the fact that, emotionally overwrought as he was, he could not possibly have acted with premeditation and malice aforethought. The trial judge further hampered the defense's efforts by refusing permission to introduce evidence in support of Wells's mental condition.

Dr. Day and Dr. Howard both had concluded that Wells was in such a state of anxiety and tension that he would react abnormally to stress. In a written report they stated that he was suffering from "an abnormal fear for his personal safety," and that any threat to it might cause him to react violently and unpredictably.

Wilkins and Curtright sought to call Drs. Day and Howard to the stand, but the judge would not permit it, ruling that their testimony would be irrelevant and not germane to the case. Having no validation of Wells's state of extreme mental stress, the jury convicted. Wells was sentenced to die. He was sent to death row at San Quentin prison in August 1947, nearly twenty years after he had first been convicted for petty thievery. Prosecutor Mundt's strategy to exterminate him seemed to be working.

However, Wells wrote to Wilkins after he arrived at San Quentin:

> You probably will not be able to understand it, but I am glad to be here. After what I went through "down below" at Folsom, I assure you it is quite a treat to be here, even though this is condemned row. I feel such a sorrow for the men here. They are so young and when they walk past, and one knows it is their last walk, and one can't do anything for them, man, what I feel inside.

Wilkins and Curtright appealed to the California Supreme Court which ruled that the trial judge had committed judicial error in excluding the medical and psychiatric testimony, but it split four to three over the issue of whether the exclusion was prejudicial, the majority voting that it was not, and it sustained both the conviction and the death sentence.

But the three dissenting justices said the exclusion of such crucial testimony was not only prejudicial but also took away Wells's right to a jury trial as the jurors could not hear his defense. Subsequent to this opinion, several jurors filed affidavits stating that had they known of Wells's overwrought mental condition they would not have found him guilty.

Though the court upheld the conviction, its decision was nevertheless historic, for it stated for the first time that the mental condition of a legally sane person should be considered by juries, and that judges should allow such testimony to be presented.

In this decision, the concept of "diminished responsibility" was first set forth. This concept enables a defendent to use medical or psychiatric testimony to show that he was not in the proper mental state to have acted with "premeditation" or "malice aforethought." This is different from the older McNaughton Rule, under which an accused can plead temporary insanity. Using "diminished responsibility," many defendants have been able to escape first-degree murder convictions, usually finding themselves convicted on lesser charges such as second-degree murder or manslaughter, neither of which is a capital offense.

Soon after I entered the *Wells* case, we appealed to Governor Earl

Warren for executive clemency. Warren denied the appeal on the grounds that Wells had been incorrigible while in prison.

We then applied to the United States Supreme Court for a review of the California Supreme Court's decision, and as a result the execution date of May 27, 1949, was postponed. At noon on January 26, 1950, the California Supreme Court turned down our final petition to stay the execution, which had been rescheduled. Wells was to go to the gas chamber at ten in the morning of the following day. C. K. Curtright, who had defended Wells at his trial, Aubrey Grossman, a dedicated civil rights lawyer, and the Reverend Henry Clement of the San Francisco Ministerial Alliance came to my office. Together we worked feverishly trying to find a way to save Wells, and at four in the afternoon we dictated a writ of habeas corpus to be presented in federal court. We phoned the court, said we had a writ to file in the *Wells* case, and Judge Louis E. Goodman agreed to wait for us. I asked Reverend Clement to gather a prayer vigil outside San Quentin.

The previous Saturday I had been awakened by a phone call from Walter Winchell, the radio commentator. Winchell said he had heard about the *Wells* case but before he got involved he wanted to know if the Communist party had anything to do with the campaign to save him. I told him I hoped the Communist party and the Republican and the Democratic parties all had something to do with it, that I thought references to the political views of those trying to save Wells's life were totally irrelevant. On Sunday I had listened to Winchell's regular broadcast, not knowing what to expect. This is what I heard, in Winchell's distinctive, staccato delivery:

San Quentin—Wesley Robert Wells is to die at San Quentin on Friday next for assaulting a prison guard. That's the law in the state of California. If you're a lifer, and you assault a prison keeper, you must die. Wesley Robert Wells has a long record I know, and all his appeals are now exhausted. He no longer has any claims on the law of the land. But a criminal, governor, no matter how low or friendless, is still a fellow man, white or black, and by laws higher than those on the books, Wesley Robert Wells still has a claim on our hearts.

Governor Warren, justice is often closer to mercy than it is to the criminal code. The prison guard Wells struck did not die. Therefore, your excellency, the condemned man owes no life to the state of California. Please, governor, reconsider this case, and commute this wicked man to a life term. . . . the late Justice Frank Murphy of the High Court always kept before him a sign on his desk, quote, "All men make mistakes. Be sure your mistake is on the side of mercy."

When we arrived at Judge Goodman's chambers, it was already past six-thirty. After reading the writ, he said, "Gentlemen, I'm sorry, but I don't feel I have any jurisdiction to intervene in this case."

As he was walking us gently toward the door I reminded him that many people had taken an interest in the case, that Walter Winchell had devoted part of his broadcast to it. He replied that he'd heard Winchell but had not been influenced by him. Referring to the Mundt letter on file with the Adult Authority, I said:

"It may not influence you, but when the state goes out of its way to keep a person in an administrative limbo so that he is falsely considered a life-term prisoner, so that at some future time he can be legally entrapped, convicted, and executed, I'm sure you would be interested in that."

"But where in your petition does it say that?"

"If it doesn't say that, Judge, it's because we've been working in hysterical frenzy for the past few hours trying to save someone's life."

After further discussion the judge sent for the assistant attorney-general so that we could argue the point. It was then seven and Wells had already been taken from death row, and placed in a cell adjacent to the gas chamber, to be executed in fifteen hours. By nine the judge had agreed to a temporary stay of execution. He called Warden Duffy to notify him of the stay and told him that Curtright, Grossman, and I would bring him the formal handwritten order later that evening. We three lawyers broke down and cried from sheer relief.

Duffy was waiting when we arrived at San Quentin. Long a foe of capital punishment, after his retirement, he devoted much time to trying to abolish it. Normally death row inmates are brought downstairs to confer with attorneys, but we were escorted upstairs. It was my one and only visit there.

We sat with a guard standing nearby in a small room adjoining death row. Wells came in with a beatific smile on his thin face. Slightly built, even after twenty years of incarceration he was articulate and dynamic. Though facing the gas chamber he remained proud, dignified, independent, and defiant, traits which the California prison system could not tolerate in a black man. He hugged us all, including the warden.

"I see that my attorneys have been working in spite of the fact that they haven't kept me posted."

That night, having faced certain death, Wells still had not resigned himself and he never became completely embittered by the harsh treatment he received. Deprived of learning a trade, he had still read a great deal, teaching himself about constitutional and appellate law. In spite of the handicaps of early childhood and almost continuous imprisonment for over twenty years, he was extremely articulate and personable—we three lawyers came away baffled that such a person should have wasted his life behind bars, victim of the degrading, racist system that not only imprisons bodies but stunts minds and souls as well.

So, although Wells did not go to the gas chamber the next day, the struggle was far from over. We argued the matter again before Judge Goodman, so we could get a permanent stay of execution. In granting the permanent stay of execution, Goodman stated:

> By deliberate and designed inactivity the Adult Authority of California kept the petitioner in an indefinite and indeterminate status for the purpose of making it possible to impose the death penalty upon him. [The Authority had been overzealous in its] attempt to reach, through the criminal process [and indeed to destroy] those whom we may regard as undesirable citizens. . . . No court or judicial officer adjudged that he should be imprisoned for life. His status at the time was strictly indeterminate.

However, on appeal by the state, the Ninth Circuit Court of Appeals reversed Goodman's ruling and, on December 31, 1952, the United States Supreme Court denied our request for a hearing. Now Wells's death sentence, already upheld by the California Supreme Court, could be carried out. For the third time Wells faced the gas chamber. All legal procedures had been exhausted; the only solution was executive clemency. To fully expose Wells's position, we mounted an extensive public campaign, asking why a man's life should be taken when he has taken no life. We focused attention on the racism in the prison system. In 1953 I filed a suit on behalf of the Civil Rights Congress and a number of leading citizens against the governor, Earl Warren, the director of prisons, Richard McGee, and the Folsom warden, Robert H. Heinze, requesting that the courts restrain them from permitting, encouraging, and continuing discrimination based on race, color, and national origin.

In opposition, the California Attorney-General argued that a prisoner's civil rights are in suspension. The court agreed. It ruled that the equal protection guarantees of the Fourteenth Amendment do not apply to prisoners, that prison officials can discriminate against them at their own discretion!

We had always known that obtaining executive clemency would be difficult. After the January ruling, Goodwin J. Knight succeeded Governor Warren who was appointed to be chief justice of the United States Supreme Court. Another execution date, April 9, 1954, now hung over Wells's head. We pressed on and gathered 150,000 signatures on petitions for clemency. Additional help came from the *San Francisco Chronicle* which, in its lead editorial on Sunday, March 21, 1954, stated:

> Justice was apparently lacking in the Adult Authority's handling of the Wells case. It can fairly be said that he was deliberately and designedly entrapped into committing his offense.

And, finally, Governor Knight acted for clemency, changing the sentence to life imprisonment without possibility of parole. When I visited Wells in his cell that evening he issued the following statement:

> I consider this a temporary victory. Actually, I am pleased to be alive and able to carry on the fight for my freedom. I have already spent nearly seven years on condemned row. I have seen fifty-five men go to the gas chamber, and I have lived among the living dead, all for a crime that I never committed, and never intended to commit.

It was a tragic irony that Knight, a former superior court judge himself, recognized that Wells had been unjustly convicted but still sentenced him to a lifetime of horror in California prisons. The clemency applied only to the death sentence, not to the conviction itself. We continued to work, through every discouragement, ourselves sparked by Wells's fighting spirit which did not diminish though now his health began to deteriorate badly. After a time it seemed to us that the only way Wells would be released from prison would be through the intervention of another governor. In 1958, when Pat Brown, a Democrat and former member of the Lawyers Guild, was elected we were very hopeful. Cecil Poole, who had been instrumental in getting me involved in the *Wells* case initially, was his clemency secretary, but, in his eight years as governor, Brown, who professed to be a liberal, refused to further commute Wells's sentence.

We made no attempt to get the next governor, Ronald Reagan, to effect clemency as after informal contacts we felt the effort would be futile and Wells himself did not want another negative decision. Despite all these setbacks, Wells never lost his essential humanity— he remained courageous, kind, and courteous. Late in the 1950s, Julius Keller, my partner, was afflicted with lung cancer. Wells wrote the following letter to him:

> We are not strangers, Julius, because I too know how it feels and what it means to await what appears to be imminent death. But don't give up, Julius. As long as there is a breath in our bodies, and a will to live, we have a chance. The best example of this is that I'm still around. Keep punching, Julius. I'm hoping and praying to see you again in the not too distant future.

Keller, who read the letter over and over until he died six months later, said that during his illness he had gained the most courage from Wells's letter, remembering how steadfast Wells had been as we worked to save him from the gas chamber.

Then in 1963, citing the concept of diminished responsibility, the California Supreme Court reversed a conviction in another death penalty case, stating, ". . . even though a defendant be legally sane, if he was suffering from a mental illness that prevented his acting with malice aforethought or with premeditation and deliberation, he cannot be convicted of first-degree murder."

If Wells had been tried in the 1960s instead of in the 1940s, his conviction would have been reversed. Many people seemed destined to benefit from the concept of diminished responsibility in what was to become known as the Wells-Gorshan Rule, except Wells himself. There were to be several Supreme Court decisions that had a bearing on Wells's case, but, in each instance, the Court would rule that its decision could not be applied retroactively to Wells's case. As a consequence, Wells remained in San Quentin, although at one point over a thousand of his fellow inmates signed a petition asking Governor Reagan for his release. The warden, Louis Nelson, agreed, but Reagan still refused to commute the sentence. With the involvement of the Black Panther party, prominent individuals, and community groups we formed another committee, headed by a local college president, to create public support to free Wells, but this effort, too, failed.

In 1974 attorneys for another prisoner serving a life sentence without possibility of parole argued successfully to the California Supreme Court that such a sentence constituted cruel and unusual punishment. The court held that the sentence also violated the equal protection clause of the Fourteenth Amendment. This decision affected only twelve prisoners, but one of them was Bob Wells. He could now petition the Adult Authority for a parole. Aided by the Delancey Street Foundation, a San Francisco self-help organization of ex-prisoners, he succeeded and, in July 1974, after forty-six years in prison, Wells walked out from behind the walls—with a smile, without bitterness. Waiting for him were myself and John Maher, president of the Delancey Street Foundation, along with a swarm of news reporters.

After hugging all of his friends, Wells said:

> The power of the people got me out, and I am deeply grateful. I believed and I believe. Man can't live without hope. I was the same man walking in that I am walking out. Sure, I'm older and wiser, and more self-controlled, but the original spirit—I still have it. And I'll have it till they put me in the ground.

Why did Wells serve those forty-six degrading, mentally and physically excruciating years in prison? For stealing a $26 suit? For trying to steal a car battery? For getting into fights in prison? For slinging a spittoon at a guard?

No, Wells was punished because he demanded equal treatment, because he protested being called "nigger" and "boy," because he pleaded to be taught a trade, because he refused to prostrate himself before prison officials, because he sought always to maintain his dignity, humanity, independence.

Kevin Wallace, of the *San Francisco Chronicle*, wrote about Wells's release from prison this way:

> He said he'd be better able to say later today what his new role at Delancey Street will be and concluded—*with much of that cool and gracious*

elegance Duke Ellington gave his signoffs—"And now I'll really appreciate it if you'll let me go."

Wells went on to become an important member of the Delancey Street community, but on the morning of January 9, 1976, barely a year and a half after achieving his hard-won freedom, he died suddenly. His spirit had been very much alive through it all, but his maltreated body just gave out.

DIMINISHED RESPONSIBILITY

A thirty-nine-year-old Armenian house painter, Lewon Melkonian, was accused of shooting and killing both his wife and his best friend. There was little question that Melkonian had committed the deed. He was charged with two counts of murder and the district attorney was seeking the death penalty. In addition, a psychiatrist had declared him legally sane. It was early 1953, shortly after the Supreme Court had denied Wells's last appeal.

As I analyzed the facts of the case I saw but one possible defense: diminished responsibility as described in the California Supreme Court ruling in *People* vs. *Wells*. Few lawyers had tried to make use of the Wells decision in the four years since it had been written, and none had successfully used a diminished responsibility defense.

From infancy, Melkonian's life had been a series of disasters: the year he was born, 1914, both his father and sister were killed in a Turkish massacre. His mother fled to what is now Soviet Armenia, but she died when he was three and he was put into an orphanage and later raised by a distant relation. When the Germans invaded Russia in 1941, he was drafted into the Red Army and captured by the Germans in 1943. Along with about fifty thousand other POWs he was placed in a fenced enclosure where he watched the men dying daily from malnutrition and dysentery. Periodically the Jewish soldiers were taken out and shot in front of the other prisoners. In desperation he dug a hole under the fence and escaped. A Russian doctor hid him and in 1944 he married his daughter, Koharig. The Germans, still in control, sent the couple to Stuttgart where they lived in a labor camp and Melkonian worked as a painter. After the war they lived for five years in a camp for displaced persons. There their three children were born and there they formed a firm friendship with another couple, the Usunians. Though Lewon Usunian, the husband, was thirty years older than Melkonian, they developed an unusual closeness, "spiritual and racial brothers," as Melkonian put it.

In 1949 the two couples came to the United States together and settled near Fresno; in 1952 the Melkonians made a down payment on a modest house in San Francisco with money Melkonian had earned as a house painter and moved into it with the children and the Usunians. It was in this house several months later that Melkonian opened the door to his and his wife's bedroom and saw, or thought he saw, Usunian, who was then seventy-five, embracing his wife. He went for his gun and shot and killed them both.

It was an arduous, lengthy trial as all the testimony had to be translated into Russian and Armenian (the accused must be able to hear and understand the testimony given by both sides and Melkonian had little English). During this time Melkonian, a quiet little man who didn't weigh much more than 110 pounds, repeatedly told me he wanted to die.

The prosecutor, Elton Lawless, handled the trial like an ordinary murder case, using no psychiatric testimony, not even that from the psychiatrist who had declared Melkonian legally sane. He presented what seemed to be a clear-cut case.

The only witness for the defense was Dr. Bernard Diamond, an eminent Bay Area psychiatrist whom I had engaged to diagnose Melkonian. We made no attempt to deny that Melkonian had shot his wife and Usunian. We would show, however, that he had been incapable, because of his mental state, of premeditated action and malice aforethought. Prosecutor Lawless argued forcibly against admitting Dr. Diamond's testimony, but I had taken the precaution of "educating" the judge, Herman van der Zee, on the concept of diminished responsibility. Previously I had referred him to the California Supreme Court decision in the *Wells* case and I had sent him a stream of articles and opinions on the legality and validity of psychiatric testimony. I also sent him a law journal article by Dr. Diamond regarding malice aforethought. After a lengthy argument, van der Zee decided to follow the guidelines laid down in the *Wells* case, overruling the prosecutor's objections.

On the stand Dr. Diamond testified that he had found Melkonian to be an acute schizophrenic psychotic, although legally sane. He explained, "In the state of California, for a person to be legally insane, he must not know the nature and quality of his act, nor know the difference between right and wrong."

I asked the doctor if Melkonian had known the difference between right and wrong; his answer was yes.

"In my opinion, Mr. Melkonian, at the time I examined him, was legally sane. My diagnosis was acute schizophrenic psychosis, reactive type, manifested by depressive and paranoid symptoms."

He further testified that, as is common among people raised in orphanages and in unusual circumstances, Melkonian had become obsessed with the idea of an ideal and happy marriage and home life. Later he had become paranoid, suspecting his wife of infidelity, fearing that his wife and friends were plotting to poison him in order to marry her to a rich Russian. Suspicious and fearful of almost everyone, he bought several guns and took to sleeping on his living room sofa with a gun beside him. He stopped eating regularly, lost sleep, and became nervous and jittery. In his mental state, as Dr. Diamond explained, everything took on a threatening aspect.

"My own feeling is that Mr. Melkonian would take certain things that actually did happen, and fit them into his own schemes—into his own mental illness—and he would react to them in a very abnormal way. He would probably embellish and elaborate on them, and these ideas had a very special meaning to him, a meaning they might not have had to a more normal person."

Thus, when Melkonian opened the bedroom door and believed he saw Usunian and his wife embracing, he went berserk.

"Melkonian was terribly frightened," Diamond said, "and again caught up in this state of emotional conflict which had been plaguing him for so many years. The need to stand up and assert himself, and to enforce what he considered his right in terms of his need for a faithful wife was balanced against his fear that if he did, Usunian would kill him.

"So instead of saying anything, he ran, in this confused, irrational state, and got his gun, which he put in his belt for protection. He was then going to confront Usunian and his wife."

Evidently, Diamond stated, Melkonian's perception was that Usunian made a threatening gesture toward him; at this, feeling that his own life, after the years of struggle, unhappiness, hardship, and confinement, was about over, he drew his gun and shot them. Then, in what Diamond described as "a sincere attempt at suicide," he turned the gun on himself but only inflicted a superficial wound. In his summing up, the doctor said:

"I would say that for a number of months before January twenty-third, this man was in a very abnormal mental state, and that he continued to be in that state until January, at which time it culminated in this acute panic. Medically speaking he is very, very ill. His actions were the result of his mental illness, and certainly not the result of any deliberation or conscious intent in any sense of the word."

The prosecutor all but ignored the psychiatric testimony, cross-examining Diamond only perfunctorily and in his final argument not mentioning it at all. I don't believe he understood the concept of diminished responsibility before or after the trial.

My own final argument took all of one court day. I gave the history of the Armenian people, the massacres, the genocide attempts. I recapitulated Melkonian's life history to the present moment when, frightened, friendless, intimidated, speaking no English, he sat before us in the courtroom. I asked the jurors to rely on Diamond's testimony but I did not ask for acquittal, instead suggesting that they find him guilty of manslaughter. As this was the first time diminished responsibility had been used for the defense in California, I was concerned that asking outright for an acquittal might tilt the jury to convict of first-degree murder. After less than three hours of deliberation, the jury returned with a verdict finding Melkonian guilty of two counts of manslaughter. Although Judge van der Zee sentenced him to two consecutive instead of concurrent terms of one to fifteen years each, Melkonian served only twelve years and was paroled in 1965. He went to live with relatives and, as far as I know, never had any more trouble with the law. It was unfortunate that he had to serve that time at all, but with my client facing a possible gas chamber I did not feel I could take the gamble of asking for acquittal, though had I done so he might have gone free. I later heard that the only controversy in the jury room was whether to deliver a verdict of manslaughter or not guilty! According to report, one juror had said, "If Mr. Garry had wanted us to acquit him he would have said so. He asked us to convict him of manslaughter." While he was in prison his children became wards of the state. Justice, were there any, would have been to send him to a place where his mental problems could be treated.

Taking the long view, however, it was a very hopeful case, the first time a diminished responsibility defense had been used successfully in a California court. Many who came after Melkonian not only escaped the gas chamber but also received lesser sentences as the concept became more familiar and was more widely understood.

THE WELLS-GORSHAN RULE

In 1957 a man named Nicholas Gorshan, a member of the International Longshoremen's and Warehousemen's Union (ILWU) shot a longshore gang boss, Joseph ("Red") O'Leary.

Gorshan, born in Russian in 1901, had come to the United States in 1923. Unlike Melkonian, his English was good. He had been a dockworker for twenty-three years. A mild-mannered, even-tempered man, known around the docks as "Sleepy Nick," he had, with a friend, consumed a fifth of gin on the night of the shooting, unusual behavior for Gorshan.

O'Leary declared him too drunk to work and ordered him off the ship. Gorshan protested that he was sober enough to work. O'Leary said he couldn't. Words flew thicker, faster, angrier. A fight broke out. The heavy-set O'Leary battered the smaller man severely while dozens of longshoremen watched. While he was down, O'Leary kicked Gorshan in the face. He was briefly unconscious. Taken to Harbor Emergency Hospital, he was given a cursory examination, treated, and released. He went looking for O'Leary and, unable to find him, went home to get a gun telling friends he was going to "shoot that son of a bitch."

He drove home, he took a .25 caliber pistol from his dresser drawer, and, before his wife could stop him, ran from the house. Back at Pier 29 he went aboard the ship but, unable to find O'Leary, headed back down the gangplank to see two cops and a union business agent coming his way. They had been alerted about his threat to kill O'Leary. Gorshan didn't seem upset by the cops' presence and the agent stayed behind them. All might have been settled amicably had not a broadly smiling O'Leary suddenly appeared upon the scene, directly behind the agent. Suddenly Gorshan pulled the gun and fired, hitting O'Leary squarely in the abdomen. He was dead on arrival at Harbor Emergency Hospital.

When I saw Gorshan in the county jail a few days after his arrest, he was filled with remorse, felt his life was over, and was contemplating suicide.

"Do they hang you?" he asked me. "I hate to hang. I hope I can go like a man." He also felt terribly alone. He believed his friends had let him down during the argument and fight. "I thought I had lots of friends until then."

He could recall only some of the events prior to the shooting, remembering that he was "cool as a cucumber" from the time he left the hospital, while looking for O'Leary, until the time he pulled the trigger. But he did not remember driving home or driving back to the pier. He did recall taking out the pistol and waking his wife. He said neither he nor O'Leary had borne a grudge against the other nor had they quarreled before. Why then did he shoot O'Leary? Gorshan claimed that when he saw the gang boss suddenly appear with a "triumphant grin," he became so angry, thinking, "Why does he have to be grinning at me?" that he instinctively pulled the gun out and fired. He had given a similar account to the police, in the presence of Cecil Poole, who would not stand for coercion. There seemed no way to fight the confession. Besides, it was exactly what Gorshan told me.

Furthermore, there were reliable witnesses to the argument, fight, threats, and the shooting. There was no denying Gorshan had fired the fatal shot. He had been lucid, coherent, sane; a plea of insanity was not feasible.

We checked Gorshan's background. He was married, had two sons, was active in the Russian Orthodox Church, sang in its choir. Gorshan said he drank only occasionally but kept liquor in his house. The only strange thing about him was his habit of first fluttering, then closing, his eyes for a few moments every so often, appearing to fall asleep. Then he would open his eyes and resume whatever he had been doing.

Dreyfus and I discussed the difficulties of the case and decided to call in Dr. Diamond, who diagnosed Gorshan as a "chronic paranoid schizophrenic of the ambulatory type." This diagnosis would let us use diminished responsibility as a defense, but had Diamond found Gorshan without serious mental problems he would have been almost impossible to defend successfully. We waived a jury trial, an unusual procedure for me, but we felt a jury would probably find Gorshan guilty and impose the death penalty. A California jury reconvenes after a first-degree murder conviction and also decides the sentence. We felt we stood a better chance trying the case before a judge alone, in this case Harry J. Neubarth.

As in the Melkonian case, the prosecutor relied on obvious evidence and witnesses, ignoring Gorshan's psyche. And once more our defense was based on Dr. Diamond's testimony alone. In describing to the judge the symptoms of paranoid schizophrenia wherein the person often has delusions and hallucinations, he said:

"The dominant disturbance is in the relationship between the thinking processes and the emotional reactions of the patient. Although many schizophrenic patients show the obvious manifestations of the disease, there are a large number of people who have all the basic disturbances of schizophrenia, but who for one reason or another, have not yet displayed its obvious manifestations. The term ambulatory refers to schizophrenics not ordinarily confined to a hospital."

We explained to the judge that this was not an insanity plea, that the accused clearly knew right from wrong at the time of the shooting. Then Diamond pointed out Gorshan's odd habit of seeming to fall asleep for brief periods, told what he experienced mentally during these times, and said that he had kept the nature of these experiences secret for more than twenty years. According to the psychiatrist's testimony which follows, Gorshan had visions during these spells, with images that seemed real to him.

> These visions are not at all like the daydreams or visions that normal people have. One of the most consistent features of the fantasies he has during these trances is that he is floating in the air, floating over the ground, over the trees, and over the telephone poles. The peculiar, or typically schizophrenic features, come in terms of the content of his visions. For example, he believes this floating is caused by a machine which keeps him up in the air. The machine is run by Oriental men who are always disfigured. They either have short arms, short legs, big heads, or sores on their faces.
>
> He is required during these trances to remain absolutely rigid because the slightest muscular movement disturbs these visions. So he does have a considerable degree of conscious control over them in that he can change them or interrupt them by moving or breaking this rigidity. Frequently he is frightened to death to do this, because, if he changes them, they only change for the worse.

The content of the visions was often of a bizarre sexual nature in which women turned into men with enormous sexual organs. In other hallucinatory moments, Gorshan fantasized that he was undergoing open heart surgery and that his heart had been removed from his body and connected to a special pumping machine. He also described being in a gold room where a man in dark glasses changed into a boy, and, when Gorshan tried to touch the boy on the shoulder, his hand went right through him. Nevertheless, the boy acted as if the touch had hurt him.

When Diamond had questioned Gorshan about the meaning of his visions, he had become quite confused and puzzled. He started talking about his religious beliefs and upbringing in the Russian Orthodox Church.

> He believes very literally in the struggle between the devil and God, and he believes that the agents of the devil are actually around us all the time and influence us. It is his belief that these visions are experiences which are forced upon him by forces of the devil, often disguised as women, and these voices try to make him "go for bad things," as he puts it.

Gorshan also believed that the female devil's agents were trying to tear apart his genitals.

> If these ideas were to occur in a normal waking state, you would have a very typical schizophrenic psychosis, somebody who would be medically and legally insane, so disturbed he would have to be confined to a mental institution.
>
> Many schizophrenic patients, as a way of preserving their own contact with reality, adopt various ways of dealing with their abnormal thoughts. One patient will suppress them completely and translate them into action; another will isolate these unusual ideas so they're way off on the periphery of their lives.
>
> A more unusual, but not unheard of method is to do what Mr. Gorshan has done; that is to confine the delusional thoughts to these trance-like states, so that, at least intellectually, he knows they are not real, but sometimes he acts very much as if they were real.
>
> It is important to realize that the term ambulatory schizophrenia does not mean someone who is potentially a schizophrenic. It means someone who is actually schizophrenic but has not broken contact with reality, at least during the major portion of his life.
>
> Schizophrenic ideas are very peculiar, and there is a specific sexual content to them. They always involve certain abnormal sexual ideas and the individual struggles with the abnormal and the sexual ideas. These usually come from without, they appear to be imposed upon the patient, and he tries to escape from them.
>
> I think it would be difficult, if not absolutely impossible, for anyone to make up this kind of material for the purposes of simulating insanity. They would have to be almost schizophrenic to try to pretend they were having these kinds of delusions.

The material Diamond brought out about Gorshan was fascinating, something no one would ever have known, but it was useless unless we could tie his delusionary state to the killing of O'Leary, so I questioned him about the connection.

The connection is this. This man's contact with reality has been breaking down for some time, for perhaps a year or more prior to the shooting. Gorshan has been showing signs of concern over what he believes to be his failing sexual powers. About a year ago, he consulted a physician because he thought his sexual powers were not what they ought to have been. Although on the surface he has apparently been able to have normal sexual relationships, he himself has not felt they were normal and has worried a great deal at the loss of his potency.

With the loss of potency there has been an increase in these perverse thoughts so that his fantasies have been coming more often. Most patients faced with a loss of sexual potency try to be a man in other ways.

This past year Mr. Gorshan's work has assumed a very special meaning for him. In his mind, the only way he has of proving that he is still a man and not the sexually abnormal individual his fantasies tell him he is, is to put a good deal of emphasis on his ability to work and to be an adequate longshoreman.

I think this reached a crisis on the night of the shooting, and I think it accounts for what he describes as his cocky attitude. When O'Leary accused him of being drunk, and said he had a replacement for him, these were not just ordinary words to Gorshan. They fitted in with all this previous material.

It was the psychological equivalent of O'Leary saying, "You're not a man. You're impotent. You've lost your sexual vigor. You're a sexual pervert." Then O'Leary called him a cocksucker. This produced a threatened total breakdown. Gorshan was confronted with the imminent possibility of a complete loss of his sanity. It's not infrequent. I've actually seen cases like this. In such a crisis, the individual totally falls apart.

As an alternative to total disintegration and insanity, Diamond said, such people sometimes develop an obsessive, murderous rage, which in psychiatric literature is referred to as an unassuageable anger. This becomes a dominant obsession, and the strength of the obsession is proportional not to the reality danger but to the danger of going insane.

For this man to go insane meant he would be permanently in the world of these visions and under the influence of the devil. So it is fair to say that an individual in this state of crisis will do anything to avoid the threatened insanity, and this reaction lends the strength to his compulsive behavior, so he could think of nothing else but to get O'Leary. Therefore, he went home, got the gun, and shot him.

As is usually the case in this type of event, the shooting itself releases the danger of the situation. Such an individual is, if anything, much more in contact with reality after the shooting than before.

Diamond detailed the three types of schizophrenics who commit violence. Type one is the psychotic who acts in response to delusions and hallucinations, such as a message from God. These people are clearly insane, both medically and legally. Type two appears sane, but the act of violence precipitates psychological breakdown. Type three, the category to which Gorshan belonged, consists of people who have been living on the brink of insanity for years, suffering from a psychosis. These are medically sane to the extent that they are not hospitalized and they are legally sane. The crisis occurs when their sanity is threatened.

I regard these people as legally sane under the strict interpretation of the McNaughton [insanity] Rules, because they do actually know the difference between right and wrong and they are in contact with reality before and after the events. However, I feel that they are acting almost as automatons. It is my opinion that no element of free will is involved. It's like shooting a psychological gun. Once events have pulled the trigger, nothing on God's earth can stop them.

As you saw with this man, not even the fact that the police were at his elbow, that there was no possibility of getting away with it, could stop the train of obsessive thoughts that resulted in the killing. Such an individual under no stretch of the imagination could be considered to be acting with any sort of free will.

I feel Gorshan did not commit this act intentionally, *that he did not have the mental state which is required for malice aforethought or premeditation or anything which implied intention, deliberation, or premeditation.*

Questioned on cross-examination as to the fact that Gorshan had expressed his intention of killing O'Leary, and asked if that didn't show premeditation, Diamond said:

These actions were just as much a symptom of his mental disease as was the shooting itself. I would not distinguish between the actual pulling of the gun or the driving home to get the gun, or the statements he made to the effect that "I'm going to shoot the son of a bitch." These are important parts of the same thing; the urge and need to shoot that man. This urge and need and everything derived from it are simply symptoms of his mental illness.

The prosecutor's final question was designed to knock down everything Dr. Diamond had testified to previously.

"You found Nicholas Gorshan to be mentally ill?"

"Yes."

"You nevertheless fully appreciated that for the past twenty-three years he has worked as a longshoreman, that he got along pretty well with his associates and family, evidently was a church member, a devoted father and grandfather, and that his only problem seems to be these occasional attacks as you termed them, but which he described as a period of sleepiness? Don't many people have that, doctor?"

"No, these attacks are actually quite unusual. They are sufficiently unusual so that anyone who has them is really quite conspicuous. This symptom occurs only in certain kinds of conditions, all of which are fairly serious. It occurs in schizophrenia. It occurs in certain organic diseases. If I saw a patient with these symptoms in my private practice, I would be very concerned and would immediately hospitalize him for an extensive investigation. I wouldn't dismiss it as something that just happens."

Just before Judge Neubarth rendered his verdict, he made some unofficial remarks which became part of the trial record:

I might say that until Dr. Diamond testified there was no explanation of why this crime was committed. Now Diamond, I will admit, comes up with the first explanation, the first reasonable explanation. Whether it is correct or not, I don't know, but at least he does come up with an explanation.

Now if I would follow Diamond's testimony in toto, I should acquit this man. If I were to follow his theories, there is no question that he should be acquitted.

I think that the courts, someday, will take care of these problems in a medical way. I think they are all medical problems. Defendants will come before some medical board and be treated as sick people.

Now my problem is this. Have we advanced in our legal jurisprudence to the point where I can say, "Well, these people are sick and therefore I should do so and so about them, or see that they get medical care?" Or am I bound to follow the law? I can't make the law, I can only administer it.

Normally we don't get this type of testimony. Usually we get the facts from lay witnesses and they are submitted to a jury or to a court. I don't think there are too many cases where you have psychiatrists testifying as to mental condition and thoughts, etc.

So I really compliment you in the presentation of the case, counsel, but I have the feeling that you are *too advanced*. I don't like to say that because I would like to be modern myself, but it seems to me that my hands are tied with the legal jurisprudence as it stands today.

In reaching his decision of second-degree murder, Neubarth concluded with these words, "I have all the sympathy in the world for this man. I am sure he will never commit another crime in his life."*

Nonetheless, the judge felt it was his duty to sentence Gorshan to from five years to life.

We appealed unsuccessfully to the District Court of Appeals, and then took the case to the California Supreme Court. Although it upheld the conviction, the state's highest court delivered a lengthy opinion which became another landmark in California law.

First, the opinion clearly stated that the psychiatric testimony had been correctly admitted into evidence under the guidelines of the Wells case.

Second, the court said that Neubarth's comment that psychiatric testimony was "too advanced" to consider was incorrect. What Neubarth really meant, the Supreme Court decided, was not that Diamond's testimony was incomprehensible or unacceptable as a matter of law, but that the judge himself, as the decider of the facts, did not have reasonable doubt that Gorshan lacked the intent to kill, or lacked malice aforethought when he fired the shot.

He must have so concluded [read the opinion], because he received, considered, and gave effect to the expert's testimony on the issue to which it was pertinent.

As a direct result of this case the concept of diminished responsibility is now part of California law and it is accepted in other states as well. It is sometimes known as diminished capacity and, in California,

*Gorshan was paroled after three years, the prison psychiatrists evidently agreeing with Neubarth's opinion, and he returned to his waterfront job, dying a natural death a few years later in his mid-sixties.

it is also known as the Wells-Gorshan Rule. The mental condition of the accused must now be considered as part of the defense; if a judge does not allow such evidence to be presented and does not instruct the jury that it must consider it, an appeal is almost certain to gain a reversal. The application of the concept of diminished responsibility has greatly increased the use of psychiatric testimony and has dramatically reduced the number of death sentences.

Although some critics have said that a smart lawyer could get anyone off this way, such defense cannot be attempted unless a reputable psychiatrist can be found who believes the accused has severe mental problems. Also, the jury must find the psychiatric testimony convincing and in keeping with the facts of the case. Psychiatric testimony alone does not guarantee an acquittal, or even conviction on lesser charges, but it has helped medically incompetent people to escape the gas chamber.

As the prosecutor knows that the defense can introduce psychiatric evidence, the Wells-Gorshan Rule has become an invaluable lever in the plea-bargaining process, which allows the defendant to plead guilty to a lesser charge and avoid the possibility of facing the death penalty.

THE FIGHT GOES ON

Prior to 1972, and since early in the century, most states employed the death penalty in a discretionary form under which juries and judges in capital cases had the freedom to choose between death or imprisonment after a defendant had been convicted. In 1972, however, in the case of *Furman* vs. *Georgia,* the United States Supreme Court held that this form of death penalty was unconstitutional on the grounds that it could be applied in an arbitrary and capricious manner.

Following the *Furman* decision, thirty-five states rewrote their death-penalty laws in an attempt to comply with the new guidelines. These new laws fell into two basic categories: mandatory (for example, for first-degree murder) and guided-discretion which allowed for the consideration of certain mitigating factors.

In its decisions of July 2 and July 6, 1976, the Supreme Court invalidated the mandatory statutes and upheld the guided-discretion statutes. So far, it has upheld the statutes of Florida, Georgia, and Texas and declared those of Louisiana, North Carolina, and Oklahoma as unconstitutional. It now appears that the Court will have to rule on the validity of each state law. The Court has drawn a thin line that is difficult to understand and follow.

In California, shortly before the *Furman* decision in 1972, the California Supreme Court decided that the death penalty amounted to cruel and unusual punishment and was unconstitutional on the basis of the California constitution. Chief Justice Donald Wright wrote in his opinion:

> We have concluded that capital punishment is impermissibly cruel. It degrades and dehumanizes all who participate in its processes. It is unnecessary to any legitimate goal of the state and is incompatible with the dignity of man and the judicial process. Our conclusion that the death penalty may no longer be exacted in California consistently with our Constitution is not grounded in sympathy for those who would commit crimes of violence, but in concern for the society that diminishes itself whenever it takes the life of one of its members.

Less than a year after this decision, California enacted another death-penalty law by a direct vote of the people in a statewide initiative. Late in 1976, the California Supreme Court ruled for the second time that the death penalty was unconstitutional, striking down the law created by the initiative.

In the meantime, the fight goes on.

3.

Combating McCarthyism

> There is an ominous trend in this nation. We are developing a tolerance only for the orthodox point of view on world affairs, and intolerance for new or different approaches. The Communist threat inside this country has been magnified and exalted far beyond its realities.
>
> Irresponsible talk by irresponsible people has fanned the flames of fear. Accusations have been loosely made. Character assassinations have become common. Suspicion has taken the place of good-will. Innocent acts become tell-tale marks of disloyalty. The coincidence that an idea parallels Soviet Russia's policy for a moment of time settles an aura of suspicion around a person.*

So wrote United States Supreme Court Justice William O. Douglas in 1952.

The 1950s had engendered a climate of fear in this country—fear of a foreign-based system of government—the like of which had not been seen since the passage of the Alien and Sedition Acts in 1798. In 1947 President Truman had signed an executive order under which nearly four million people in or seeking government jobs were subject to loyalty checks, required to sign loyalty oaths. In some states, teachers, doctors, lawyers also were required to sign oaths of loyalty to the United States. Failure to do so could ruin professional careers, bring on an FBI investigation.

Attorneys defending clients with unpopular political views were often ridiculed by judges or held in contempt of court. As a result, the independence of the bar was threatened. Those accused of being Communist, or pro-Communist, had great difficulty obtaining legal

*The New York Times Magazine, January 13, 1952.

counsel because attorneys found that defending such persons caused them to lose other clients; sometimes their own loyalty was called into question.

Senator Joseph McCarthy seemed to be investigating everyone who was even left-handed. The televised sessions of the House Un-American Activities Committee (HUAC) drew national attention, and one appearance before McCarthy's Permanent Investigations Subcommittee or Senator Pat McCarran's Internal Security Subcommittee could ruin a career. Often these accusations were based on very flimsy evidence or mere hearsay. Thousands were driven from both government and non-government jobs, often on spurious grounds, with information of dubious validity, without due process. Paid informers made sweeping accusations of disloyalty. And adding to the fear of the times were books like *Red Channels*, which accused scores of prominent people of being Communists or Communist supporters. *Counterattack,* a weekly newsletter run by a former FBI agent, claimed to have uncovered subversives in almost every major American industry. The FBI seemed to be everywhere, questioning people about friends, neighbors, relatives, employers, employees, teachers, pupils. A visit from the FBI to an employer often was enough to cause that person to lose the job.

All of this was exacerbated by the Cold War and by the war in Korea. The American people were told that thousands of Communists and Communist-sympathizers were loose in the country, actively working to subvert the government. In 1948–1949 twelve top Communist party leaders were tried and convicted under the Smith Act for "teaching and advocating" the violent overthrow of the government. They were not accused of taking any actions with that intent, but only of having such ideas. The courageous lawyers who defended them were all found in contempt of court and jailed from three months to one year.

The McCarran Act, which provided for detention camps, travel restrictions, and possible deportation of naturalized American citizens deemed subversive by certain government agencies, and the Mundt-Nixon Bill, which provided that the Attorney-General could declare any organization or group subversive, were serious threats to individual civil liberties, and literally hundreds of organizations came under governmental scrutiny. Though much of both of these were later declared unconstitutional by the Warren Court, they were in force during the 1950s and as a result many organizations were placed on the Attorney-General's "subversive list." People were afraid to belong to *any* organization, reluctant even to sign petitions for fear the supporting sponsoring organization might later be deemed subversive and its supporters called before a congressional committee.

Labor unions felt the pressure, too. The Mundt-Nixon Bill also provided for ten years imprisonment and a $10,000 fine for anyone who conspired to disrupt trade, commerce, or government in the United States with the intent to further the objectives of the world Communist movement. Not only did this provision inhibit a person's right to advocate fundamental political change, but it also could be used against labor unions. In addition, the Taft-Hartley Act and the Landrum-Griffin Law provoked numerous investigations into the political activities of the unions and the political views of their leaders.

Walter Reuther, president of the CIO, was prompted to remark, "These investigations have assumed all the aspects of inquisitional proceedings, where dissenters can be called to account for deviations from the certified doctrine of McCarthy."

Things might not have been as bad as in 1798–1800 when newspaper editors were arrested and jailed under the Sedition Act, congressmen were threatened with indictment for writing to their constituents, and lawyers who defended them charged with sedition and denounced for propagating dangerous principles—but it looked as if they were.

THE ROSENBERG TRIAL

It was in 1950, just five years after the end of World War II and the change in status of Russia as our ally in that war to the new condition of the Iron Curtain and the Cold War, with fear of Communist infiltration seeping across the country, that Julius and Ethel Rosenberg were indicted, tried, and convicted on charges of conspiracy to commit espionage, a capital offense. Specifically, they were accused of transmitting atomic secrets to Soviet agents.

Though I was not directly involved in the trial, the outcome made me angry and suspicious. I sent for a complete transcript. Later I made a trip to New York and did some research on my own. I am of the opinion that the execution of the Rosenbergs and the eighteen-year imprisonment of Morton Sobell, their co-defendant, was one of the worst miscarriages of justice in American history.

The transcript is full of crucial errors made by the defense—though they should not be held completely at fault. Such were the times that the defendants could not find experienced, competent trial attorneys to represent them. Though they tried to engage left and liberal lawyers and even approached a number of conservatives, everyone seemed to be running scared, afraid that defending the Rosenbergs and Sobell would taint their reputations: they had seen what had happened to those who had represented the Communist party leaders.

Finally, the Rosenbergs retained Emmanuel H. Bloch, a sincere and dedicated lawyer, but one who had specialized in civil not criminal work and who had done very little trial work. Bloch asked his seventy-year-old father, Alexander, to assist him, and the elder Bloch became counsel for Ethel Rosenberg and helped to engineer one of the worst blunders I've ever heard about in an American court. In their eagerness to avoid trouble for themselves, the Blochs waived many of their clients' rights, making it easier for the government to railroad them into the electric chair. Edward Kuntz and Harold Phillips, who represented Sobell, had rarely practiced in federal court. And none of the defense lawyers had ever tried a capital case before!

The trial, lasting from March 6 to March 29, drew little organized support; the Communist party and leftists in the New York area deliberately disassociated themselves from the defense.

It was incredible to me that such an important and complicated case could be tried in such a short time, and I was astounded to find, upon reading the transcript, that the selection of a jury took only a day and a half, that the defense had conducted no investigation into the backgrounds of the prospective jurors.

Judge Irving Kaufman seemed to be almost an adjunct to the prosecution. It is the judge's responsibility to see that the defendant is properly represented, that his or her rights are protected, and he should have realized that the defense attorneys were woefully unprepared.

The defense appeared to be so intimidated—by Judge Kauffman, the prosecutors, Irving Saypol and Roy Cohn, and by the negative political atmosphere—that it virtually conceded the government's version of the case. The defense was further hampered by the complete discord that existed between the Blochs' and Sobell's attorneys.

From the transcript, it was obvious to me that the defense had done insufficient research on atomic energy; it had not tried to determine if in fact an "atomic secret" still existed in 1945, the time of the alleged conspiracy to transmit the secret. There were other errors.

David Greenglass, Ethel Rosenberg's brother and a key witness of the prosecution, was a student machinist with a limited education and no scientific training working at Los Alamos in September 1945 when, he said, he passed a sketch of the atomic bomb to Julius Rosenberg. The original sketch could not be found. Five years later, according to testimony, he drew another, from memory. As Cohn was about to submit this second sketch into evidence, Emmanuel Bloch requested that it be shown in camera. This means that only the judge, the jury, and the lawyers can see it and such evidence cannot be reviewed on appeal.

Startled, Judge Kaufman said, "That is a rather strange request coming from the defendants."

"Not a strange request coming from me at the present," was Bloch's reply. Evidently he was afraid that he himself might be indicted if he insisted that the sketch be made part of the public record.

In complying with Bloch's request, the judge commented, "As a matter of fact, there might have been some question on appeal. I welcome the suggestion coming from the defense because it removes the question completely."

It certainly did, and it complicated the Rosenbergs' appeals enormously. The sketch was a crucial point in the trial. It was supposed to be a cross-section of the atomic bomb, but, as described by Greenglass, it was ludicrously simple. However, the Blochs did not question Greenglass on its details nor did they even try to verify that the sketch was actually a drawing pertaining to the bomb. By the time of the trial the sketch had been declassified by the Atomic Energy Commission and the Russians had developed their own atom bomb. Nonetheless, Alexander Bloch had stated, quite piously, "I'm an American first and a defense counsel second. I move that this testimony be given in camera." Not only did this attitude forfeit the defendants' right to a public trial, it lent an aura of credibility to the government's case. The Blochs' desire to protect "national security" was expressed in front of the jury who must have then concluded that the sketch was genuine, that there was reason to keep it from the public. Sobell's attorneys objected to these concessions but the judge would not listen.

Later it was almost revealed that the sketch was not, as Greenglass had claimed it was, a complete description of the bomb.

"Would you say as a scientist, and as a graduate engineer," Emmanuel Bloch asked a government witness on cross-examination, "that a machinist without an engineering degree or any scientific training would be able to accurately describe the functions of the atom bomb and its component parts?"

Judge Kaufman interposed "objection sustained" before the prosecutors had even objected. Bloch asked another question in a similar vein and, again, before the prosecutors could open their mouths the judge said, "objection sustained."

Browbeaten, Bloch gave up at the point where an experienced trial lawyer would have made an "offer of proof," that is, present evidence to show that a man with Greenglass's limited background couldn't possibly have understood how the bomb worked nor been able to redraw the sketch from memory five years later.

Dr. James Beckerly and Charles Dennison, high-ranking Atomic Energy Commission officials, were in the courtroom during the trial, but Bloch did not try to question them. He could have asked them if a "secret" to the composition of the atom bomb still existed in 1945. It is now widely believed that the Germans were working on an A-bomb during World War II, and that the Russians captured either their research, or the scientists doing it.

Nine months after the Rosenbergs were executed, Dr. Beckerly, director of the AEC classification office, said at a meeting of industrialists in New York, "It is time to stop kidding ourselves about atomic secrets. The atomic bomb and the hydrogen bomb were not stolen from us by spies."*

It seems obvious why Beckerly did not speak up sooner, but why the defense never interviewed him or any other well-known atomic scientists remains a mystery to me as does their failure to examine Harry Gold, another key government witness, who had just been sentenced to thirty years for spying.

After the Rosenbergs were sentenced to die there was a worldwide campaign to save them, in which I took an active part. I flew to New York to meet with Emmanuel Bloch and with other attorneys whom I had persuaded to attend. At that meeting I raised the above points and I told Bloch that I could well understand why he had been

*The New York Times, March 17, 1954.

frightened and had felt isolated during the trial.

He told me that, until the Rosenbergs were sentenced, most of the lawyers then in the room had avoided him, not wanting to risk being tainted by association. He had thus been forced to work alone and, with his limited experience and resources, he had done the best he could. In the interest of saving the Rosenbergs' lives, I urged him to tell the courts he had been intimidated during the trial and had been prevented from doing the research and investigation needed for a competent defense. He said he would make such a motion, which was necessary to get around the problem of the appeals courts repeatedly saying, "but learned counsel intentionally did thus and so." By not contesting certain actions, Bloch had waived appeal on those points.

It was not my intention to have him humiliate himself; I only wanted to get the record straight, and have it reflect what really had happened, in order for us to get around the legal roadblocks. But the Supreme Court refused to hear the Rosenberg and Sobell appeals, and the decision of the lower courts was upheld.

A week before the Rosenbergs were to be executed, Dr. Harold Urey, one of the nation's foremost atomic scientists and a developer of the atom bomb, sent the following telegram to President Eisenhower:

A man of Greenglass's capacity is wholly incapable of transmitting the physics, chemistry, and mathematics of the atomic bomb to anyone. The prosecution's contention that he could depends upon the blowing up of patently perjured testimony.

Urey never received a reply. He tried to see Attorney-General Herbert Brownell, but Brownell refused to see anyone connected to the defense or to appeals for clemency, although appeals came from French President Vincent Auriol, from Pope Pius XII, from members of the British Parliament, and from thousands of people all over the world.

A Supreme Court justice has the power to grant a stay of sentence, after which a case is usually returned to the lower courts. On June 17, 1953, just two days before the execution was scheduled, Justice William O. Douglas ordered such a temporary stay. Defense attorneys had argued that the Rosenbergs should have been tried under the Atomic Energy Act of 1946, in which a jury's recommendation is needed before a death sentence can be imposed, rather than under the Espionage Act of 1917, under which a judge, acting alone, can impose it. Douglas felt the argument was a substantial one and should be further studied.

However, the next day Chief Justice Fred Vinson reconvened the entire Court, which had already started its summer recess, and the full Court set aside the temporary stay. Justice Hugo Black, who joined with Douglas and Justice Felix Frankfurter in dissenting, wrote:

> The government argues that this Court has the power to set aside the stay. I think this is doubtful. I have found no statute or rule which permits the full Court to set aside a mere temporary stay entered by a justice.

Francis E. Walter, member of the House Judiciary Committee, expressed a similar view, but it, too, went unheeded. The Rosenbergs were executed a day later.

It is impossible to say what the outcome would have been had the Rosenbergs and Sobell been able to retain fearless, competent, vigorous, independent counsel, not concerned for its own personal reputation, above fear of disbarment or public ridicule. All attorneys face tremendous difficulties trying cases in highly charged political atmospheres, but with a strong defense the defendants would have at least had the semblance of a fair trial. And there probably would have been grounds for a review later on, had not the Rosenbergs already been dead, their rights irresponsibly waived by their attorneys.

AFTERMATH

Within months of the Rosenberg execution Attorney-General Brownell opened a government campaign against the National Lawyers Guild. This was an apparent effort to further intimidate lawyers, many of whom had taken part in the campaign to save the Rosenbergs from execution, which had nearly been successful. In a speech to the American Bar Association (ABA), Brownell announced that he was moving to place the Guild on the subversive list.

The announcement itself was in violation of Brownell's own procedures, drawn up several months before. One requirement was that no public announcement could be made for ten days after the organization was first charged, to give it a chance to respond. Four days later, Brownell repeated the statement in another public speech, compounding the violation.

Earlier in 1953, the ABA adopted a resolution calling for disciplinary investigation of lawyers who refused to testify before congressional committees and of lawyers who had been accused by the committees of being members of Communist party cells. This resolution made it doubly difficult for people with left-wing affiliations to get able legal representation, for it sent the few attorneys not already intimidated running for cover. This was as true on the West Coast then as it had been in the East a few years before.

As president of the San Francisco chapter of the Guild, I participated in the fight to resist these arbitrary actions and to preserve the independence of the bar. The Guild waged a legal fight against the Attorney-General's action for five years and, when Brownell resigned in 1958, to be replaced by William P. Rogers, all charges against us were dropped. But by then our membership had dropped to a record low—it had sickened me to see how much fear the attack on the Guild's integrity had produced; the members had immediately resigned in droves, even though they knew it would take lengthy legal proceedings to make Brownell's designation final. Those lawyers who remained members showed great courage, and in the 1960s our membership was swelled by thousands of young activist lawyers joining our ranks.

It was during this period that I defended a group called Californians for the Bill of Rights. This organization was threatened with the subversive designation, but instead of answering the questions of the Justice Department we attacked their allegations as being "vague, incoherent, and ambiguous," contending that the organization was not in violation of public policy. The Justice Department responded with an amended set of interrogatories, but I replied that my clients stood on their previous statement and pointed out that the questions did not meet the guidelines laid down in the United States Court of Appeals case, *National Lawyers Guild* vs. *Brownell*. That was the end of that. We never heard from the Justice Department again and my client was never placed on the list of subversive organizations.

Legislation was proposed in the California assembly to require lawyers to sign loyalty oaths. I joined with other attorneys to fight this and after a vigorous campaign we succeeded. During the 1950s California's judges and teachers had to take loyalty oaths, but lawyers did not. At this time I also represented people called before McCarthy's subcommittee and defended many persons whose jobs or reputations were in jeopardy because of the government's loyalty apparatus.

During a four-year period in the late 1940s and early 1950s nearly two thousand people left government service while their loyalty was being investigated. Eighteen hundred whose cases had been forwarded by the FBI to loyalty boards resigned. Five hundred and seventy were fired.

LOYALTY CASES—THE 1950s

Mrs. A was a clerk in the San Francisco office of the United States Treasury Department, drawing a yearly salary of $2,600. Abruptly, she was suspended without pay. She was sent a questionnaire. One question was, "To what extent, if any, do you assist or cooperate with your husband in connection with his activity for the Communist party or related organizations? Give full details."

She replied that she and her husband no longer lived together, that she had separated from him and saw him infrequently, that she was unfamiliar with the organizations to which he belonged.

Another question was, had she ever attended meetings of the Communist party or any Communist political organizations. A third, had she ever been a member of the Communist party or a related political group. Both her answers were no.

In the space provided for her to comment on her loyalty to the United States, she wrote, "I consider myself a loyal citizen of the United States. I respect and obey the laws of my country and am proud to say that I am an American."

She was ordered, in spite of this document, to appear at a hearing before a loyalty board. I represented her. The hearing lasted an entire day and all kinds of hearsay (which would have been inadmissible as evidence in a court) were brought in. Under oath, she testified to her husband's conduct and in due time was cleared and reinstated in her job.

Shortly thereafter I began her divorce proceedings and obtained legal separation. Three years after the first hearing, she again was suspended without pay. President Truman had signed a new executive order regarding federal employees. The old order required that "reasonable grounds" exist before an employee could be considered disloyal; the new order, however, stated that the government need only show "reasonable doubt" for a summary dismissal.

Mrs. A received a second questionnaire similar to the first. Most of the questions pertained to the husband from whom she was now divorced. Six months after the second suspension we had a second hearing. The board cleared her once more, but now her case had to be reviewed by a loyalty review board whose function it was also to determine if she was a loyal citizen. This board also cleared her and one year after the second suspension she was reinstated in her job.

Eighteen months later Mrs. A received yet a third notification from the Treasury Department—this one ordered her to attend another hearing based on a new executive order signed by President Eisenhower slightly altering the criteria for loyalty. Again she was suspended, again subjected to a long, grueling examination, again cleared. It was several months after this third hearing and *six years* after the first suspension from her job that she was finally judged permanently loyal.

Mr. B was a respected businessman. President of the California Society of the Sons of the American Revolution, he lived in a city near San Francisco and had been a highly decorated major in the Marines during World War II. He left active duty in 1946, but continued on inactive status as a reserve officer until 1952 at which time he received a letter from the Secretary of the Navy asserting that his loyalty was in question, that he was to be discharged under less than honorable conditions. The attached list of questions was mostly about his first wife's political activities and his own connections to the 1948 presidential campaign of Henry Wallace, the Progressive party candidate.

Following active combat, Mr. B had resumed his business career, been divorced and had remarried. His only political activities had been campaigning for Henry Wallace, who had been Secretary of Agriculture from 1940–1944 in the Roosevelt administration.

He told me that he could easily answer the questions submitted to him, but that as a matter of principle he felt he should not do so, believing that they were a violation of his constitutional rights to freedom of speech and of political expression. He had strong feelings about these basic rights, feelings that had impelled him to volunteer for combat duty, and in conscience he could not answer the questionnaire. It was with extreme reluctance that he resigned his commission in the Marine Corps. In his letter of resignation he stated that he had had great pride in being an officer and had cherished his reserve commission. The Navy, however, would not allow him to resign; it ordered a hearing. This was conducted like a court-martial, with officers of higher rank than the accused sitting in judgment.

Prior to the hearing I made a two-hour argument to the board contending that it did not have the legal right, either under military law or the United States Constitution, to proceed with charges of disloyalty against Mr. B. I argued that the new executive order was not applicable to a person not at the time a government employee and I told them that if they were squeamish about his reserve officer status they had only to accept his resignation.

I first quoted from a Supreme Court decision which held that no agency of government has the power to inquire into the political, economic, or social views of any citizen, and then I moved to exclude all the evidence that was about to be offered against my client on the grounds that I would not be allowed to cross-examine those who were going to testify against him.

The motion was denied, but not one witness appeared against Mr. B. Much information about his and his former wife's alleged associations was read into the record, but there were no witnesses. He was asked numerous questions about his views on a wide range of subjects, whether he had ever been a member, a prospective member, or in contact with any organization on the Attorney-General's subversive list, but he refused to answer the questions on constitutional grounds. He did, however, make the following brief statement to the board.

> I feel that the kind of position I have been put in here, and the kind of information that has been brought up, and the kinds of questions asked me have not been getting at loyalty at all. I don't believe anyone has the right to invade my thoughts, or my right to associate with anyone, or to read what I want to read. It is an entirely un-American kind of thing, and this thing I'm being put through is entirely un-American.

Nevertheless, Mr. B was discharged from the Marines under less than honorable conditions, without a single witness confronting him and without his counsel's being able to cross-examine his accusers. I was confident that the decision would be overturned in federal court. I had succeeded in doing just that for another former officer whose offer to resign had been similarly refused. The federal court had said in that case:

> The validity of such proceedings, lacking in the normal essentials of due process, must rest upon the executive finding that they are required for

national security. Since the plaintiff [the officer] offers to separate himself from military service, no requirement of national security justifies the summary administrative proceeding.

I was optimistic about obtaining a favorable federal court ruling, but Mr. B refused to allow me to sue on his behalf, saying that filing such a suit, with the attendant publicity, would probably cause his community to lose respect for him and would certainly destroy his business. He asked me to do nothing further. Such was the withering effect of the loyalty procedure.

These cases represented the rule rather than the exception. A Yale professor, John Peters, was fired as a consultant to the public health service in 1955, because there was reasonable doubt as to his loyalty. Peters was never told why he was dismissed, so he appealed to the Supreme Court. The government, represented by Assistant Attorney-General Warren Burger, refused to divulge the information upon which the firing was based, or to prove there was valid information at all.

Burger argued that considerations of public security justified withholding the names of informants, even from the Supreme Court. Justices Frankfurter and Black demanded the information, but Burger and the government held their ground, and the majority Court upheld the firing. Warren Burger is unfortunately now chief justice of the United States, appointed to that office in 1969 by President Nixon. Under his leadership the Court has set about to dismantle the great work in civil liberties and civil rights it did in the 1960s under Earl Warren.

THE HUAC HEARINGS IN SAN FRANCISCO

Given my activities during the 1950s, I was not surprised when, in May 1957, I was supoenaed to appear before the House Un-American Activities Committee at its hearings scheduled the following month in San Francisco. Subpoenaed, too, were Barney Dreyfus and Julius Keller. We had just formed the law firm of Garry, Dreyfus, McTernan, and Keller along with Frank McTernan who was a top Bay Area labor lawyer. (Keller died a few months after we established the partnership; Al Brotsky, a fine labor and civil rights attorney then joined us.) The subpoenas arrived about a week after we opened our new offices on Market Street.

As the date for the HUAC hearings grew closer, I began to feel that they would produce some fireworks. In Los Angeles several months before, the committee had provoked an uproar by insulting several lawyers representing clients before it, not permitting attorneys to object to the way in which the hearings were conducted, and by tossing lawyers who objected in any way out of the hearing room.

As a result, Joseph Ball, president of the California bar, attacked HUAC's method of operation in a public statement.

> Grossly offensive remarks directed against the witness were made and threatened the lawyer's right to appear on behalf of his client and the client's right to be represented by a lawyer of his choice. This conduct menaced the very independence of the bar.

It was the first time that an organization as prestigious and as powerful as the California bar had dared censure the committee's actions. This infuriated committee members, who responded by attacking the bar, a bad mistake which resulted in further criticism of HUAC in the media.

HUAC hearings were like a traveling circus. A few days before it arrived it would leak the names of the people it had subpoenaed to the press. The local papers generally played up the hearings and they frequently were televised. The purpose of a congressional investigation or hearing is to develop new legislation, but, in all its years of existence, no major piece of legislation ever emerged from HUAC. Its main effect was to hold people up to public ridicule, prevent them from taking part in political activity, and force them from their jobs or businesses.

In its advance publicity for the San Francisco hearings, HUAC stressed that it was going to expose a network of Communist professionals in the Bay Area, particularly Communist lawyers. Forty-seven people were subpoenaed, including writer Jessica Mitford, KCBS news commentator Earl Hartman, *San Francisco Examiner* reporter Jack Eshleman, architect Sidney Brisker, concert pianists Lev and Frances Shorr, and a large number of attorneys, including Dreyfus, Keller, and Garry.

Within days after they testified, Hartman and Eshleman lost their jobs even though they answered many of the committee's questions. However, HUAC suffered a number of reverses while it was in San Francisco. Only twenty-eight of the forty-seven people subpoenaed actually testified and the committee left town early.

Two days before the hearings were to start, William Sherwood, a forty-one-year-old Stanford University biochemist and cancer researcher took his own life by poison. The distraught man, who left a wife and four young children, wrote a suicide note in which he said:

> My life and livelihood are now threatened by the House Committee. In two days I will be assassinated by publicity. I have a fierce resentment against being televised. This committee's trail is strewn with blasted lies and the wreckage of youthful careers.

The widely reported news of Sherwood's suicide, coupled with the criticism from the California bar, did not give HUAC the most favorable climate to operate in. Sherwood had asked the committee to postpone his appearance so he could deliver a scientific paper in Canada. HUAC's response was to schedule his testimony for the day *before* he was to give the paper. Sherwood concluded they were trying to humiliate him before his scientific colleagues and took his own life. His wife said he had not been politically active for years, although in his youth he had participated in some antifascist demonstrations.

The day after Sherwood's death the Supreme Court handed down three decisions that amounted to a strong rebuke to HUAC. The Court reversed the contempt of Congress conviction of John T. Watkins, a United Auto Workers organizer who had refused to tell HUAC about past associates of his who might have been Communists. The Court said the committee had exceeded its authority in attempting to force Watkins to talk.

The Court at the same time overturned the Smith Act convictions of fourteen California Communist party leaders, freeing five of them outright and ordering new trials for nine others. Finally, the Court set aside the 1951 firing of John Stewart Service, a foreign service career officer who lost his job when the top loyalty review board decided he wasn't loyal enough. The Court ruled that Service had been cleared by the State Department and that that clearance was sufficient for him to retain his job.

Then, during the middle of the San Francisco hearings, Sam Rayburn, Speaker of the House of Representatives, said that HUAC was acting in violation of House rules by televising its hearings. The committee continued to televise the San Francisco hearings anyway, saying it was waiting for a formal written order from the Speaker. This allowed it to finish in the same circus-like atmosphere in which it had begun.

Barney and I retained James C. Purcell to advise and counsel us during our appearance. It was important to know what questions to answer and when to take the Fifth Amendment. The committee's procedures were so erratic and unpredictable that witnesses had to be extremely careful. If they answered some questions but refused to answer others on Fifth Amendment grounds, it could be determined that, by answering the initial queries, the witness had waived Fifth Amendment rights. A number of witnesses had already received contempt citations in precisely this way.

So it was necessary to have another lawyer present, one not directly involved in the questioning, who could gauge the committee's behavior, although the most perceptive observer could not always intuit what the committee might do. Many people who took the Fifth Amendment during these hearings did so not because they were ashamed of anything they had done or of any organizations to which they had belonged. They took the Fifth because if they admitted membership in the organizations, the committee would then demand the names of other members.

This put the witness in the position of either being a stoolpigeon or facing contempt proceedings. Therefore, many chose to remain silent, especially about organizations with which they had not been connected for years. It was the only legally sound position left after the Supreme Court ruled that the First Amendment defense of the "Hollywood Ten" was insufficient.

Sometimes a denial of membership in left-wing organizations didn't do a witness much good. Eshleman emphatically denied that he was a Communist party member and told HUAC he was not at all in sympathy with it. Nevertheless, he was fired. His denial simply was not enough. He had been accused by HUAC and dismissal, the Hearst-owned paper obviously felt, was mandatory. As it would take years of worry, job discrimination, legal expenses, and uncertainty for anyone falsely accused to set the record straight, it was much easier to take the Fifth Amendment and refuse to answer.

Early in the hearings, HUAC brought in its "friendly" witnesses, who had once been members of the Communist party or who had joined it at the instigation of the FBI. Jack Patten, who accused Dreyfus and me of being party members, was an ex-professor at San

Francisco State College. Patten—using the standard HUAC method of broad, loosely phrased accusations which were combined with the technique of guilt by association—claimed that he had seen me at certain educational gatherings of the "professional section" of the Communist party. He did not say he knew me to be a party member, only that he had seen me, along with a great many others, at these educational gatherings.

Simple cross-examination would have forced Patten to say if he knew me to be a party member or merely harbored the suspicion that I might be one. He could have been pinned down as to *how* he knew, *when* he had seen me, and under *what* circumstances. Of course, HUAC did not allow cross-examination of its friendly witnesses. The accused never got the chance to confront his accusers. Patten also stated that I was often quoted by what he described as a Communist newspaper, the *People's World.*

Patten had a history of psychiatric problems and based on his testimony alone Dreyfus and I had been subpoenaed. That we had both been officers of the Guild and had defended many leftists was probably reason enough for the committee to call us. My representation of the Civil Rights Congress and Bob Wells, my committee work to save the Rosenbergs, my Progressive Party congressional candidacy, and my participation in the California Labor School were later cited in a report of the HUAC as proof of my Communist affiliations.

In midweek the newspapers called me for a comment on Patten's testimony. I said, "If he placed me in the Communist party with him, he's a liar, and I'll want an opportunity to cross-examine him."

Dreyfus testified before I did on what turned out to be the last day of the hearings. Quietly but firmly he challenged the committee's authority to question him and he invoked the First and Fifth amendments when asked about his political affiliations past and present. But, with nothing but contempt and disdain for the committee, its members, and the way it operated, I had decided on a more aggressive approach.

When I entered the hearing room I had with me two important references, the recent Supreme Court decision in the Watkins case and our family Bible, in which my father had recorded my birth. I told HUAC I was proud to have been president of the San Francisco chapter of the Guild for three years. Committee counsel Frank Tavenner then read clippings from *People's World* about my Guild activities. Objecting vehemently, I said, "I highly resent you picking up this information from *People's World* when the same information is available to you in *The Recorder*," the official newspaper of the San Francisco courts.

"How many members of the National Lawyers Guild were members of the professional section of the Communist party?" he asked.

"I object to the jurisdiction of this body to ask a question like that," I replied. "I want to ask its relevance."

Tavenner began saying, "Under the ruling of the Watsons case . . ."

"It's the Watkins case," I interrupted. "Let's get the record straight."

"Mr. Tavenner is only trying to explain it to you," explained Congressman Gordon Scherer.

"He is confused," I told him.

Since Tavenner had brought up the Watkins case, I used the opening to read most of the decision. Watkins had been quite willing to talk about his own political past, but he would not reveal the names of people he knew had long since left the Communist party. He had also refused to take the Fifth Amendment, feeling that there had been nothing illegal about his past political activities. With the financial help of the United Auto Workers union, for whom he worked, he appealed his case to the U. S. Supreme Court. In its majority opinion, the Court wrote:

> The Bill of Rights is applicable to investigations as to all forms of governmental action. Witnesses cannot be compelled to give evidence against themselves. They cannot be subject to unreasonable search and seizure. Nor can the First Amendment freedoms of speech, press, religion, or political belief be abridged.
>
> We have no doubt that there is no congressional power to expose for the sake of exposure. The public is, of course, entitled to be informed concerning the workings of its government. That cannot be inflated into general power to expose where the predominant result can only be an invasion of the private rights of individuals. . . . It would be difficult to imagine a less explicit authorizing resolution. Who can define the meaning of "un-American"? . . . No one could reasonably deduce from the charter the kind of investigation that the committee was directed to make.

Reading the lengthy decision took so long that I was accused of trying to filibuster the hearings.

At another point, I tangled with Scherer, an Ohio Republican who had been the committee member most vocal in deploring the statement issued by the California bar. Mindful of what I had just read about the lack of congressional power to expose people, I said:

"Mr. Chairman, I charge you with having brought me up here solely for the purpose of exposing me to ridicule and scorn and for no valid legislative purpose." As there was no immediate response, I continued, "Did you not bring me here for the purpose of exposure?" There was still no response, so I asked Scherer, "May I read your opening statement?" He dourly answered no, but a while later I told him that his opening remarks "made it clear it was your purpose to expose lawyers." Scherer finally responded, "It was the criticism of lawyers like yourself and the conduct of lawyers like yourself that I was criticizing."

During the course of lengthy questioning I had refused to answer any inquiries about political affiliations, citing the First Amendment right to political belief and the Fifth Amendment right against self-incrimination.

"Have you advised the community of your membership in the Communist party?" Scherer asked.

"I want to refer to the Holy Bible, the book of Matthew . . ."

"Just a minute Mr. Garry," interrupted Congressman Robert McIntosh, a Michigan Republican. "It's not necessary to read the Bible. We have access to it. Just cite the chapter and verse for the record."

"Mr. McIntosh, it's the twenty-seventh chapter, the eleventh verse through the fourteenth."

The reference was the passage:

And Jesus stood before the governor: and the governor asked Him, saying, Art Thou the King of the Jews? And Jesus said unto him, "Thou sayest."

And when he was accused of the chief priest and elders, He answered nothing.

Then said Pilate unto Him, Hearest Thou not how many things they witness against Thee?

And he answered him to never a word; insomuch that the governor marveled greatly.

Scherer broke into my reading with, "Don't the Communists deny that book, the Bible?"

I leaped to my feet in anger and shouted, "Mr. Chairman, I happen to be a Christian. My people have been Christians for thousands of years. And I resent insinuations like that from you or anyone like you! What the Communists do with regard to their God is their business, and what I do with regard to my God is my business, and not yours!"

Purcell said the committee might use my shouting as the basis of a contempt citation, so I stood up again to apologize formally though I certainly did not feel apologetic.

Scherer ordered the committee's investigator to get the tape of our exchange, implying that he might seek a contempt citation but he did not. Tavenner asked several more questions which I refused to answer. I was excused and advised to sign a voucher to collect the nine-dollar witness fee. I declined. "I suggest you use the money for some worthy cause," I said.

"That's the first time I've heard an attorney cite the Bible as a legal reference in any kind of a proceeding," I overheard Scherer say as I was leaving. It had been a difficult week for HUAC.

I was excused late Friday afternoon and the hearings were adjourned for the weekend. But the next morning I was surprised to read in the newspaper that the committee had decided abruptly to end its San Francisco investigation. Headlined "S.F. RED INQUIRY ENDS IN NEW ROW," the front-page story in the *Chronicle* read as follows:

A defiant lawyer-witness protested at such length yesterday afternoon against any inquiry into his associations that the House Subcommittee on Un-American Activities finally decided to leave town.

At the end of the televised four-day hearings, one of the congressmen said the recent decision of the Supreme Court in the Watkins case "obviously has slowed the committee's work." Nineteen witnesses who had been served with subpoenas were not called to testify.

Charles R. Garry, former president of the San Francisco chapter of the National Lawyers Guild, was asked about his political affiliations at the hearings. . . .

Sometimes shouting and finally waving a copy of the Bible during an angry discussion about Communists and religion, Garry accused the committee of calling him only "for ridicule and exposure."

On that note, HUAC crawled out of San Francisco.

4.

Students on Trial

In June 1959, HUAC released the names of over a hundred California teachers subpoenaed for its San Francisco hearings. It then postponed the hearings, leaving the teachers no way to defend themselves against the unfounded allegations. The hearings were rescheduled, postponed again, and finally canceled in October. HUAC had, however, sent its files to state education officials and some teachers lost their jobs. Then HUAC issued a new batch of subpoenas returnable on Thursday, May 12, 1960.

The Episcopal Diocese of California, the California Federation of Labor, the San Francisco Central Labor Council, the Society of Friends, the American Federation of Teachers, and over seven hundred Berkeley, Stanford, San José, and San Francisco state college faculty members condemned HUAC's return to the Bay Area.

On the Berkeley campus, where student activism was still in its infancy, the Students for Civil Liberties circulated a petition calling for cancellation of the hearings and abolition of HUAC. They obtained two thousand signatures in four days. Encouraged by the response, the students scheduled a rally for May 12, planning a march to City Hall to picket and view the hearings.

The rally, march, and picketing took place without incident, but when the students tried to enter the hearing room they discovered that only those with white cards issued by HUAC's staff were allowed inside. They waited all afternoon but few got in.

The next day, Friday, about two hundred students returned and waited all morning in vain to see the committee in action. Inside the hearings had turned into a farce. Witness after witness defied the committee and several were bodily removed from the hearing room.

At the afternoon session after only a few of them got in, the impatient students began chanting *Let us in! Let us in!* Police ordered them to leave, but they sat down and began singing "We Shall Not Be Moved," a hymn identified with the civil rights movement. An officer suddenly turned on a firehose and began spraying the students. A second hose was engaged and within seconds pandemonium ensued. The sitting demonstrators were soaked and everyone else was ankle deep in the water that covered the marble floors and went cascading down the main staircase. Police began pushing the students backwards; in the melee there was a lot of pushing, slipping, sliding, falling. Some demonstrators left voluntarily, but some remained. Police dragged, threw, or pulled them down the stairs, some by their feet so that their heads bounced on each step. In the midst of this confusion, several policemen leaped on a student, pummeling and kicking him. They then dragged him back toward the hearing room. His name was Robert Meisenbach, a junior English major at Berkeley. Although sixty-three others were arrested, they were charged with misdemeanors; Meisenbach was charged with a felony, assaulting a police officer with a deadly weapon. The allegation was that he had wrested a club from Officer Ralph Schaumleffel and beat him with it.

The State Judicial Council called me to say one of their young lawyers, Marshall Krause, had been arrested at City Hall. I went to get him and when I saw everyone being brought in soaked to the skin, I became so incensed that I bailed out the sixty-four students as well, without consulting my partners, my firm guaranteeing $30,000 in bail during that afternoon and evening.

The incident was reported locally in banner headlines with the media dubbing May 13 as "Black Friday." The next day about five thousand people ringed City Hall in a chanting picket line. Effects of Black Friday were felt all the way to Washington, D.C., where the *Washington Post*, calling HUAC "wandering minstrels," editorialized:

> There is only one thing wrong with this minstrel show. It stinks. It makes a shabby joke out of the investigating power of Congress. It demeans the House of Representatives. It perpetrates a cynical con game on a lot of gullible Americans.

Judge Albert Axelrod dismissed all charges against the sixty-three charged with misdemeanors, but that left Meisenbach facing a felony count. The lawyers who had been defending the students had a meeting and chose me and Jack Berman, a former assistant district attorney, to defend Meisenbach.

J. Edgar Hoover, director of the FBI, released a report charging that Communists had instigated the City Hall demonstration, that the students had been unwittingly used by "a few Communists using mob psychology to turn peaceful demonstrations into riots."

Right after the charges against them were dismissed, fifty-eight of the students issued a rebuttal which stated, "Nobody incited us, nobody misguided us. We were led only by our own convictions, and we still stand firmly by them."

The Hoover report also claimed that the violence had been precipitated by a demonstrator jumping a police barricade and grabbing an officer's nightstick, causing the rest of the crowd to surge forward, leaving the police no alternative but the firehoses.

In September HUAC came out with a similar version of Black Friday in a different medium. It had subpoenaed footage of the hearings and demonstrations and created a film called "Operation Abolition," which was shown all over the country. Its theme was that the drive to abolish the committee was part of an orchestrated Communist plot and that the students had been manipulated into riot.

Filled with inaccuracies, distortions, and innuendo, the film transposed the sequence of events so that it appeared the trouble took place before, not after, the hosings. Footage showing police clubbing demonstrators was omitted. The slanted narration claimed that only pro-Communist newspapers had reported excessive police force, but actually the *San Francisco Chronicle, Oakland Tribune,* and *New York Times* all had reported it.

The *Washington Post* called the film a propaganda movie with "a mendaciously distorted view of the demonstrations, a flagrant case of forgery by film." Berkeley students and the ACLU prepared and printed a rebuttal. The controversy raged into the spring of 1961. "Operation Abolition" played to overflow student audiences, but its overall effect seemed to make them more interested in activism. Radical leaders said the film had been an excellent organizing tool.

From the point of view of Meisenbach's defense, the key inaccuracy was the prosecution's charge that Meisenbach, a former high-school high jumper, had vaulted over the police barricade and grabbed Officer Schaumleffel's club.

THE TRIAL BEGINS

It was April 1961 before Meisenbach came to trial. The judge was
Harry Neubarth who had heard the Gorshan case, though this would
be a jury trial. We figured, in the face of the publicity, it would be
tough to find twelve unprejudiced jurors, but we looked forward to
the trial, having worked hard in preparation. An additional incentive
was that, if Meisenbach was acquitted, HUAC's credibility would slip
to a new low.

First we did a photo search, enlisting the aid of students, friends,
relatives. We found more than a hundred different shots. Then we
had an artist render a large map of the inside layout of City Hall with
its huge marble staircase leading up to a second-floor rotunda, off
which there were several lobbies. On the third and fourth floors
there were galleries leading to offices, courtrooms, and a library. The
ornate post-Renaissance-style building was topped by a huge dome.
From the foot of the staircase the entire dome could be viewed.
Everything was built around this central open area.

We had all prospective witnesses locate exactly where they had
been on the map; by the time of the trial we knew not only the exact
sequence of events but also what could be seen from where. Using
the concept of demonstrative evidence we also had built a wooden
replica of the City Hall interior, six by eight feet, to use as a visual
aid in the courtroom along with the map.

Today there are discovery procedures by which a defendant can
see in advance all the evidence gathered by police and prosecution
against him. There is reason for this: a criminal trial is not a game—
lives and, at the very least, freedom are at stake. In order to prepare
an adequate defense, the defense attorney, who comes into the case
long after the police and the district attorney, must have access to the
evidence against his client. Unfortunately, some prosecutors still try
to withhold this information. Sometimes police reports are sup-
pressed or destroyed. But in 1961 the discovery process was not as
formalized as it is now, and a major problem was that we could not
obtain legally all the evidence against Meisenbach. Although Judge
Neubarth ordered the district attorney's office to turn over all reports
to us, they sent only two. One was Officer Schaumleffel's; the other
by Patrolman Thomas Walsh. Both men were to be prosecution witnesses, but, in contradiction to the Hoover report and the HUAC

film, neither police report claimed that the riot had been triggered by a student jumping a barricade and grabbing an officer's club.

This information had been provided by the San Francisco Police Intelligence Unit. We went to court to get the additional reports but Tom Cahill, chief of police, and Inspector Thomas Fitzpatrick, head of intelligence, denied there were other reports. So, before we got to court we knew that the police were withholding the reports of Inspector Michael Maguire—who had been in charge at City Hall on May 13—and Cecil Pharris, an assistant inspector. We knew because we had obtained photostatic copies of the reports in the same way resourceful lawyers always had obtained such information before the discovery rules took effect—we paid for it. (This was another reason the courts formalized discovery: attorneys wanting information could always get it by paying for it.)

A week before the trial Judge Neubarth summoned the prosecutor, Walter Giubbini, Berman, and myself to his chambers and laid down the ground rules. There would be no admission of evidence concerning "Operation Abolition" or the Hoover report. Evidence would be strictly limited to what had happened at City Hall on May 13 as, he pointed out, the trial was only to determine whether or not Meisenbach had assaulted Schaumleffel with a police billy.

Judges and prosecutors frequently try to keep the political elements out of important cases. This keeps the defense from raising the political issues directly while allowing the prosecution to convey political attitudes by innuendo. However, in this case I believe that Neubarth was simply trying to keep the trial from becoming a circus, because the controversy was still very much in the news.

We had thought picking a jury would take days, but to our surprise we found twelve reasonably unbiased people in less than two hours, ten of whom were women, mostly middle-aged.

As Berman and I were both trial lawyers, we had to divide the trial responsibilities. Only one of us could make an opening statement, only one cross-examine each prosecution witness, only one question each defense witness. We were both itching to get a chance at Schaumleffel on cross-examination so we asked Carolyn Anspacher, a reporter, to toss a coin. Berman won the toss and with it the opening statement and the cross-examination of Schaumleffel.

Both opening statements were brief. Prosecutor Giubbini merely outlined what he hoped to prove, namely, that in the middle of a melee Meisenbach had grabbed the club of the falling Schaumleffel and beaten him with it. He made no mention of any leaping of the barricade, maintaining it was the students' disruptive behavior and the clubbing of the officer that had provoked the incident.

Berman countered dramatically, saying that the entire incident was caused by Inspector Michael Maguire, "the sadistic man solely and singly responsible for the incidents," who had ordered the hoses turned on the students. He said that the evidence, including our photos, would show Meisenbach at the back of the crowd of demonstrators, peacefully on his way out of City Hall when Schaumleffel tackled and beat him.

Schaumleffel, stocky, sandy-haired, thirty-one-years old, a San Francisco cop for twelve years, was the prosecution's lead-off witness. His testimony, as elicited by the prosecutor, went as follows:

The incident began shortly before 1:00 P.M. when the students began pushing against the wooden barricades a short distance from the hearing room. A surge knocked over the barricades at one point, but a handful of policemen managed to push back the two hundred students and replace the barricades. At this point a firehose was brought in. Schaumleffel tried to get the students to calm down but was answered with catcalls. Then there came a second surging of the crowd in which several students got past the barricades. Schaumleffel got cut off from the other officers and began pulling out his club, but he lost his balance, fell, and someone grabbed the club out of his hand. Still off balance, trying to retain his footing, he saw Meisenbach with the club raised over his head. Although three or four feet from him, Schaumleffel charged Meisenbach and tackled him near the waist, but, just before he hit Meisenbach, the club came down and struck him on the left side of the head. He nevertheless managed to subdue Meisenbach and, with the help of other officers, handcuffed him. At the close of testimony, Giubbini had Schaumleffel draw an X on a diagram of City Hall at the spot where he was when Meisenbach supposedly struck him. He placed the X well in front of the barricade.

After this testimony it was our turn to punch Schaumleffel's story full of holes. Berman asked Schaumleffel when Meisenbach had first taken off his glasses. He replied that he had first noticed them only after Meisenbach was handcuffed. Berman handed him a newspaper photo showing Meisenbach down, trying to protect his face with his arm, holding his glasses in one hand, unhandcuffed, with six policemen standing over him. Berman asked if Meisenbach had been subdued at this point.

"No, he was not completely subdued, sir. He continued to fight vociferously and very strenuously until we had the handcuffs on him."

"With six officers surrounding him, as is demonstrated here?"

"They were not surrounding him, sir."

Berman requested that the picture be shown to the jury.

To us it clearly showed Meisenbach only trying protect himself. To say, as Schaumleffel did, that he struggled vigorously, with six cops standing over him, simply did not ring true, especially with the quiet, academic-looking Meisenbach sitting just a few feet from the jury, wearing his thick, horn-rimmed glasses. This also cast doubt on Schaumleffel's overall credibility.

During the more than two-hour cross-examination, Berman continued to contradict Schaumleffel.

"You related today in your direct examination certain remarks you alleged you heard people make to the effect of 'Let's get the cops,' 'Storm the doors' and 'Let's go.' "

"Yes."

"Did you ever mention these remarks either in your police report or in your testimony before the grand jury?"

"No, I did not."

"So this is the first time you've mentioned these statements, is that correct?"

"Yes."

Under further questioning Schaumleffel said that at one point several students succeeded in getting over the barricade, that during this surge the barricade was knocked over, the police forced back.

"At any time, up to this point, had you ever seen Robert Meisenbach?"

"I don't believe so, sir. No."

Schaumleffel said he and twenty other officers had great difficulty pushing the two hundred students back a short distance.

"Isn't it true there were student monitors controlling the group at this time?"

"No sir, that is not true."

"Didn't everyone immediately in front of the barricade sit down?"

"No, sir."

"Isn't it true that the majority of the people in the area marked lobby were sitting down?"

"No, sir."

"Did the alleged Meisenbach incident take place before the hoses were turned on?"

"I don't know sir, because I don't know when the hoses were turned on."

I handed Berman another photo showing water coming from a hose. Schaumleffel was not visible, probably because he was behind the hose, but Meisenbach was clearly identifiable.

"Do you see Robert Meisenbach in that photograph?"

"I see a person who could be Mr. Meisenbach."

"The man with the pipe and the glasses leaning against the pillar, is that right?"

"Yes, that's correct."

"Now that you've seen this photograph, could you testify under oath that your altercation with Mr. Meisenbach took place after the water was turned on?"

"Yes, I would so testify. Yes."

This was a major breakthrough. Another part of the official version of the incident stood refuted.

Berman pressed on asking Schaumleffel if he had ever discussed the case with Inspector Cecil Pharris. Berman then picked up Pharris's report.

"Did you tell Pharris, 'At approximately 1:20 P.M. Officer Ralph Schaumleffel was attacked by the crowd and had his police baton taken from him.' Did you tell him that?"

"Not in those exact words, but substantially that, yes, sir."

"Did you tell him: 'This baton was used to strike the officer in the head by one Robert J. Meisenbach. This seemed to arouse the crowd and they tried to get through our barricades and lines to force their way into the hearing room. General rioting then ensued. The mob was driven back to the landing at the top of the grand staircase with the help of firehoses.' Did you tell Mr. Pharris that?"

"The first sentence only, sir."

"The next sentence about arousing the crowd and trying to get to the barricade and then turning on the water?"

"That is not my . . ."

"That is Mr. Pharris's? You don't know anything about that?"

"Right."

"He made it up?"

"No, I didn't say he made it up."

"Well, we do know the incident between you and Meisenbach took place after the water was turned on, not before, don't we?"

"Yes."

"Of that we're certain?"

"Yes."

"Did you ever mention that either in your police report or in your testimony before the grand jury?"

"I don't believe I mentioned the water at all, sir, on either of those occasions."

Once again Berman showed Schaumleffel the picture of the fire-hose spraying the students.

"Is it not true that everyone in front of that hose and in front of that barricade is sitting down?"

"Yes, that's true. Most of them."

"So that when the water was turned on, the majority of people in front of the barricade were sitting down, is that correct?"

"According to that picture, but I don't know that the picture indicates when the water was turned on." Berman confronted him with another picture that showed the students sitting down as the hoses were being turned on them. Both photos showed Meisenbach at the rear of the crowd, leaning against a pillar.

A debate about the water followed.

"With a big firehose turning out X gallons of water a minute, the floor got pretty wet, didn't it?"

"When I was finished with my struggle with Mr. Meisenbach, it was quite wet, yes."

"Before the struggle. Was the floor wet then?"

"I don't know, sir."

"Are you telling me you were surrounded by hundreds of people, the water is turned on, and you don't know whether the floor was wet?"

"That is correct, sir."

We then showed Schaumleffel several news photos of the hosing, the lobby full of water, and the drenched students, but he maintained that he wasn't aware of the water until after he finished fighting with Meisenbach. All our witnesses had told us Meisenbach had been attacked on the staircase as he was leaving City Hall. Schaumleffel claimed he finally subdued Meisenbach on a staircase landing after grappling with him up in the lobby and rolling down the stairs.

Once a witness starts lying, he has to continue lying to cover the original deception. By going over his story very carefully and using him in the photos, Berman caught numerous contradictions. We even produced a picture of Schaumleffel holding the right side of his head, rather than the left side he said he had been hit on.

"Isn't it true that the lobby area had been completely cleared of civilians before you ever came in contact with Meisenbach?"

"No, that is not true, sir."

"That is not true?"

"No, sir."

Then he had to explain why, if Meisenbach was the first person taken into custody as he claimed, there were no paddy wagons available.

"I am not denying that they were there. I say there were none available. They were all filled and in use when I had need for one."

His answer seemed to prove what he had denied, that most of the students already had been arrested and put in paddy wagons before Schaumleffel ever came in contact with Meisenbach—which would have made it difficult for Meisenbach to ignite the incident. We would point this out during our final argument.

"Is there any mention in here [his grand jury testimony] of the fact that there were two surges toward the barricades?"

"I don't believe that was mentioned before the grand jury. No."

"So you made that up for the trial, is that right?"

The prosecution objected and was sustained.

We left court that afternoon satisfied, but we had scarcely questioned Schaumleffel about the alleged assault. Over dinner we discussed the testimony and later picked up the copy of the daily transcript. Then we both went home to sleep. At 2:00 A.M. we met in my office. One read the transcript circling and underlining significant passages. The other dictated these on tape.

Early that morning a secretary typed this reduced version of the transcript. From it we were able to see other areas where Schaumleffel was vulnerable. I use this gutted transcript technique whenever a transcript is available. Not only does it help in cross-examination but also it's invaluable in preparing the final argument. Several thousand pages of testimony are reduced to several hundred.

On the night of May 13, KPFA, the Pacifica station in Berkeley, had reported that a policeman had told a news photographer that Schaumleffel wasn't struck by a club at all but had slipped and hit his head on the marble floor. Berman asked Schaumleffel if the report was true. He denied it vigorously.

"The truth and fact of the matter is, that you were pretty confused about the entire incident?"

"I was confused about the overall incident, but not about the particular incident of being struck on the head by Mr. Meisenbach."

Berman read from a newspaper clipping: " 'I don't know completely, exactly, what took place.' Did you make that statement on May 13, 1960?"

"I did."

" 'Several of us were knocked down, and when I was down . . . I had my club in my hand.' Did you make that statement on May 13, 1960?"

"I probably did, sir, if you have the transcript of something."

"Well, you had the club in your hand when you were knocked down, is that right?"

"No. As I testified yesterday, I was taking the club out. It could have been in my hand. It could have been halfway out of my pocket. I'm not sure of the exact position of the club."

"Well, your recollection was much clearer, was it not, at about two-fifteen or two-thirty on the afternoon of May thirteenth than it is today, isn't that correct?"

"No, that is not correct, sir."

"You have a better recollection today?"

"I have a better picture of what happened. At that time I was, as I said, I was injured, I was quite confused, and I was dizzy."

Before finishing we wanted to make an important point in this trial to help further discovery procedures. To this end we used the cross-examination to show that Schaumleffel was biased because he had refused to talk to the defense's representative before the trial. Following his refusal, we had gone to court over the matter and Neubarth had ruled that the district attorney could not prevent officers from talking to the defense but that it was each policeman's individual decision to do so or not. Our representative had returned to Schaumleffel with a letter from us to the effect that he could have both an attorney and a certified court reporter present when we questioned him, but he refused a second time. The district attorney said that he had not instructed Schaumleffel not to talk to us. Schaumleffel said that he had asked his friends, and they had advised him to talk only to the district attorney.

After hammering in this point, Berman retraced Schaumleffel's every move from the moment he stepped out from behind the barricade, having him mark his various positions on a diagram to show exactly how he had stumbled through two hundred people on a slippery wet marble floor. He claimed to have tripped and lost his

balance, that his club was taken from him and passed back to Meisenbach. He said that he had seen Meisenbach with the club when he
was four feet from him.

"You had to move forward against him to get hit, didn't you?"

"No, sir, I did not."

"At a distance of four feet, Mr. Meisenbach hit you without throwing that club?"

"Mr. Meisenbach was advancing toward me so I don't know
whether he could have hit me from four feet or not."

"Now you tell us that Mr. Meisenbach was advancing toward you,
is that correct?"

"That's correct."

"In your testimony yesterday morning, in your testimony yesterday afternoon, in your testimony before the grand jury on August 6,
1960, in your official police report, in your discussion with any one
of the twenty-five policemen you have mentioned, have you at any
other time before this very minute stated that Mr. Meisenbach was
advancing toward you?"

"I have never so stated under oath in those exact words."

Asked why he didn't back up to avoid being hit, he said he was
hemmed in by demonstrators. Yet he had just explained how easily
he'd made his way going forward through the crowd.

"Was this statement made in your presence either by yourself,
Inspector Pharris, or Inspector Maguire to members of the FBI?"
Berman asked, reading from part of the Pharris report, words that
had appeared substantially in the Hoover report and were on the
melodramatic soundtrack of "Operation Abolition."

" 'One of the demonstrators provided the spark that touched off
the flame of violence. Leaping a barricade that had been erected, he
grabbed the officer's nightstick and began beating the officer over
the head. More surged forward as if to storm the doors, and the police
inspector ordered the firehose turned on.' "

Schaumleffel, over Giubbini's vociferous objections, was permitted
to answer.

"That statement was never made in my presence."

"That was not made in your presence?"

"No, sir, and it was not made by me."

"Or in your presence?"

"Or in my presence. That's correct."

That, we thought, pretty well placed the Hoover report and "Operation Abolition" in the garbage pail where they belonged. It was noon when Schaumleffel left the witness stand. We had cross-examined him for almost five hours. His direct testimony had taken thirty minutes.

FALSE WITNESS

Berman told me that a witness for the prosecution whose name we did not recognize—John W. Stansfield—was in the intelligence unit office upstairs. I went up to take a look. He was a middle-aged man dressed in a blue suit and he was preening in front of a mirror, fixing his tie, smoothing down his hair with the palm of his hand. He seemed to enjoy looking at himself. A former naval officer and federal narcotics agent, he now had his own private investigation service. He had told Giubbini that he had been standing on a third-floor gallery and had observed the alleged incident.

Under direct questioning he swore that he had seen a policeman with arms folded push his way through the crowd in a straight line. About twenty-five feet from the barrier, the officer had slipped or tripped and fell to his knees. As he started to rise, a man had emerged from behind a post, grabbed a club, and hit the officer over the head. The officer had grabbed his assailant about the knees in a football-type tackle and held on until other officers came to his assistance. Giubbini asked him to mark the spot where he saw the officer struck. Then he turned him over to me for cross-examination.

There were obvious contradictions between his testimony and Schaumleffel's. He had placed the officer in a different position than the officer placed himself. Against the officer's strong testimony that he had been struck from the front, he claimed that Schaumleffel had been struck from behind. His version had the officer transversing the lobby erect and in a straight line, whereas Schaumleffel's own testimony was that he was in a crouch and moved in an arc.

Even so, it was necessary to totally discredit Stansfield's credibility. Furthermore, I knew he was lying. I decided to attack.

"How old are you, sir?"

"I'll be fifty years old on August twenty-fifth of this year."

"And where do you live?"

"I told you that, Mr. Berman."

"Oh, excuse me, Mr. Witness. I didn't mean to hurt your feelings. Are you ashamed of where you're living?"

"Not at all."

"Well, then tell me where you are living."

"I live at 810 Gonzales Drive."

I led him to talk about his background, establishing that he had been working as a chief welfare investigator in a neighboring county when he had suffered a heart attack following which he set up the private investigation service from his home. This brought out his strong law-enforcement background. Then I asked:

"When did your first find out you were going to be a witness in this case?"

"On the first day of April, this year, 1961."

"How did you happen to be contacted as a witness?"

"On the twenty-eighth of March, I dropped by to say hello to Inspector Fitzpatrick, whom I have known for a number of years."

"You had known Inspector Fitzpatrick for a number of years?"

"Since I was the chief investigator for the twelfth Naval District for the General Courts-Martial in 1945—'44, '45, and '46."

"Knowing him that well, you also know he is head of the police intelligence unit, is that right?"

"Yes, sir, that's true."

Stansfield claimed that during his visit with Fitzpatrick another man in the office made a remark about the City Hall incident, prompting Stansfield to say, "I was out there that day Tom, and saw that thing and was appalled by it." Fitzpatrick then asked him what he saw.

"I saw the whole thing from the third floor," Stansfield said. "I saw that fellow strike the officer!"

Fitzpatrick supposedly asked him why he hadn't come forward before. "I didn't want to get involved," Stansfield explained, citing his ill health. However, Fitzpatrick convinced him to talk to someone from the district attorney's office. He agreed, he said, because, "this is a man's duty as a citizen." A few days later, Giubbini and Pharris went out to his house to talk to him.

"When Mr. Giubbini came out to see you on April first, did he bring with him a public stenographer?"

"He did not."

"Did he bring with him a secretary?"

"He did not."

"Did he bring with him a recording device?"

"He did not."

"Did he bring with him a pad and pencil to take some notes?"

"No, sir."

According to Stansfield's testimony, Giubbini had not brought pictures or a diagram of City Hall. Pharris likewise had arrived empty-handed, and the only other people present were his mother, his wife, and his two daughters; he went to City Hall a few days later and a photo, already placed into evidence, was taken to show where he had been standing when he witnessed the alleged assault.

"Mr. Stansfield, how did you happen to be in city hall on May 13, 1960?"

"Why, Mr. Garry, I have occasion to walk around the city. As I say, I'm not too well. I had been to a luncheon the day before and the subject of the riot and demonstrations was discussed. I thought, I'll go out there and take a look at it. I haven't anything else to do."

"Now you say that the day before May thirteenth, that would be May twelfth, you had been to a luncheon, is that right?"

"That's right. I eat lunch."

"Lunch was at what time, around noon?"

"Lunch was at the special agents luncheon on the top of the telephone building, with all the special agents of the various commercial companies here in the city represented. There were telephone company special agents, my old friend Walter Vervay, Mr. Lawrence of the P.G.&E., Mr. Hayden of the telephone company, people I have known for a long time. Lunch was at twelve noon."

"And at that time you say they were discussing the fact that there was a riot at City Hall?"

"No. That there had been a demonstration. If I used the word riot, it was inadvisable."

"I asked you, sir, how you happened to go to city hall on Friday, May thirteenth, and I believe you said you went there because you had heard that there was a riot going on. Now you're willing to recant that, is that right?"

"I'm not willing to recant that I heard that there had been a demonstration at the City Hall on May twelfth. The fact that I was interested is because I had heard that there had been some trouble there on the twelfth and therefore I went on the thirteenth to see what was going on."

"Were you shown pictures of Mr. Meisenbach?"

"I didn't need to be shown any pictures, no."

"Isn't it a fact, Mr. Stansfield, that while you were sitting right here where Mr. Giubbini is sitting, just before the court session commenced, that Robert Meisenbach had to be pointed out to you?"

"That is not a fact. It is not true."

"Have you seen Mr. Meisenbach's picture in the paper in the last four or five days?"

"I don't recall it. I haven't read about this."

"You have not read anything about this case?"

"Headlines. I'm not particularly interested in this case."

Having earlier witnessed something he called frightening and appalling, so much so that it was still on his mind ten months later when he visited Fitzpatrick, he now stated that he had little interest in the case! I had the gut feeling that he had not even been in City Hall on May 13. I suspected that, in semi-retirement as he was, and ill, he needed something to keep up his status with his friends, since he was no longer involved in real law-enforcement work. What better way to put himself in the spotlight than by helping the prosecution win this important case?

"Did you read anything in reference to the fact that Mr. Meisenbach was the person who is on trial in this case?

"Well, I read the name."

"You didn't see his picture?"

"I do not recall seeing Mr. Meisenbach's picture in the paper."

"Do you subscribe to any newspaper in this home of yours?"

"I subscribe to the *San Francisco Examiner.*

"Did you see Mr. Meisenbach's picture in the *Examiner?*"

"Well, if it was in there, I didn't see it. I don't get to read the paper every day."

"Too busy?"

"Oh, that's a rather personal question. I don't know whether I'm too busy or not. I just haven't read the paper in the last few days."

"As a matter of fact, this case has been quite important in your life, isn't that right?"

"As a matter of fact, this case never even occurred to me until the twenty-eighth day of March, this year."

I wanted to show the jury that he had a heavy personal stake in the trial, that he was no impartial witness motivated by a pure sense of citizenship.

"You have been an enforcement officer for a number of years, isn't that right?"

"Yes, sir, and it's no disgrace."

"And you've been in the armed services."

"And I'm proud of it."

"And you've been in the narcotic enforcement section?"

"I have."

"Then on May 13, 1960, with that kind of background and tremendously proud of it, when just at noon the day before you'd had lunch with all these big names, you, with that kind of background, see a man assaulting a police officer with a nightstick, and you remain silent until March 28, 1961? Is that your testimony? And you want this jury to believe that cock-and-bull story?"

Giubbini objected strenuously, and Judge Neubarth asked me to remain calm. He could see that I was about to explode.

"I think I'd better take a tranquilizer," I quipped.

"I wonder if that would help," the judge observed drily.

After a few more questions, I asked Stansfield to mark on a diagram of City Hall the spot where Meisenbach allegedly struck Schaumleffel. I also asked him to mark where the barricades were, and where the scuffle ended. His marks were not in the same place as Schaumleffel's.

"Did you see an incident out here Mr. Stansfield, where a student was thrown by a group of officers, thrown right down here, and laid prone here?" I indicated points on the diagram.

"No, Mr. Garry. From where I was standing I doubt very much if you could see that area in there."

"Did you see police officers picking ladies up and throwing them down these steps?"

"No, sir."

"Did you see any police officers using nightsticks on students?"

"No, sir, I did not."

We had pictures of the police doing all these things, and, one by one, we offered them into evidence.

"By the way, did you see any water being turned on, Mr. Stansfield?"

"No, sir, I don't recall any water."

"In other words, in all the time that you were there, you saw no water whatsoever?"

"Well, I can't recall about the water. I might have seen splashes of water, but I saw no one stream of water or anything like that that everybody talks about. I didn't see any of that. I was asked whether or not I had seen any stream of water. I did not see any stream of water."

I was pretty sure that few jurors would put any faith in Stansfield's testimony, but, just to clinch things, I had him point out how much of the lobby he could see from where he was standing. It was evident that he could not see the entire area from his vantage point. There was a question about the number of people packed into the small area he claimed he could see. He said there had been about 125 people.

"How many people would you say are in this courtroom right now?"

"I would say there are two hundred people in this courtroom."

"Judge, how many people are in the courtroom? Do you have any record of it?"

"One hundred and eight," was the reply.

To wind things up, we had Stansfield demonstrate exactly what he saw. At first he played Schaumleffel, then I did, at his direction. Then I had Meisenbach move in the way Stansfield said he saw him move. When it was all over, Stansfield had described a set of movements that differed significantly in several important ways from what Schaumleffel said had happened. After bringing out that Stansfield also had refused to talk with defense investigators, I concluded the cross-examination.

THE PROSECUTION RESTS

Giubbini now brought on real-estate broker Albert V. Morris, a non-practicing attorney. Morris had written a letter to a local minister congratulating him for publicly defending HUAC. In it he had told the minister that he had had an unobstructed view of the riot from a fourth-floor perch outside the City Hall law library. As Morris said he had not communicated either with the police or the district attorney, it presumably was not until he wrote the Reverend Curtis Nimms, a month before the trial, that Giubbini knew he existed. Nimms had turned Morris's letter over to the prosecutor who interviewed him.

Morris's tale differed in important ways from what Schaumleffel and Stansfield had testified previously—Schaumleffel was attempting to lead a student out of the lobby when another student raced out from behind a post and tackled him. (He marked a place some distance from the spots Stansfield and Schaumleffel had pinpointed earlier.) The two students wrestled the officer for the club, one of them eventually grabbing it and hitting Schaumleffel over the head with it several times. (Both Stansfield and Schaumleffel had said there was only one blow struck.) Before Morris took the stand we had Meisenbach remove his glasses. Giubbini asked him to identify the assailant, but Morris was unable to pick Meisenbach out.

Morris's account contradicted the previous witnesses on other points. He had the assailant racing through the lobby as if it were empty. He said Schaumleffel was hit on the right side of his head, and that Schaumleffel had his club in his hand when it was wrested from him, which the officer had repeatedly denied.

As Schaumleffel had never claimed he was trying to arrest anyone when he was attacked, what Morris described was significantly different from what Stansfield and Schaumleffel had depicted. Toward the end of cross-examination, I played the picture game with him that I had with Stansfield. No, he hadn't seen the police use clubs. No, he hadn't seen them throw any students down the stairs. No, he hadn't seen the firehoses turned on. Every picture seemed to surprise him. Since Morris had so effectively contradicted Schaumleffel and Stansfield, we let him off the stand reluctantly.

As with Stansfield, Giubbini made no attempt to rehabilitate his witness through redirect examination.

Hadley Roff, of the *News-Call-Bulletin* summed up the first week of testimony this way:

> So far prosecution witnesses haven't been able to agree to much other than that Patrolman Ralph E. Schaumleffel was struck by the young student during the melee. But on almost every other essential detail, the witnesses . . . differ widely in their accounts. Their dissimilar stories, however, do tote up to a grave refutation of the charges leveled against Meisenbach in FBI Director J. Edgar Hoover's report on the riot.

The doctor who had examined Schaumleffel was unavailable, but Giubbini put on the ambulance steward who had taken Schaumleffel to the hospital. Reading from hospital records, the steward said the officer had suffered a bruise with some swelling on the *lower back part* of his head. There was no break in the skin, no bleeding. Schaumleffel apparently received no treatment, because the records showed only he was examined and advised, then released. No X-rays were taken and no medical evidence of injury to Schaumleffel was offered. With that, the prosecution rested.

WITNESSES FOR THE DEFENSE

We started bringing on the witnesses, none of whom had been involved in the demonstrations.

First was Joseph F. Lewis, an attorney who had been in City Hall to represent two clients subpoenaed by HUAC. Lewis was a member of the central committee of the Santa Clara County Democratic party and the central committee of the California Democratic party. He had been only a few feet from the hearing room when he saw the students sitting in front of the barricade, chanting and occasionally singing. He left for a few moments to make a phone call, and when he returned he saw the firehoses coiled on the floor.

"I saw no surge toward the barriers. I saw no one leap the barricade. I saw no student hit anyone over the head. In fact, I saw no student violence whatsoever." As he was six feet four inches tall, and most of the students were sitting down, he had a good view.

Our next two witnesses, Sandra Levinson and Jane O'Grady both were graduate teaching assistants, one at Stanford, the other at California (Berkeley). Neither saw any student surge, or anyone jump the barricades, nor did they see an officer stumble and move forward in the way Schaumleffel had described. They did not see Meisenbach. O'Grady did observe several policemen lift a seated student and throw him down the stairs. Both women were extremely effective.

Fred Haines, a reporter for KPFA, testified that he observed Inspector Maguire trying to keep out even those students who had obtained white cards. He also said that after Maguire hosed the students, motorcycle cops wearing boots and helmets waded into the crowd and began beating people with clubs, and pushing them down the steps.

During cross-examination Haines said that Sheriff Matthew Carberry, incensed by the committee's arbitrary rules, promised the students he would get a sizable number of them admitted to the afternoon session. When it appeared that only a few would get in, the students sat down to show that they didn't intend to use force to get inside. Haines had told us in my office that he heard Maguire say, long before the hosing, that he intended to "clear these bums out," but this was deemed hearsay, and he wasn't permitted to reveal that to the jury.

Elwood Murray, a young schoolteacher from Sierra County doing advanced work at San Francisco State College, had walked into City Hall just in time to be blasted in the face with a firehose. He saw policemen repeatedly beat students and also observed two officers slip and fall in the water. One was wearing a regular police cap (as was Schaumleffel). This man moved out in front of the barricade, slipped, fell on his backside, possibly hit his head, and quickly regained his feet. The second officer was a motorcycle cop who wore a helmet. This policeman lost his club while beating a student and retreated behind the barricade. Two students raced for the club, and one of them flung it into a vacant part of City Hall. He could not identify either student.

The day ended with Murray still on the stand. Giubbini went over Murray's testimony microscopically in an attempt to discredit it, but he was unable to do so.

The next day we continued to present witnesses who had been close to the scene. Professor Mervyn Cadwallader, a San José State sociologist, said there had been no violence before the hoses were turned on.

"Did you see a student vault the barrier and take a policeman's club?"

"I did not."

"And hit the officer?"

"I did not. I saw no violence before the hoses went on."

Four students followed, and they portrayed vividly the violent and irresponsible way the police had behaved. Kelvyn McGoughey had tried to register a protest with Maguire, but before he could finish he was hosed from a distance of eight or ten inches. Then he was seized by several other officers and thrown down the stairs, suffering a deep gash in his head. Another student took a photograph. Maguire vaulted the barricade and herded him into a corner where he was subsequently hosed. No one had seen Schaumleffel emerge from behind the barricade and trip. A photographer (who had heard another officer say that Schaumleffel had actually hurt his head in a fall) was not permitted to testify. His story was deemed hearsay because he had not himself heard Schaumleffel say it.

Then we brought on witnesses who actually had seen Schaumleffel beat Meisenbach. The most telling was Douglas Kinney, a graduate student working in the City Hall law library. He said he saw a hatless Schaumleffel grab Meisenbach, who was on his way out, and, with the aid of several other policemen, beat him around the head three or four times with a club.

Kinney, a former naval lieutenant, raced down the stairs to try and prevent any further beatings and took down the badge numbers of two officers. Then he ran back up to the law library and typed out a statement.

Barbara Reese, a secretary for the carpenters' union witnessed the same incident, although she couldn't identify Meisenbach as the victim.

Finally, Gerald Gray, another Berkeley graduate student, had seen Meisenbach pick up the loose club that had bounced down to the staircase landing and toss it softly into an empty part of the lobby, just before he was set upon by a policeman.

Giubbini could not shake our witnesses. They had all been right on the scene, much closer than either Morris or Stansfield, and they were all telling the truth. When they didn't see something, or didn't know, they said so. They didn't invent answers. These witnesses set the stage for Meisenbach himself to testify.

My direct examination was brief. Like all the witnesses who had preceded him, we had him mark the spot on a diagram where he had been and then, using a cardboard figure, trace his movements on the wooden model. He said that when the hosing started he first stood behind the pillar, then started edging toward the stairs. A second hose was turned directly on him as he started down the staircase.

"I started down the stairs to the gallery landing. While at the top, I saw two policemen throw a man down the stairs to my left. I started down and I stumbled."

"What caused you to stumble?"

"The marble floor. The stairs were slippery. I reached the bottom, the gallery landing."

"And then?"

"I stepped on a club, an officer's club."

"What did you do when you stumbled on the officer's club?"

"Well, I picked up the club and tossed it into this area."

I had Bob demonstrate just how he tossed it, underhanded, in a straight line.

"Why did you toss it?"

"To get it out of the way."

"Was the area filled with people?"

"Oh, no, no. There were no people there."

Meisenbach said he tossed the club ten or fifteen feet, then turned to leave, but he had got no more than a few steps when he was jumped from behind by a policeman whom he learned later was

Schaumleffel. He said Schaumleffel hit him several times, once squarely in the face, with a club.

"Did you at that time or any other time strike Officer Schaumleffel, either before you were tackled or afterward?"

"No, I did not."

"Did you at any time lay a hand on Officer Schaumleffel?"

"No, I did not."

"Or any other officer?"

"No, I did not."

"Did you have your glasses on at the time that you were grabbed by Officer Schaumleffel."

"On this point I'm confused. I know that they were not on at the time Schaumleffel was on top of me, because I either took them off then, or took them off some place before. I can't be definite about that."

The pictures showed Meisenbach with his glasses in his hand. Other witnesses who wore glasses had testified that they had to remove them when they got wet. Meisenbach's eyesight was so bad that without his glasses everything was blurry. It seemed unlikely he could have walked down the stairs without them.

He had been dragged up the stairs to the lobby, and there was beaten again, this time by Schaumleffel and several other officers. His teeth were pushed through his upper lip. He was handcuffed and pushed against a wall in a sitting position and left there with blood streaming out of his mouth. At one point he asked a cop to stop pulling on his arm because he didn't want to lose his glasses. "To hell with your glasses," the cop had replied. Bob's glasses were broken anyhow as well as a replacement pair he always carried in his breast pocket. The next day he had black and blue marks all over his body.

"Did anything else happen to you?"

"Not that I can recall. I was confused."

"Did you have something happen to you physically?"

"Yes."

"What?"

I could see he was crying, even though he kept his face down. When he recovered, he looked up and said,

"I had a bowel movement."

I turned him over to Giubbini for cross-examination.

The prosecutor tried hard to break the story, to catch him on details, but under his close questioning small points emerged that lent more veracity to his testimony.

Giubbini implied that Meisenbach would have been more seriously injured if he had been struck in the face with a club, but he gave several vivid descriptions of the clubbings, so the prosecutor finally quit.

We put on three character witnesses, all former teachers of Meisenbach's from his high school and Modesto Junior College.

Then the jury was escorted to a bus, and they, along with the attorneys, Judge Neubarth, Meisenbach, the press, and public, took a tour of City Hall. We had Bob stand next to the pillar our photos showed him near and puff on his pipe, just as he had done before the hosing started.

REBUTTALS—THE FINAL ARGUMENT

Monday morning Giubbini called eight rebuttal witnesses and put Schaumleffel back on the stand. All the rebuttal witnesses were cops, but their testimony was not significant. It seemed to be the police department's last-ditch effort to avoid taking the blame for the incident.

The next-to-last rebuttal witness was Cecil Pharris. On cross-examination, Berman read portions of his report aloud, pointing out contradictions between it and testimony given in the trial.

"It is true, is it not, that you discussed with Officer Schaumleffel the fact that somebody had taken down his badge number?"

"No, it is not."

"And it's further true, Mr. Pharris, that at that time you had a discussion with Schaumleffel and it was agreed that somebody had to be arrested to explain the brutality on Meisenbach?"

"As I recall, sir, Mr. Meisenbach was already in custody, was he not?"

This did not answer the question, but as Judge Neubarth was anxious to bring the trial to a close, Berman did not persist. We knew Pharris was slippery on the witness stand—it might take hours to pin him down. We felt we had given the jury a reason why Meisenbach had been charged with the felony.

We now had the right to put on our rebuttal witnesses, witnesses who could call into question what the prosecution rebuttal witnesses had said. We only used one, James R. Toombs, a former junior college student then working as a newspaper carrier for the *Chronicle*. Toombs said he had been standing on the staircase landing on his way out of City Hall, Meisenbach to his right and behind him. He saw

Schaumleffel, club in hand, coming at him rapidly.

"He was either swinging the club or losing his balance," Toombs said. "About six to eight feet away from me, he went down in front of me, all the way down to the floor. The club went out of his hand, past my right in the vicinity of where I have indicated Mr. Meisenbach was.

"The officer fell with his left knee underneath him and his left arm clasped so that his head was very close to the floor."

According to his testimony, Schaumleffel had been ten feet from Meisenbach when he fell. Meisenbach had picked up the loose club and tossed it away. Schaumleffel had had some trouble regaining his balance on the wet marble, but when he did he charged between Toombs and a friend and tackled Meisenbach.

"Did Mr. Meisenbach at any time strike Officer Schaumleffel?"

"It was impossible for him to strike Officer Schaumleffel because . . ."

He was about to explain that Meisenbach had his back to Schaumleffel, but Giubbini's furious objection cut him off. The objection was sustained because, under the rules of evidence, witnesses can only say what they see: they are not permitted to draw conclusions from what they've seen or heard.

"Could it have been possible from the way that Mr. Meisenbach was located at that time for him to have struck Officer Schaumleffel in the back of his head or any part of his body?"

Once again Giubbini said the question called for the witness' conclusion, and Judge Neubarth sustained him.

On cross-examination the prosecutor could not shake his story at all. He implied that Meisenbach threw the club at Schaumleffel, but Toombs was quite precise, saying the officer was down on his side when Bob lofted the club in a direction away from him. With that explosive bit of testimony, both sides rested.

The next day was devoted to final arguments. Dismissing most of our witnesses as biased, Giubbini claimed that if *his* witnesses told different stories it was because the human memory sometimes plays tricks. He said that Meisenbach was a liar, that if he had been hit in the face with a club he would have suffered at least a broken nose or black eye.

"There's been a lot of lying going on in this courtroom," I said in rebuttal. "More than that, there has been deliberate perjury by the prosecution witnesses."

We had had artists make huge blow-ups of key testimony. The contradictary accounts given by Schaumleffel, Stansfield, and Morris were highlighted on big cards, along with portions of the Pharris and Maguire reports, and placed in front of the jury.

I told the jurors I didn't believe that John Stansfield was ever in City Hall on May 13, 1960, that his testimony was a complete fabrication. I could see several jurors nodding their heads in agreement. I pointed to Pharris's statement about a student jumping a barricade: "Did you hear anybody testify that that happened?"

I asked if there had been any testimony to corroborate the statement that a "mob had stormed the doors" of the hearing room. (These phrases were spread all around me. All I had to do was point at them.) I told the jury we purposely went beyond extablishing a reasonable doubt.

"We have gone on the offensive and prosecuted the people who have accused us. This incident never would have happened if it weren't for a man named Maguire."

I reminded them Maguire had been in charge at City Hall, that it was Maguire who wouldn't let the students in, who ordered the hosing. I recalled the testimony that Maguire himself had leaped the barricade.

"Meisenbach was the victim of a diabolical, horrible mix-up by one stupid cop."

The next morning the judge read his legal instructions to the jury. The courtroom atmosphere was extremely tense; lines of people waited outside. The jury went out to deliberate early in the day and we spent the intervening time biting our nails.

We saw the jurors go to lunch. When they came back, they were laughing and joking. We didn't know what to think. Despite our confidence, we were still nervous. It had been an emotional trial; big issues were at stake. Had it been a simple assault case, we would have tried it in a few days, but we had been in court for almost three weeks. Two o'clock came with no word. Two-thirty. Nothing. Three o'clock. Still no verdict.

Finally, at three-fifteen, the jury came back and the clerk read the verdict to a hushed courtroom.

"The jury finds the defendant Robert J. Meisenbach, not guilty . . ."

The rest was drowned out in cheers and applause. Spectators jumped up and down and embraced. Meisenbach's parents hugged me and Jack Berman. It was a great victory, not only because he was justifiably acquitted but because the verdict also served to further discredit HUAC.

Afterward, we asked the jurors what had taken them so long, as the evidence seemed so overwhelmingly in our favor.

"Oh, we had a verdict in ten minutes. We just hammed it up a bit like you fellows did during the trial."

That night, the student defense committee threw a party at the Old Spaghetti Factory in North Beach. People of all political persuasions came—lawyers, students, artists, priests, political activists, and four jurors. It was a wonderful celebration and the beer flowed freely all night.

Besides contributing to the downward slide of HUAC, the Meisenbach case was a rally point for the student movement of the sixties. It was fun to try, because the evidence on our side was so strong, but other cases I tried later in the sixties would not be that easy, or much fun.

5.

The Police
vs. Huey P. Newton

"Charles," said the voice on the telephone, "a brother is shot and in the hospital. He's charged with murder. I'd like you to defend him."

And that was how, through the urging of my friend Dr. Carleton B. Goodlett, physician and publisher of a black community newspaper, I got involved with Huey P. Newton, and the Black Panther party. I'd seen the banner headlines that late October day in 1967 announcing that a man named Huey P. Newton had shot and killed an Oakland policeman early that morning, and, somehow, as I had read the story, I'd had a feeling that I'd be called to defend him.

At that point I knew very little about Newton and even less about the Panthers. Beverly Axelrod, the attorney who had secured Eldridge Cleaver's release from prison, arranged for me to see Huey Newton in Highland Hospital in Oakland, the halls of which were full of heavily armed policemen. When they learned my purpose there, they looked at me with hostility and distrust. I had to go through several high-ranking officers before they would permit me to see Huey.

Shot in the stomach with a high-velocity bullet, he had lost much blood. Trachea tubes in his nose kept his lungs clear, and he was trying to shake off the effects of several days of sedation. Beverly introduced us, and Huey asked me to represent him. He told me the police threatened him constantly, saying, "You goddamned nigger, we're going to cut off this tube and save the state the trouble of gassing you." I had felt the depth of their hostility in the halls, and I had no trouble believing this, that it might even be carried out. So I suggested that we hire private nurses to watch Huey around the clock.

A few days later—on the grounds that there he could get better medical attention and be more secure—Huey was transferred to San Quentin. We protested, and he first was returned to Highland Hospital and then removed to an isolation cell in the county jail. For eleven months he was kept away from other prisoners, confined to a small stuffy cell.

I went to visit him. I wanted to get to know Huey, to understand the Black Panther party, its origins, its purposes. Huey suggested I read, among others, the writings of Malcolm X, Frantz Fanon's *Wretched of the Earth,* Richard Wright's *Listen, White Man, Listen.* Thus, over the Christmas holiday, I began my education in black history, deepening what had previously been only a superficial understanding. I re-read the works of W.E.B. DuBois, such as *Souls of Black Folk, Black Reconstruction, Black Folk Then and Now,* gaining new insight from them after my talks with Huey.

To offset the negative publicity the case had already stirred up, I arranged a series of press conferences so Huey could talk about the black liberation movement and explain why the Panthers felt that blacks should carry guns (for at that time it was legal in California to carry a gun in the streets if the weapon was not concealed), to tell why the Panthers had patrolled the black neighborhoods, armed, insisting that the police not harass black people. They would walk up to cops who were harassing people and say:

"Don't try to intimidate them. Arrest them if that's your job. We'll be down to bail them out."

They told the community:

"Submit to an arrest. Don't give any arguments. Give only your name and address. We'll bail you out."

They carried tape recorders as well as guns—to have a record of what actually transpired on the steets.

This approach had engendered considerable hostility from the police and, to combat it, they had drawn up a list of Panther vehicles and a list of the people patrolling in them. Newton's name topped the list; he had been stopped more than fifty times before the October shooting.

In addition, the powerful *Oakland Tribune,* published by former Senator William F. Knowland, was proceeding on the assumption that Newton was guilty of killing Officer John Frey. Although the defense had a right to request a change of venue,* we elected to remain in Alameda County, concluding that no other would be better in terms of pre-trial publicity. Also, nearly forty percent of Oakland's population was black; they at least would understand what the Black Panther party was all about.

ATTACKING THE GRAND JURY SYSTEM

The grand jury was born in England to serve as a buffer between citizens and governmental tyranny. But, by the early 1900s, the British had found out that the system only encouraged unfair governmental prosecutions and, in 1930, it was abolished by Parliament. But grand juries survive in the United States. In California, prosecutors may use them at will. There are no guidelines governing what cases may be brought before a grand jury. In 97 percent of felony cases, a complaint is filed in municipal court and a preliminary hearing is held. Both the accused and his lawyer can attend, and the defense attorney can cross-examine the prosecution witnesses. The judge then decides if there was probable cause that the accused committed the felony and sends the case to trial, or he dismisses the charges for insufficient evidence or on constitutional or legal grounds. But people brought before a grand jury cannot bring counsel into the room with them, nor can attorneys cross-examine witnesses. In addition, grand juries were selected from among friends and acquaintances of judges earning $35,000 a year or more.

Therefore, an early legal move of ours was to attack the composition of the all-white grand jury which had indicted Huey. We moved to dismiss the indictment on the grounds that the grand jury did not represent a cross-section of the county's population. We held that it had been hand-picked from among the "cronies" of the judges, a deliberate choice of wording on my part that irritated the judges considerably. Newton's people—the working poor, the unemployed, those on welfare—were not members of grand juries. Our motion to throw out the indictment was turned down, but we had shown the public that the judicial system was not as impartial as it was made out to be. We also had given additional impetus to the criticism of the

---

*A change of venue is to have the trial held in another county because of alleged inability to secure a fair trial in the original county (where the incident occurred) due to negative public opinion or publicity.

grand jury system by some of our leading jurists who hold that it is an unhealthy, unwise system that should be abolished.

The case was to come to trial on April 10, 1968. From a transcript of the grand jury hearing, I learned Newton had been indicted for the murder of Officer John Frey, for assault with a deadly weapon on Officer Herbert Heanes, and for kidnapping Dell Ross, a young black man.

Heanes was the only eyewitness and he, with no defense lawyer to challenge him, had told the grand jury he never saw a gun in Newton's hand.

Ross's testimony to the grand jury ran as follows. He did not see the shooting but heard a series of shots as he sat in his car with a friend near Seventh and Willow at about five that Saturday morning. His friend jumped out to investigate, leaving the passenger door open, and two young black men jumped in—one in front, one in back—ordering him to drive to another part of Oakland. He protested, and the man in the back, who seemed to be bleeding and holding his stomach in pain, pointed a pistol at his head, saying, "Drive me to Thirty-second and Chestnut."

The man in front said, "You shot two dudes," to which the man in back replied, "I would have kept on firing if my gun hadn't jammed." Ross drove several miles, then they jumped out and disappeared down an alley.

This was the basis for the kidnapping charge, which was almost as serious as the murder charge. California no longer had the death penalty for kidnapping, but a conviction could mean a twenty-five-years-to-life prison term.

Heanes told the grand jury that Frey had stopped Newton's car shortly before five, that he himself had arrived as a backup to find Frey writing a ticket and Newton sitting in the driver's seat with another black man beside him.

According to Heanes's testimony, Frey then placed Newton under arrest ordering him out of the car, and they walked past Frey's car to the rear of Heanes's car where a scuffle broke out. Heanes heard several shots. When he drew his gun, he was shot in the right arm. Shifting the pistol to his left hand, he fired directly at Newton's midsection. Shortly after firing he was shot twice. Though blacking out, he remembered crawling to Frey's car and radioing for help. He then lost consciousness but revived long enough to tell arriving officers, "Huey Newton did it," and to say he may have wounded him. With that, he blacked out again.

The testimony of a badly wounded officer recalling what he saw at a distance in predawn darkness was sufficient to indict Newton for murder and hold him without bail. None of the grand jurors asked any questions—although they have that right—nor did the judge.

PRE-TRIAL INVESTIGATION

After studying the grand jury transcript, we began our investigation with a discovery motion for the list of prospective prosecution witnesses. None of the police witnesses would talk with us, including Heanes, who said, "Whatever I have to say, I'll tell you from the witness stand."

We did interview police criminalist John Davis, a man of integrity and a first-rate scientist.

Davis had concluded that Frey had been shot five times. Three bullets struck him from the front and two were fired into his back at close range. One of the latter bullets had caused massive bleeding in his chest cavity, killing him. He determined by analyzing the gunpowder on Frey's uniform that the bullets were from two different .38 caliber pistols; some were from Frey's own gun, while the others were probably from Heanes's gun.

The analysis showed flake and ball powder both present. Flake powder is used in standard .38 caliber police bullets and the unexpended rounds in Heanes's revolver were filled with flake powder. Frey's gun was missing, but the bullets found in his gun belt were not standard. Frey had been using high-velocity bullets, which do far more damage than the standard police bullet, and these rounds were packed with ball powder.

Two 9-millimeter shell casings were found at the scene and a 9-millimeter bullet was found in the Volkswagen, but no gun was found to match them. *This indicated that someone else at the scene had been shooting, probably at Heanes, because Frey was only hit by .38 caliber bullets.*

After the interviews, we began investigating the actual scene, usually at five, the approximate time of the shooting. I was always accompanied by several Panthers so that people wouldn't be afraid to talk to me. Reading the transcript, one got the impression that there were just four people present in a lonely part of town. Actually, the opposite was true. Although the south side of Seventh Street was deserted, the north side was teeming with activity because directly across from the south-side construction site were all-night soul-food restaurants, bars, a pool hall, and several houses of prostitution—an area where people congregated after hours. Newton had been going to one of the restaurants when Frey had stopped his car. Once the fracas started any number of people could possibly have shot Frey.

Frey had only been twenty-three, and a policeman for less than two years when he stopped Huey. We learned he was a racist and a bully, was disliked in the black community. We found people willing to testify to that.

All calls from patrol cars to police headquarters are taped: we subpoenaed the tapes. They showed that Frey spotted Newton's car at 4:51 and stopped it moments later.

"It's a known Black Panther vehicle," Frey had said as he requested information on it.

A bloody law book, a volume of California criminal codes, had been found at the scene. It was placed in the trunk of a police car by investigating officers, probably on the supposition that it belonged to Frey or Heanes. When the book was opened, Newton's signature was on the inside cover and a stamp indicated he had purchased the book at Merritt College, where he had been a student.

The book, found behind the second police car (the one on which Heanes had said Newton and Frey had fought), indicated that Newton had been holding the book. It would have been difficult for him to hold a thick book and a large revolver at the same time. The crime lab had made no effort to determine whose blood was on the book, nor had they conducted tests to determine if either Newton or Frey had fired a gun. The police had access to Newton and to Frey's body within an hour of the shooting, and the mobile crime lab could easily have conducted such tests.

As the trial date approached, we began to assemble our defense team. Fay Stender, a member of our firm, became co-counsel and assisted me during the trial. In addition, we had two volunteer attorneys, Ed Keating, former publisher of *Ramparts,* and Alex Hoffman of Berkeley, and two legal assistants, John Escobedo and Carlton Innes.

During this time the Panthers had been trying to make people aware of the forthcoming trial, of Huey's role in the Black Liberation Movement. Bobby Seale and Eldridge Cleaver were in demand as speakers, and wherever they went they spoke of Huey, police oppression, and the need for blacks to attain self-determination and personal dignity. The slogan FREE HUEY became a rallying cry to

Black Panther party chapters springing up all over America. Despite these efforts, however, we felt that too few people really understood the aims and goals of the Black Panther party. We therefore encouraged Huey to give interviews, and I personally spoke to anyone who sought me out, for we had to counter the notion that the party was nothing but a gang of angry young blacks running amok with guns. There were serious reasons for the guns, and we wanted this known and understood. This was a political case—the defendant on trial for his beliefs as much as for the alleged crime—and in such instances it is vital to project the right image of these ideas in interviews and in speeches outside the courtroom, but also in the trial itself. To do otherwise only plays into the prosecutor's hands and is an invitation to disaster.

TRAGEDY INTERVENES

Only six days before Newton's trial was to begin, on April 4, 1968, Dr. Martin Luther King, Jr., was shot and killed in Memphis, Tennessee. The black community in Oakland erupted in explosive anger.

Soon, heavy police patrols roamed through the streets and the black sector of Oakland looked like it was under occupation. Riot-equipped police stood on almost every corner. Those who ventured outside were stopped and searched.

And then, on April 6, just two days after the assassination of Dr. King and four days before the trial I received a telephone call telling me there had been yet another shooting in Oakland. The seventeen-year-old treasurer of the Panthers, Bobby Hutton, had been killed. Several Panthers had been wounded, others had been arrested. Two policemen had been wounded.

When I arrived at the Oakland police station I discovered that the wounded included both Eldridge Cleaver and Panther Warren Wells. Arrested also were David Hilliard, the Panthers' chief-of-staff and five other Panthers. They were being held on $100,000 bail each.

To further complicate matters, Cleaver's parole was to be revoked; he was to be returned to prison as soon as his wounds healed. Hutton had been shot in the head as he and Cleaver had tried to surrender.

There was no choice but to attempt to postpone Newton's case. Due to the huge amount of adverse publicity concerning this second shooting and the hostile atmosphere it had produced, we were able to get a postponement until July 15. Our firm had already committed itself to defending the Panthers who had survived the April shooting, as well as to try to get Cleaver out of prison. Cleaver was desperately needed for our effort to get the Panther story abroad—not only was he an accomplished public speaker, but also he was in demand since his book *Soul on Ice* had been published to wide acclaim. However, the Adult Authority, acting arbitrarily and without a hearing, as was its wont and right, had revoked Cleaver's parole, making him ineligible for bail.

Early in June we filed a writ of habeas corpus contesting this decision. Our petition came before Raymond Sherwin, an extremely able jurist who was a superior court judge in Solano County. We charged the Adult Authority with disgraceful treatment of patrolees, citing its nearly unlimited power, against Cleaver's excellent parole record (his parole officer was going to recommend he be taken off parole at the end of the year). We gave evidence to show that Cleaver was employed (by *Ramparts*), was the author of a best-selling book, was economically self-sufficient, had married. We contended he had been imprisoned on political grounds without benefit of a trial, that he was entitled to the presumption of innocence. The courtroom was crowded with those who had come to lend their support, including prominent writers and political figures.

Judge Sherwin ruled that the Adult Authority's action had indeed been arbitrary, that it appeared to be based more on Cleaver's speeches and writings than on anything else, and he ordered him released immediately on bail.

That evening there was jubilation among us—not only because we had secured Cleaver's release, but also because, for the first time, a judge had had the temerity to challenge the Adult Authority and overrule it.

THE JUDGE

The Newton case was assigned to Monroe Friedman, known as a no-nonsense judge, who, at seventy-two, acted as if he were on the Supreme Court.

Had he wished, Friedman could have declined to try the case, by citing his seniority or his age. We, on the other hand, could have challenged him preemptorily as in California each side has one preemptory challenge regarding judges. Judges can also be disqualified for cause; for example, several were removed from the Angela Davis trial because of the defense's contention of bias.

Though I felt Friedman wanted to see Newton convicted, and I knew he could be strict and haughty in court, I felt he would let us try our case fairly—we could live with him. There were worse, more biased, less competent judges in Alameda County, and I had heard via the courthouse grapevine that there were several of these waiting in the wings. Some attorneys operate on the theory that an incompetent judge is preferable at the trial level, that he will make errors that can be used on appeal to reverse a conviction. But only one in a hundred cases is overturned on appeal, and that's an awful chance to take.

THE TRIAL—FIRST DAY

The atmosphere that surrounded the beginning of the trial on July 15, 1968, can only be described as terrifyingly tense. Not only had King been killed, but also Robert Kennedy had been assassinated early in June. The FREE HUEY campaign had resulted in a lot of public support, and, on opening day, thousands gathered outside the courthouse. A contingent of Panthers in black leather jackets and black berets led the crowd in a series of chants. Although these demonstrations took place at a side entrance, getting into the courthouse still wasn't easy. Outside, heavily armed sheriff's deputies patrolled. Every door leading in was locked. No one was admitted without proper identification. More than a hundred news people vied for the twenty-eight seats accorded to the media. Each person, except the lawyers, who entered the courtroom was searched thoroughly. During recesses the courtroom was locked and armed deputies guarded the halls. I had never before encountered such a highly strung trial atmosphere, and I was fearful it would inevitably effect the attitudes of the jurors.

As every trial in the United States is supposed to be public, I made a motion to move the trial across the street to the Oakland Auditorium to accommodate the media and spectators, for there were fewer than thirty seats available to the public, but Judge Friedman turned me down.

A MOTION FOR THE DEFENSE

I made a second motion, this one crucial. It concerned an earlier conviction of Newton for assault with a deadly weapon—a felony. Previously, Huey had had several scrapes with the law, all minor except this one, the result of a fight at a party. He had defended himself in the misdemeanor trials, and, emboldened with his legal successes, he defended himself in the felony trial, something the trial judge should not have permitted. Naturally, he was no match for the experienced prosecutor, and he was convicted, being sentenced, however, only to three years probation, which was to have ended on October 27, 1967. Technically, therefore, he was an ex-felon, and as such could draw a longer jail term even if convicted on a lesser charge. We had to challenge this conviction on the grounds it had been illegally obtained, that Newton had not been represented by a lawyer at the trial nor on appeal. If the prior felony conviction was allowed to stand, it could be used to attack Huey's credibility when he testified. If a defendant has only been convicted of misdemeanors, the prosecution may not bring his arrest record into the trial. However, once convicted of a felony, his entire past, misdemeanors, felonies, etc. can be used against him if he testifies.

Furthermore, we learned that the prosecution was planning to contend that Huey was still on probation when Frey stopped his car, and in an attempt to avoid having his probation revoked for possessing marijuana, Huey shot Frey. Therefore, we argued at length that the 1964 conviction be disallowed, but Judge Friedman and presiding Judge Lewis Lecara both turned us down.* During the noon recess, we took the matter first to the District Court of Appeals in San Francisco, and then to the California Supreme Court, but were denied once more. We had asked that recent federal court decisions requiring that a defendant be advised of his right not to testify be retroactively applied to Huey's 1964 case.

THE VOIR-DIRE

The voir-dire is the part of the trial when prospective jurors are questioned about their qualifications to sit on the jury. The purpose is to uncover bias or vested interest. In California, the voir-dire takes place before the entire jury panel; when one juror is questioned, the others can hear. This enables them to formulate their answers in advance.

When the first jury panel of forty-five persons came in, we challenged it in its entirety on the grounds that blacks, other minorities,

*Ironically, several years later in 1971, in a cooler emotional climate, another Alameda County judge declared the felony conviction null and void.

and the poor were inadequately represented. After this, we made moves to prove that it would be impossible to pick an unbiased jury in Alameda County. To this end we made three motions.

As the master jury panel is drawn from voter registration lists, we first heard the testimony of Jan Dizard, a University of California sociologist who had made a study of voter registration patterns in Alameda County. His findings showed the lowest percentage to be in West Oakland, the predominately black community where Huey Newton lived. Then we cited the Kerner Report, which had just been released, on the 1967 urban riots. The report concluded that "white racism" was a primary cause and that it was prevalent everywhere in American society.

Our second motion referred to the history of the Fair Housing Act, passed by the California legislature in 1963, which prohibited property owners from refusing to sell to certain persons because of race, color, or national origin. The act was repealed by the voters in 1964 by a general margin of two to one, but in Alameda County the margin had run as high as nine to one.

The third step was to call in Dr. Bernard Diamond, on whom we had successfully relied before. Dr. Diamond was by now a professor of law and criminology at the University of California, and he testified that it would be impossible to determine, in the time allotted to each individual during the voir-dire (less than an hour) whether a person was prejudiced. He went on to explain that no human being is totally without bias but said that once aware of the bias the individual can make the appropriate allowances so as not to color his judgment.

However, all the motions were turned down by Judge Friedman so there was nothing to do but start picking the jury, and the voir-dire began.

We had accepted that we would not get an unbiased jury, and in preparation for the voir-dire we had drawn up a list of 290 possible questions to make the jurors aware of their own racism and to educate them to understand racism in America and how it oppresses those who suffer from it.

A number of sociologists and psychologists had volunteered to sit with us through the voir-dire to consult about the acceptability of each juror.

As we had expected, the prosecutor, Lowell Jensen, saved his preemptory challenges for the few blacks on the panel. Each time,

I would rise and state, "Let the record show that Mr. or Mrs. X is a black person."

Fortunately for us, about a week before the trial began five young black men had gone on trial in another Alameda County courtroom. The district attorney had systematically challenged every black juror. When the jury selection ended, the judge, George W. Phillips, declared a mistrial on the grounds that the prosecutor obviously had been racist in selecting jurors. This had an effect on the prosecution's strategy in our case. They decided to leave one black person on the jury, a man named David Harper, a lending officer at the Bank of America in San Francisco. His wife was head of security at the bank's main office in Oakland. They lived in a predominately white part of town. However, it looked as if Harper would be more likely to sympathize with the prosecutor than with Newton.

Jensen was also challenging Berkeley people and those with reservations about capital punishment, for cause. After the grand jury challenge, we had filed a motion on jurors' attitudes toward capital punishment as we knew the prosecution would challenge prospective jurors opposed to the death penalty, for cause.* Our aim was to obtain a ruling allowing people opposed to capital punishment to be on the jury panel. At the very least, we hoped to force the prosecution to use its preemptory challenges to remove them. As the defense could not challenge for cause those who *favored* the death penalty, this seemed only equitable. We had high expectations because of the Witherspoon case.†

To bolster our argument, we asked Dr. Hans Zeisel, Professor of Law and Sociology at the University of Chicago, to fly to California

---

*There are two types of challenges: for cause and preemptory. Each side gets the same fixed number of preemptories, twenty in the Newton case. To exclude jurors for cause, however, you must prove bias or prejudice, though there are no limits on challenges for cause. It was common practice for prosecutors to move to exclude opponents of capital punishment for cause, and for judges routinely to grant such motions.

†Tried by a jury from which all death penalty opponents had been excluded, Witherspoon had been convicted and sentenced to die. The Supreme Court reversed his conviction because of the exclusion, saying that prospective jurors in capital cases had to be asked: "Despite your opposition to capital punishment, could you consider it?" If they answered affirmatively, the Court ruled, they could not be excluded for cause.

to offer expert testimony on the difficulties of a defendant getting a fair trial from a pro-death-penalty jury. Dr. Zeisel, co-author of *The American Jury** had been studying juries since 1953. He testified that jurors favoring capital punishment were likely to vote guilty on the first ballot, that they placed far greater credence in authority figures —policemen, doctors, government officials—than in those lacking such credentials.

The motion was denied, but I believe that the mere fact that we filed it, supported it with expert testimony, and cited the Witherspoon decision had a positive effect on the attitude of the trial judge.

When Jensen challenged a juror the judge would ask, "Aren't there any circumstances upon which you would ever vote for the death penalty?" If the answer was no, he would ask further, "Can't you think of some outlandish situation in which you could vote for the death penalty? What if someone killed your child?" If there was a slight hesitation, or if the person said he might consider it, Friedman would deny Jensen's challenge for cause.

Our biggest problem was to weed out the covert as well as the overt prejudices. We knew that people with anti-Panther biases were trying to get on the jury. We also tried to find out which ones really understood the Panther party and which believed the stereotype. It wasn't easy. Thirteen of the first twenty had a friend or relative in law-enforcement work, yet some of these claimed they could be impartial. And so it went. Into the third week, when Jensen had used six fewer preemptories than we had, and we had only three left, Fay Stender and one of our consulting sociologists suggested that we accept the jury as it was constituted. But I opposed the suggestion. We went on until we had exhausted our preemptory challenges and beyond—for days we were without any preemptories and as a result I finally accepted a jury with a few people on it I would not want to have lunch with let alone have them decide Huey's fate. Nevertheless, it was a better jury than we had when it was first suggested we stop. The final panel consisted of seven whites, one Asian-American, three people with Hispanic names, and David Harper, the one black juror.

**The American Jury*, Harry Klaven, Jr., and Hans Zeisel (New York: Little Brown & Co., 1966).

THE KIDNAP VICTIM

Early in the voir-dire I learned that Dell Ross, the black man who had told the grand jury two black men forced him to drive them away from Seventh and Willow streets on the morning of October 28, 1967, had been located by our investigator. Besides being the only black witness against Newton that we knew about, he was the only person who claimed to have seen a gun in Newton's hand.

He came to my office on a Saturday morning. I informed him I was taping the conversation and that I would play back the tape in case there was anything he wanted to change. After I replayed the tape I advised him to get a lawyer to represent him at the trial.

SURPRISE WITNESS

With jury selection ended, we finally received the complete list of prosecution witnesses we had been demanding for months. Immediately we understood why Jensen had been so reluctant to release it! On it was a witness who had not testified before the grand jury, who was not a police officer. His name was Henry Grier, and he was a black bus driver, a veteran of twenty years in the Navy, who claimed to have seen the entire incident. In a statement given to the police ninety minutes after the shooting, he had identified the man who shot Frey. Clearly Jensen was placing his hopes for a first-degree murder conviction on this man's testimony. Grier was the perfect disinterested witness, but he was a puzzle to us. We had come across no mention of a bus during our pre-trial investigation. There was no mention of a bus in the testimony of four policemen who went before the grand jury, none in a dozen police reports. Jensen had been hiding Grier from us, so we went looking for him, but until the day he walked into the courtroom he could not be found. We tried calling him, but his phone had been temporarily disconnected. We had someone sitting on his doorstep from the afternoon we received his statement, but neither he, nor any member of his family ever showed up.

DEATH THREATS

It was August before we were ready with opening statements, and by then the tensions had reached fever pitch. Right-wing and law-

and-order groups were demanding that Huey be sent to the gas chamber; left-wing and liberal organizations were demanding he be set free. All the Bay Area police departments were stirred up by the case and its attendant publicity.

At the beginning of the trial I received numerous death threats. These came with such regularity and were so vituperative that the Panthers decided, over my vociferous protests, to provide me with a twenty-four-hour body guard. After a few days I found that my protection was interfering with my work and, after a long discussion with Huey, I persuaded him to withdraw them. Then, late one evening as I was leaving Oakland after a long day working on the voir-dire, I was pulled to the curb by what I thought to be a police car. I stepped outside and the three men in ordinary civilian dress inside the car began calling me, among other things, a cop-killing lawyer —getting out of the car, they said they were going to teach me a lesson. I hadn't forgotten my days in Selma: I quickly bashed two of their heads together and the three jumped into their car and drove off.

Moments later an Oakland police sergeant came by. I told him what had happened but he did not believe me. I was certain the trio were off-duty cops. I could tell by their mannerisms, their clothes, their shoes, the way they talked, but I did not pursue the matter for I was equally certain that I would get no cooperation from the Oakland police.

OPENING STATEMENTS

Monday, August 5, 1968: Jensen, more emotional than usual, said he intended to prove that Newton had willfully, intentionally, and maliciously killed Frey and that, after killing Frey, he had shot Heanes; that, while escaping, he had commandeered an automobile and its occupant, kidnapping the driver. He hardly mentioned the Black Panther party, telling the jury that the two police officers had been shot while on normal patrol duty.

My opening statement followed Jensen's.* I told the jury about Huey's family and his background. His father was a minister, but worked as a laborer to maintain his family of seven children of which

---

*In California, the defense attorney can make his opening statement right after the prosecutor or later on when he opens the defense case. I always like to follow the district attorney, to take the sting out of his remarks.

Huey was the youngest. Though Huey had finished high school he had there learned neither to read nor to write, teaching himself those basic skills after leaving school and going on to Merritt College where he became active in the Black Liberation Movement. Afterward, he had entered law school and then he and Bobby Seale had founded the Black Panther party, which had first been called the Black Panther Party for Self-Defense. I read the party's entire ten-point platform into the record, ending with point ten, which read: *We want land, bread, housing, education, clothing, justice, and peace.*

The jury learned from me that because of its position on police brutality and its insistence on implementing the constitutional right to bear arms, the Panther Party had become a hated symbol to the Oakland police.

"The Oakland police made a list of all Panther automobiles. The evidence will show that they took pictures of people who were active, especially Huey Newton, the founder and minister of defense. The result was . . . that there wasn't a single person in the Oakland police department who didn't know the name Huey Newton, didn't know him by his picture."

I reviewed the events of the morning of the killing, noting that Frey had radioed, "I'm stopping a known Panther vehicle."

"The evidence will show that Officer Frey stopped Huey Newton for no reason whatsoever. It was entirely unnecessary, and was a form of harassment. . . . This case was nothing more than a conspiracy to destroy the Black Panther party."

My opening statement lasted two hours.

THE PROSECUTION'S CASE

Dr. George Loquvam, the first witness, was the autopsy surgeon. He testified that Frey had been shot five times. One bullet grazed his elbow, two entered from the front, two from the back. The bullet that killed him was fired into his back and caused massive hemorrhaging.

On cross-examination, I asked Dr. Loquvam to trace the trajectory of the bullets that passed through Frey's back. They had passed upward through his body, exiting from his chest. As will be seen, this seemingly minor point was crucial to our case.

Cross-examination of Roland DeHoyas, the first policeman on the scene after the shooting, was brief, but hit an important point in the prosecution's case.

"What did you do with Officer Frey's gun?" I asked.

"I never saw his gun."

"Did you look for it?"

"No, sir."

"You were the first person on the scene?"

"Yes, sir."

A major problem for Jensen was that Frey's revolver was never found. Officer Heanes, when called to testify, tried to help him out. Heanes had told the grand jury, "Mr. Newton spun around and I heard some shooting." He then volunteered that he never saw a gun in Newton's hand. At the trial however, he stated that "Newton turned around and started shooting," a remarkable feat for a man without a gun. Jensen never asked him if he saw a gun in Huey's hand. Heanes also neglected to mention on direct examination that he blacked out several times during the incident.

Heanes testified that when he arrived on the scene he found Frey in his patrol car writing out a ticket. Just in front was the tan Volkswagen occupied by two black males. Frey had told Heanes that the driver of the car had identified himself as LaVerne Williams, but when Heanes went to the car and asked, "Mr. Williams, do you have some more identification?" the driver immediately had informed him that he was Huey P. Newton. Seconds later, Frey came up and told Newton he was under arrest for failure to identify himself and for giving false information to a police officer. Newton got out of the car and began walking back toward the patrol cars with Frey following. (Newton is five feet ten inches and weighed 165; Frey was over six feet tall, weighing well over 200.) Heanes said that when Newton reached the second patrol car he suddenly spun around and shot at Frey. The two men were at arms length, Newton facing Heanes and Frey with his back to Heanes. Heanes attempted to draw his own revolver but when so doing he was shot through the right arm. He then saw Frey lunge at Newton and the pair begin wrestling on the trunk of the second patrol car. He heard several more shots, shifted his pistol to his left hand, and, down on one knee, aimed at Newton's midsection and fired. The passenger in the Volkswagen threw his empty hands in the air. Seconds later Heanes was shot in the chest, but managed to radio for help before blacking out.

My cross-examination was designed to get our theory of the shooting over to the jury—namely that Heanes himself had shot Frey with a wild bullet.

"Officer Heanes, did you shoot and kill Officer Frey?"

"No, sir, I did not."

"It is a fact though, isn't it, that you shot Officer Frey?"

"No, sir."

"Isn't it a fact that you fired two shots from your gun?"

"I recall firing once."

"There were two shots expended, were there not, sir?"

"I have been told this, yes."

"What happened to the other shot?"

"I have no idea, sir."

"Now when you say you shot Huey Newton in the midsection, did you see whether your aim had taken hold?"

"No, sir, I did not."

"As a matter of fact, when you made that shot, the only person who fell . . . was Officer Frey, isn't that right?"

"I didn't see anybody fall."

"You never at any time saw a gun in the hand of Huey Newton, did you, sir?"

"No, sir, I did not."

Then I had Heanes demonstrate how, while down on one knee, shaken by a bullet wound, he had transferred the gun to his left hand and fired from about thirty feet. I asked him to place Newton in the same position, to place me where Frey had been. We positioned ourselves in front of the jury box following Heanes's directions. It seemed that Heanes could have hit Frey as easily as he could have hit Huey.

"You were rendered unconscious?"

"I don't know whether I went unconscious or not. I have a lapse of memory. I fired the shot and the next thing I recall was lying in the police car."

"After you fired, Newton was standing up and so was Frey, isn't that right?"

"Yes, sir."

"And Huey Newton did not have any firearm in his hand?"

"I did not see one."

Cross-examination of Heanes lasted almost an entire day. He admitted that Newton had done nothing to warrant being placed under arrest, and this cast considerable doubt upon Frey's motivation in writing out a ticket. Heanes said he saw a vehicle registration but no license in Frey's possession.

"Why didn't you ask to see Newton's license?"

"I was already under the impression that he didn't have one."

During our investigation we had discovered that the police had the ticket that Officer Frey had begun to write out but did not complete. In the space for offense Frey had written NIP (not in possession of a driver's license). The ticket was written against LaVerne Williams, whose name was on the registration, but the address Frey had written down was 881 47th St., which was Huey's address, and which was on his driver's license. How could Frey have gotten that address if not from the license? The radio tapes showed he made no request for the address. We entered the ticket into evidence to impugn Frey's motives.

"What was Officer Frey writing a ticket about?"

"I have no idea."

"As a matter of fact, you and Officer Frey were trying to find some excuse to write a citation on him, isn't that right?" Here Jensen objected; Judge Friedman ordered me to reframe the question.

"Did the two of you discuss trying to find some violation to cite Mr. Newton for?"

"No, sir, I did not."

"Did you ask Frey why he was attempting to cite Mr. Newton?"

"No, I did not."

"Then as far as you knew, when you went to Frey's car, there had been no violation of any kind?"

"At the time I arrived, I was not aware that any violations had occurred."

"When did you frisk Mr. Newton and the passenger?"

"I didn't frisk either of them at any time."

"Why didn't you?"

"Well, everything had gone so calmly, I didn't feel any need to."

"You already knew who Huey P. Newton was?"

"I had seen his picture, yes."

"You knew, did you not, that you had to take certain precautions with the Panthers, according to the information you had received from your superiors?"

"I would take those precautions I deemed necessary."

The deeper we got into cross-examination, the more Heanes's credibility was strained. He said he was unsure of the color of Newton's coat. He first called it tan, but when I pressed him, he said it might have been brown. I had the coat brought in. It was black.

I asked if Heanes had got a good look at Newton. He said he had.
"He had a heavy beard at the time, isn't that right?"
"I don't believe so."
I showed him two pictures taken the morning of the arrest. Huey
had begun growing a beard and hadn't shaved for a week.

Heanes claimed he had no idea of the identity of the man in the
passenger seat. We believed the prosecution didn't yet know who the
man was. Even I didn't know. Only Huey knew, but he hadn't told
me because he didn't want to bring the man into the case unless it
was absolutely essential.

Heanes said he had not seen Newton reach between the front seats
of the VW and pick up a law book just before he got out. We brought
the book in, but Heanes said he had never seen it.

"He [Frey] didn't tell you why he was placing Huey Newton under
arrest, did he?"
"No, he did not."
"As a matter of fact, you were surprised that he placed him under
arrest, isn't that right?"
"No, I was not surprised."
"Because that's the way Officer Frey would act, isn't that why you
weren't surprised?"
"Not necessarily."

Frey had a reputation as a racist, a hothead, and a troublemaker,
not only in the black community but in the police department as
well. We would question every police officer about this who testified.
Our theory was that Frey deliberately provoked the incident by
trying to find some way he could arrest Newton, then shot him in the
stomach, touching off the general round of gunfire in which the
officer was killed.

"Why didn't you go and talk to the passenger when Newton
walked away, if that was your purpose?"
"Because I was watching Officer Frey and Newton walking toward
the cars."
"You knew Officer Frey was trying to do something to Huey Newton, isn't that right?"

Jensen just about had a fit. "Object to that your honor," he cried
out indignantly. Judge Friedman asked me to reframe the question.

"Was there something about Officer Frey's conduct toward Mr.
Newton that made you cautious and worried, so you did not carry out
your intent to talk to the passenger?"

Heanes pretended he didn't understand the question.

"Were you cautious and worried?" Judge Friedman interjected.

"Not by anything I thought Officer Frey might do."

"Was there something that worried you about what Huey Newton might do?"

"Not particularly. It's just standard procedure to cover an officer when he's walking somebody to a car."

It is not standard procedure, however, for policemen to place a suspect under arrest, especially one who has been publicly identified with guns, and neither frisk nor handcuff him. Only five months before, the Panthers had invaded the California legislature carrying weapons, and Huey Newton had been widely quoted about the black community's right to self-defense. So it seemed highly illogical that he'd be placed under arrest and not be either frisked or handcuffed, the more so as two white cops were arresting a black man in the heart of the ghetto. A frisk, of course, would have revealed whether Newton was carrying a gun.

Heanes had to admit that he didn't know where the original shot, the shot that had caused him to draw his weapon and which he believed Newton fired, came from.

"You thought he [the passenger] had shot you in the arm, isn't that right?"

"No, I did not."

"Then why did you turn around on him?"

"At that point there was gunfire and I was a little nervous about anybody in that area."

"It's a fact, is it not, sir, that you did not know where the gunfire was coming from?"

"I had an opinion as to where it was coming from."

"But you didn't know, did you?"

"I couldn't say for a fact, no."

Clarence Lord, the police radio operator at the time of the shooting, brought the tapes of the radio transmissions between Frey's car and police headquarters to court. From these tapes we were able to establish that Newton and his unidentified passenger were sitting in the borrowed Volkswagen from approximately 4:51 until 5:00 A.M., that the shooting occurred at about 5:06, and that there was an interval of about fifteen minutes between Frey's initial transmission about stopping Newton and Heanes's urgent call for help.

Officer Tom Fitzmaurice, the next witness, described the bloody scene at Seventh and Willow. As he removed Heanes from Frey's car, Heanes gasped, "Huey Newton did it." Fitzmaurice put this information on the police network along with Heanes's supposition that Newton was wounded. On direct examination, Fitzmaurice said Heanes had told him he thought he had hit Newton, and he said the same thing on cross-examination. I pulled out the police report he had filed only hours after the shooting; in it he had written that Heanes said, "I shot him but I don't know if I hit him." I had him read that part to the jury.

This was a consistent pattern all through the trial. Testimony was continually changed, evidence was sometimes tampered with. This was never more evident than with Henry Grier, Jensen's surprise witness.

Jensen led Grier through a superficial account of what he was supposed to have seen. He testified that, as he drove his bus west on Seventh Street from the corner of Willow, his headlights had picked out a policeman walking toward him holding a civilian by the arm, that he had been only three or four feet from them when he saw the civilian reach into his shirt and pull out a gun. The civilian and the officer struggled for the weapon and during the struggle the civilian fired the gun at another officer standing behind the first. As his bus passed the struggling men, he brought it to a stop, called the dispatch office to report the fight, and turned to his right in time to see the civilian fire several shots into the first officer, who fell forward. Then the civilian fled across Seventh Street.

At the end of direct examination, Grier stepped from the witness stand and walked to the defense table, and put his hands on Huey's shoulders to identify him as the gunman.

CROSS-EXAMINATION OF WITNESS GRIER

Grier was still a mystery to us. We knew only that he had been employed by AC Transit for two years. When I asked him where he had been all this time, I ran into a storm of objections from Jensen. Finally we ascertained that he had been given leave on the basis of an agreement between the bus company and the district attorney's office. He had then been put in protective custody at Lake Merritt Hotel, right on the lake, not far from the courthouse.

"Did you feel you needed protective custody?"

"No, sir, I didn't."

"Nobody was threatening your life?"

"No."

I let Grier retell his version of the incident once more, stopping him on a few details, but not really challenging him. I had him use me to show the jury how he had seen Newton turn and fire. He spun me around in the opposite direction from which Heanes had described, but I didn't call him on it.

He said it had been dark that Saturday morning, the weather hazy and overcast, but that hadn't affected his vision. He saw four people near the VW—two policemen and two civilians outside the car—when he first passed the scene going toward the starting point of his route, two blocks to the east. He was very sure of the time because he had a railroad watch that kept him on schedule—his run was to have begun at 4:58, and he was certain he was on time.

On the witness stand Grier made some subtle but important changes from his original statement to the police of which I had a copy. After an hour and a half of questioning, I started to bore in on him, asking him to describe the civilian who he said had shot Frey.

"He had on a dark jacket and a light shirt."

"Didn't he have a light tan jacket and a dark shirt on?"

"No, sir."

"I want you to think about this before you answer it. I'm going to ask you again. Isn't it a fact that the person you have described as the civilian had a dark shirt and a light tan jacket on?"

"No, sir. The outer garment was dark."

"How tall was the civilian?"

"From up in the coach, sir, to look down at an angle like that, I wouldn't dare say, sir."

"Isn't it a fact that the civilian was under five feet?"

"I do not know, sir."

"Would you say the civilian was heavy-set, thin, or otherwise?"

"I didn't pay close attention, counselor."

"Mr. Grier, you know that you're under oath, do you not?"

"I do, sir."

"Mr. Grier, you made a statement to Inspector McConnell on October 28, 1967, at about 6:38 A.M., didn't you?"

"That's right, sir."

"And in that statement, didn't you tell Inspector McConnell that the person involved was under five feet?"

"I could have, sir."

Grier was saved by the afternoon recess, but the next morning I hit him with another discrepancy asking if his bus hadn't been 90 or 120 feet (thirty or forty yards) from the shooting rather than the ten to thirty feet he had estimated the day before. Grier denied he'd been so far away. Once more I read from his statement.

" 'I saw the officer walking one guy toward the second patrol car and this guy was short, sort of a small-built fellow. Just as I approached to within thirty or forty yards, I noticed the man going into his jacket. . . .' "

In those two sentences lay three contradictions—the difference in how far away he was, his description of the man's size, and that the man had gone into his shirt for his gun. This last was a subtle but important difference.

Grier testified the assailant was of medium build. He denied having originally described the man as a little "pee wee fellow." I again read from his statement.

"Was he husky?" McConnell had asked.

"No," Grier had answered.

"Slender?"

"Sort of a pee wee type fellow, you might call him."

We caught him again on the question of a beard. Grier insisted the assailant was clean-shaven. The jury had already seen pictures of Huey, taken hours after the shooting, with a week's growth of beard.

Grier was positive that the man whose picture he'd picked out for Inspector McConnell was the man who had done the shooting, so I read his original answer to McConnell.

"I wouldn't say positive it was him, but they do resemble."

How Grier happened to pick out Newton's photo and why he couldn't properly identify the color of his clothes soon became apparent.

"Mr. Grier, you were shown five or six pictures, isn't that right?"

"That's right, sir."

"Then you were shown one with Huey Newton wearing a black shirt, isn't that right?"

"I don't recall, sir."

"Is this the picture that was shown you?"

"It could have been, sir."

"And you were also told that this was the wounded man, weren't you?"

"I was told, yes, sir."

"Were you told that the man in the picture was wounded and had been at the scene? Did Inspector McConnell tell you that?"

"I don't recall, sir."

"You just got through telling me you were told that."

"I was, sir."

So while the recording machine was off, McConnell had led the willing Grier into an identification of Newton, although it was plain that Grier's earlier description of the man at the scene in no way fit him. Grier continued to contradict himself as we questioned him. He said Frey had fallen forward on his face and was lying prone when shot in the back by the assailant. In his previous statement, however, he had said that Frey fell backwards and landed on his back. Obviously, a man lying on his back cannot be shot in the back, so that, too, had to be changed.

Grier also had to twist logic and probability to place himself closer to the scene. He said at the trial that he saw the shooting and the scuffle through his front windshield, then through the side door of the bus when he pulled parallel to Frey. He testified that he moved his bus past the scene slowly, bringing it to a halt just in front of the Volkswagen where Officer DeHoyas pulled in front of him. Since Grier claimed to be so close, I asked him a few questions which showed that although he couldn't describe either officer's face he nevertheless claimed he could identify Huey.

I asked him if any bullets or ricochets had hit the bus. He said none had. Now, all the other vehicles at the scene had been hit in some way, either by bullets or ricochets, but somehow this big bus, only two or three feet from the shooting, was unscathed.

Toward the end of cross-examination we received Grier's personnel file; in the eighteen months prior to the shooting he many times had been cited for being off-schedule. His assurance the day before that he was always on time was proved untrue by notations about his habitual non-adherence to schedules. We placed his records into evidence so the jury could examine them and see that Grier often ran ahead of schedule.

We never could understand Grier's motivation in giving fraudulent testimony. Perhaps he thought it might improve his position at the bus company or possibly one of his children might have been in trouble with the police. The changes in his story were too significant to be mere innocent embellishments—he had changed his story to make it dovetail with the prosecution's version of the shooting.

Jensen followed Grier's testimony with seven police witnesses.

Only Lt. Rowland Forte, who had searched the Volkswagen and found a live 9-millimeter bullet and a brown paper bag containing two matchboxes of marijuana had significant testimony. The bullet would be left to criminalist John Davis to discuss, but the marijuana was important because the prosecution was trying to claim that Huey shot Frey because he did not want the VW searched, because as an ex-felon on probation he could be sent to prison if found with marijuana in his possession.

Forte said he found the matchboxes in a paper bag under the driver's seat of the VW in a search that took place in a police garage nine hours after the shooting. He removed the matchboxes and placed them in an evidence envelope which he handed to a criminalist for evaluation. The paper bag in which the matchboxes were found was missing; Forte thought he might have inadvertently thrown it away. As there was no attempt made to find fingerprints on the bag before it was discarded, we were confronted with more missing evidence. The police made no effort to ascertain to whom the marijuana belonged, evidently assuming that it belonged to Huey, a supposition Jensen clearly expected the jury to believe.

DELL ROSS'S TESTIMONY

Dell Ross's testimony was especially important to the prosecution. He was black, he was the only person who claimed to have seen a gun in Newton's hand. You can imagine Jensen's surprise when at the trial the following took place:

"Now, on Saturday, October 28, 1967, at about five o'clock in the morning, where were you?"

"I was here in Oakland."

"At what place in Oakland?"

"I refuse to answer that question on the grounds it would incriminate. I don't want to say anything wrong."

"I ask the court to direct the witness to answer."

"Were you in Oakland about five o'clock on the morning of October 28, 1967?" asked Judge Friedman.

"I refuse to answer that question on the grounds of the Fifth Amendment," Ross answered looking straight ahead.

"There is no showing whatsoever that there is a Fifth Amendment privilege," Jensen fumed. "In addition to that, the witness has testified before a grand jury."

Pandemonium broke out in the courtroom. Doug Hill, the young attorney Ross had engaged, tried to get himself recognized, but Judge Friedman refused to allow him to speak. Finally the jury was sent from the courtroom and Hill argued that Ross could not be forced to testify just because he had testified to the grand jury, that if Ross were to testify he would incriminate himself. Therefore, he had a right to take the Fifth Amendment.

As the legal argument raged, the trial came to a standstill. Dell Ross sat quietly off to one side, listening to the judicial storm he had touched off. It had been established that he no longer owned the car Huey allegedly commandeered, that he had been working in a bowling alley, living in a cheap hotel. He now was in a very difficult legal position: as the victim of the alleged kidnap he couldn't claim the Fifth Amendment, but, if he now stated that he had lied to the grand jury, he could be indicted for perjury. On the other hand, if he was to testify that he hadn't been kidnapped he could be indicted as an accessory to murder. After hours of arguments, Judge Friedman stopped the trial and said it wouldn't continue until the Ross matter was settled.

The next morning Jensen moved to grant Ross immunity from prosecution and Friedman granted the motion. The immunity, however, had a catch. Though Ross couldn't be prosecuted for anything he might say that would incriminate him, he still could be indicted for perjury if his testimony proved to be untrue. He could also be cited for contempt of court if he continued to refuse to answer Jensen's questions.

Ross was called back to the witness stand but he refused to say more than that he had once owned a 1958 Ford convertible and had been in Oakland on October 28, 1967. When Jensen tried to question him further, he refused to answer, citing the Fifth Amendment. Over my heated objections, Jensen then began asking Ross all the questions he had answered before the grand jury.

By this time Judge Friedman was pleading with Ross to answer: "Mr. Ross, you cannot be prosecuted for anything you testify to in this matter. Do you understand that?" he said, and Ross nodded affirmatively. Friedman then asked Ross if he intended to refuse to answer all questions pertaining to the morning of October 28, 1967. Ross said he did.

"All right," said the judge. "Do you understand that it is the duty of the court then to find you guilty of contempt and send you to jail?"

"I can understand that," Ross said.

"You do understand?" Judge Friedman repeated, as if Ross were not quite intelligent enough to comprehend what was happening.

"I can understand that," Ross replied evenly.

Friedman seemed satisfied that he had done all he could to make the witness talk. He had begun to explain the contempt sentence when Jensen interrupted him.

"May I ask this, your honor?" Jensen spoke directly to Ross, who was now slouching down in the witness chair.

"Mr. Ross, do you remember what happened on the morning of October 28?"

I could see what Jensen was getting at and immediately rose to object, but Judge Friedman cut me off. He, too, had seen what Jensen was suggesting.

"If he doesn't remember," the judge said, shrugging his shoulders, "it may be that is his answer."

I tried to object again, but Ross must have sensed that the judge and the prosecutor were leading him through a legal loophole.

"I can't remember what happened," he said quickly before I could fully state my objection.

"The witness says he can't remember what happened," Friedman declared with an air of resignation. "Now that is not the same thing. Now the fact is that you don't remember what happened that morning. Is that it?"

"I can't remember anything that happened eight or nine months ago."

Ross was now on safe legal ground, and I had no objection to that. I had no interest in seeing him go to jail. Someone can be found in contempt if they refuse to answer, but they can't be jailed if they don't remember what happened. Jensen and the judge had thrown Ross a legal lifeline, and intuitively he had grabbed it. That was fine with me, but I knew what Jensen would do next, and that I wanted to prevent.

Throwing a key witness in jail would have done the prosecution no good at all. It would have cast a pall over their other witnesses. Furthermore, Ross was black and jailing him would only confirm a central thesis of the pre-trial part of our own case—that a black man could not receive justice in Alameda County. That was another reason Jensen was not anxious to send Ross to jail.

Jensen now began reading from Ross's grand jury testimony, ostensibly to refresh his memory. Even if Ross continued not to remember, this device would enable Jensen to read all of Ross's grand jury testimony to the jury. I knew Jensen was trying to use this gimmick, and I objected, citing a recent higher court decision overturning a conviction for exactly the same thing the judge and prosecutor were now attempting to do.

Friedman read the case I cited very quickly, but he ruled that Jensen could read all the testimony before the jury to see if Ross remembered any of it. This allowed the jurors to hear highly prejudicial information which ultimately would have to be stricken from the record, which theoretically would have no bearing on the case. The jurors heard statements which Ross had attributed to Huey—"I'm too mean to die," and "I would have kept on shooting if my gun hadn't jammed"—though they would be told to disregard them.

We could not cross-examine Ross because he was refusing to answer all questions, but when Jensen finished reading the grand jury testimony I showed Ross the picture of Newton which Grier had identified. I asked him if he had ever seen it before.

"I don't remember seeing no picture like that before."

Then I asked him if he recalled being in my office in San Francisco on the morning of July 28, 1968, at about 9:25.

"I can't remember."

"He can't remember that either?" Judge Friedman commented as if amazed. "That was just a few weeks ago. Do you remember being in Mr. Garry's offices?"

"I don't know. I don't know where his office is at. I go in a lot of offices."

Of course Ross remembered being in my office, and of course he remembered what had happened down at Seventh and Willow. Jensen knew it, Friedman knew it, we all knew it. Ross's lawyer had even informally told the judge that Ross remembered but was really pleading the Fifth Amendment. The whole thing was a travesty.

We then hooked up a tape recorder and began playing the tape I had made in my office. I am asking the questions and Ross is answering them.

Q. I understand that you made a statement to the police before you testified at the grand jury. Is that correct?

A. Yes. That's correct. Ask me a few words.

Q. All right. Now was the statement that you testified to in the grand jury correct and true?

A. I take the Fifth Amendment because I couldn't be positive.

Q. In other words, what you're saying to me is that you don't believe that the testimony that you gave to the grand jury was true. Is that right?

A. That's right, because at the time I was too frightened to talk. I had a warrant on me at the time.

Q. You had a warrant on you?

A. That's true.

Q. What kind of warrant?

A. It was some parking tickets.

Q. And you were scared and you went along with whatever they had you say. Isn't that right?

A. That's right, because I'm just awful. Everywhere I've been, I've been treated kind of cold. I'm not proud about what I said to them.

Q. All right. Let me ask you this. In this police report it says that the man with the light skin and bushy hair got in the back seat. He had been hurt and he pointed a black pistol at you and said, "I want you to drive me over on Thirty-second Street." Is that true? Or not true?

A. Well, it's not true because the dark-skinned man had a gun in his—I can't call what it is.

Q. Inside of his pants?

A. Yes.

Q. All right. Now when you talk about the dark-skinned man, he's the man who was sitting next to you. Is that right?

A. That's right.

Q. The passenger who was sitting next to you?

A. That's the passenger sitting next to me.

Q. Now the man in the back, the light-skinned man, did he have a gun at any time that you saw him?

A. No, I didn't see him with no gun. He was kinda out.

Q. He was kind of what?

A. He was kind of out like.

Q. In other words, he was sick?

A. I would think something was wrong with him.

Q. He wasn't talking at all?

A. He didn't say anything at all that I can remember and I didn't pay no attention to him because I was driving. I didn't look back in the car.

Q. Now, he didn't say "I just shot two dudes," did he?

A. He didn't say anything.

Q. Did he say that he'd been hit in the stomach? Did he also say that he stopped shooting because his gun jammed? He didn't say anything like that, did he?

A. The man haven't said anything that I can remember.

We provided each juror and every media representative with a complete transcript of the tape. Even from the little Ross had said in court it was plain that the voice on the tape was his.

Ross was excused. He left the courtroom a free man. As soon as he stepped down I moved for acquittal on the kidnapping charge because now there was no evidence to sustain it. None of the grand jury transcript was admissible because Ross didn't testify at the trial. Friedman had no choice but to grant the motion. The charges now were reduced to murder and assault with a deadly weapon.

The final prosecution witnesses were its experts, principally criminalist John Davis. Davis told the court pretty much what he had told me months before, that the two bullets which had entered Frey's back, one of which had caused death, had been fired from extremely close range and probably came from Frey's gun. This was brought out in detailed elaborate testimony, illustrated with color slides. Frey's shirt had been embroidered around the bullet holes for emotional impact, and was shown to the jury.

THE PROSECUTION RESTS

We had no quarrel with Davis about the bullets, though I got him to say that Frey's bullets were a high-velocity type not normally used in police work because they are so lethal. Our major point of contention was over what had not been done.

Davis said the law book had never been given to him for either fingerprinting or an analysis of the blood on it. I asked if he or anyone working under him had tried to take fingerprints off the matchboxes of marijuana. He said no. The final question concerned paraffin and Neutron-Activation tests, means of determining if people had fired weapons. Davis said that no test of any sort had been made to determine if Newton had fired a handgun. Davis said the paraffin test was considered unreliable, as nitrates, the substances found on the hands of persons who recently have fired guns, could also be found on the hands of persons near a shooting. He said that the Neutron-Activation test was a good idea but not yet fully developed. He had sent one sample from an earlier case to San Diego, where police were conducting experiments with it, but had been dissatisfied with the results.

We concluded that the crime lab was given only part of the evidence to analyze, the part that would tend to incriminate Huey. Tests that might have pointed to his innocence were not run.

One of Jensen's final witnesses was Mel Torley, Huey's probation officer. Torley said that, although Huey's probation was scheduled to end on October 28, 1967, he had had a meeting with him several weeks earlier and could not be sure of the exact date he said the probationary period would be over. On cross-examination he stated he might have told Huey his probation ended on October 27, 1967.

The prosecution had called more than twenty-five witnesses, most of them minor. Grier and Heanes were the main hope for a conviction. Dell Ross's grand jury testimony was to be excluded, but who could tell what effect it might have on the jury?

THE DEFENSE

A BUS RIDER

Our first witness was Tommy Miller, a young man who had been on the bus. Grier was driving at the time of the shooting. Miller's testimony tended to show that Grier could not have seen what he claimed he did. He recalled that the shooting began just after the bus had passed the cars, that it had been awfully dark in the vicinity. (Because of construction, there were no street lights on the south side of Seventh Street.)

Miller said that when the shots rang out he and another man dove for cover near the back seat. When the shooting stopped, looking out of the back window he could see one policeman lying in the street. All this time, Miller stated, Grier was at, or near, the front of the bus. If Miller was at the rear of the bus, how could Grier have seen the shooting through the front windshield?

Jensen tried to shake Miller's story but couldn't get anywhere. Under pressure, his testimony got stronger because Miller also recalled seeing a civilian up against the car as if he were being frisked, something Jensen was eager to avoid. Miller cast doubt on Grier's veracity simply because his testimony made more sense than the bus driver's. It didn't seem likely that Grier would stop the bus right in front of a shootout. The normal instinct—especially for someone who had spent twenty years in the Navy—would have been to get the bus and passengers to a safe spot and observe from there.

OFFICER FREY'S REPUTATION

Our next witnesses were all black people who had had trouble with Frey. One by one they portrayed him as abusive, provacative, hostile, gun crazy.

Belford Dunning, an insurance agent, had been threatened by Frey at Eighth and Willow the night before the Newton incident. During the exchange with the middle-aged man, Frey had removed the strap on his holster and lifted his gun halfway out, causing Dunning to remark, "You're gonna make trouble in this area acting like that."

Frey had allowed sixteen-year-old Daniel King to be beaten in his patrol car. He had carried on a running feud with the family of Luther Smith, attempting to get their car towed away from in front of their own home, calling one son "you little black nigger" and another a "son of a bitch." These incidents all had happened within a year of the Newton shooting.

We traced Newton's movements on the evening before the shooting. Law-school graduate Don Hopkins had talked to Huey in a bar early in the evening, and Huey had said, "I've had this parole [probation] thing hanging over my head for three years—now it's gone." Others recalled seeing him at several parties later in the evening, including a celebration of the end of his probation.

THE UNKNOWN PASSENGER

Before the trial, Huey had been extremely reluctant to tell me the name of the man who had been in the Volkswagen with him, saying he'd already caused his friend enough trouble. And, in all the hullabaloo, the identity of the passenger had been virtually overlooked. Newton had been charged with murder and the speculation centered on whether he had killed Frey. I understood Huey's feelings in the matter and I had not pressed him. From the beginning of the trial, however, it bothered me that the prosecution did not bring up the name of the passenger, obviously a person who would know a lot about what had happened. I could only conclude that they simply did not know who he was. As we began our defense, I told Huey I needed to know the man's name. He told me, but insisted that he not be used as a witness if it would place him in any kind of jeopardy. I convinced

Huey that his friend could take the Fifth Amendment as Ross had done, if he wanted to, but it was important to show that there had been someone else in the car and to show who that someone was.

His name was Gene McKinney, and we subpoenaed him. On Wednesday, August 28, he was called to the stand. He had brought his own attorney, Harold Perry. I questioned him.

"Were you a passenger in a Volkswagen driven by Huey Newton on the morning of October 28, 1967, in the area of Seventh and Willow, Mr. McKinney?"

"Yes, I was."

"How were you dressed on that occasion?"

"Can't remember . . ."

"I would like to advise my client not to answer," Perry said, objecting to the question.

"Well, he has already answered it," Judge Friedman observed.

"Now, Mr. McKinney, on that morning at approximately five o'clock, did you by chance or otherwise shoot at Officer John Frey?" I continued.

"I refuse to answer on the ground that it may tend to incriminate me."

Jensen leaped to his feet demanding that McKinney be forced to testify.

"I ask that the question now be read to him, and the court direct him to answer."

The question was read, but Perry answered, "He refuses to answer on the grounds that his answer might tend to incriminate him."

"He gets up here and has said he was there," Jensen screamed, nearly beside himself. "He is asked a question about shooting, and now he says he can claim the privilege of the Fifth Amendment."

There followed a long legal argument between Jensen and Perry. Then the judge ordered me to ask McKinney another question.

"Mr. McKinney, did you at that time and place shoot, or fire a weapon, at Officer Heanes?"

"I refuse to answer on the grounds that it may tend to incriminate me."

"I have no further questions, your honor."

Friedman ruled that McKinney could be cross-examined about the one thing he had testified to, namely that he was in the car with Huey at the time and place of the shooting.

"Mr. McKinney, on October 28, 1967, when was it that you first came in contact with Mr. Newton?" asked Jensen.

McKinney refused to answer. The judge ordered him to, but still he refused. Friedman once again went through the routine of explaining how he could be sent to jail for contempt of court, but McKinney refused to budge. This time there was no offer of immunity, no legal loophole was opened. Ten minutes after he took the stand McKinney was on his way to jail where he remained for six weeks until a higher court overruled the citation.

BRIBERY?

Three young black men who ran one of the Seventh Street hotels had been cited for running a disorderly house and were ordered to appear at the district attorney's office. When they arrived, a member of the staff asked them if they knew anything about the Newton case, if they could provide information about the missing guns, saying he would make it worth their while to do so.

We wanted the jury to hear this because we felt it likely that Henry Grier had received and accepted a similar offer, which might explain why his story had been changed so drastically. Friedman listened to their testimony with the jury out of the courtroom and then ruled that the jury could not hear the testimony. One man had identified Jensen as the source of the money offer; another, his chief investigator.

"I will tell you what is involved, your honor, and I am going to talk bluntly. These people are charged. Three of them are brought to the district attorney's office on the pretense that they're running a disorderly house."

"That is quite a charge, that they were charged when there were no grounds for it," said Friedman.

"Then on that pretense, the district attorney and the district attorney's chief investigator come in and want to bribe them."

Jensen hotly denied the charge, calling the accusation flatly false and Judge Friedman exclaimed:

"Mr. Garry, you must stop! There is a point at which even *you* must stop, Mr. Garry! It's not bribery to hire people to get information for you. I fail to see the point."

THE ACCUSED AS WITNESS

I had deliberately not discussed the shooting with Huey before the trial. One reason was that I wanted first to complete our independent investigation. Another was that Huey had said he had lost consciousness soon after being shot and did not remember much, being, no doubt, in a state of severe shock after the bullet had penetrated his body. The investigation had convinced me that Huey was innocent, and we had developed our own version of what probably had happened the morning of October 28, 1967. Now, two days before I was to put him on the witness stand, Huey and I discussed the specifics of the shooting for the first time.

I always take writing paper with me when I have to interview a client in jail. I make sure the backing is a hard book cover which I carry with me when I leave. Afterward, I burn all the paper in an ashtray and flush the pulverized remains down the nearest toilet. These precautions are necessary because prison officials are notorious for bugging visiting rooms and taking legal documents away from defense lawyers.

I came away from the interview convinced Huey would make a fine witness—articulate and personable, he thrived on dialogue and argument. The sort of repartee that goes on in a courtroom would suit him well. In addition, he was one of only four people who could claim to be eyewitnesses; the others were Grier, Heanes, and McKinney. I was sure he would prove far more credible than either Heanes or Grier.

However, putting him on the witness stand created certain problems. Jensen could bring in his past record—there was the felony conviction and a series of minor arrests, mainly for fighting, when he was a youth. More serious were things Huey had said in interviews, and written in the Panther newspaper. In particular, there were an essay and a poem written a few months before the shooting that made reference to both guns and policemen. If Huey testified, Jensen could question him about anything he had written or had been quoted as saying.

I began the direct examination with the question, "Mr. Newton, did you kill Officer John Frey?" As I questioned him I stood to the rear of the jury box so that he was talking to the jury as well as to me. I wanted the jurors to see his face clearly because I felt that if they did they would not doubt his sincerity.

"No, I did not," he answered.

"Did you shoot, wound, Officer Herbert Heanes?"

"No, I did not."

"Did you on the morning of October 28, 1967, know about any

marijuana or any other type of drug in your vehicle?"

"I did not."

"Did you at any time ever have in your possession any narcotics of any kind, particularly marijuana?"

"I did not have any narcotics in my possession at any time."

"Have you at any time ever used marijuana in any form?"

"I have not."

"Where were you born?"

"Monroe, Louisiana."

"How old were you when you came to California?"

"I came to Oakland at the age of one or two."

I asked him to explain the black liberation movement.

"The black liberation movement is a movement to free blacks from exploitation and oppression. Black power is the means by which blacks will free themselves from the oppression of the ruling class in North America. To give you more of an insight, I could go into the historical context of the black liberation struggle."

He was impressive on the subject of black history and he spoke eloquently about war and slavery in Africa for several minutes. But when he began to talk about the European conquest of Africa, Jensen objected. Friedman ordered us to go on to another question.

"What does the Black Panther party stand for?"

"The Black Panther party stands for the liberation of black people from the brutality we have received and are still receiving in the Western World. The need for the party was stimulated by historical happenings which I am not being allowed to explain."

Jensen objected successfully to any talk about the general philosophy of the Panther party or the reasons it was formed, but Huey was to be allowed to read the party's ten-point platform and program, of which he was the co-author.

Huey read point number one: *We want freedom. We want the power to determine the destiny of our black community.* Then he got up, walked to the blackboard near the witness stand, and wrote the same words he had just spoken on it as a prelude to explaining point one of the party's ten-point platform. Under the rules of evidence, a witness may explain his response after he answers the question. However, each time Huey tried to elaborate on a point in the Panther program, Jensen objected and Friedman sustained him; but, since Huey naturally talks rapidly, he often got the information across before Jensen could formulate his objection.

We were able to give the jury a fair indication of the party's philosophy, but not so full an explanation as we had hoped for. Occasionally Judge Friedman interjected a comment, and this led to some interesting interchanges between the judge and Newton, including a legalistic dialogue over whether the Fourteenth Amendment guarantees a defendant the right to a trial by a jury of his peers.

After he went through the ten-point program, Newton gave a history of the Black Panther party. Originally called the Black Panther Party for Self-Defense, it was patterned after the Lowndes County Freedom Organization in Alabama, which had used the panther as its symbol.

"The black panther does not attack anyone. It will back up first, but if attacked it will certainly use self-defense."

He said that on his orders the Panthers had stopped their armed patrols several months before the shooting. (In response to Panther activities, the state gun laws had been changed abruptly, making open carrying of guns in urban areas illegal.)

He went on to say that the party had always been a political organization, that it was involved in community organizing, was running candidates for political office.*

"Mr. Newton, is the Black Panther party a racist organization?"

"The Black Panther party stands against racism. One of our chief purposes is to wipe out racism in this country and throughout the world. We have been victims of racism for many, many years and it is not a thing we want to promote."

"Can a white person join the Black Panthers?"

"White people can be affiliated with the Black Panther party, but because of the political dynamics now present in the black community, it's necessary that we maintain a cultural, economic group based upon our heritage. We would welcome a person like old John Brown, if you remember him, but usually white people are concerned with a whole different set of political and economic problems that are very different in nature from the situation in the black ghetto."

"Did you ever consider yourself as someone who had been convicted of a felony?"

*Huey was then the Peace and Freedom party congressional candidate, Bobby Seale and Kathleen Cleaver were running for the California assembly, and Eldridge Cleaver was the Peace and Freedom presidential candidate.

"No."

"Were you told by your probation officer that your probation would terminate on October 27, 1967?"

"Yes, I was."

"When were you told that?"

"About two weeks before my arrest."

He then began to relate exactly what had happened the day before the shooting, right up to the incident itself, a story no one had heard before.

After eating breakfast with his family that Friday morning, he was picked up by another Panther and driven to San Francisco State College. There he spoke to an afternoon meeting on The Future of the Black Liberation Struggle. He spoke and answered questions for two hours, sharing the platform with Dr. Harry Edwards, the sociologist who later organized the 1968 boycott of the Olympics.

After the talk, Huey returned home, ate supper, and walked over to the house of his fiancée, LaVerne Williams. He wanted to go out and celebrate the end of his probation, but she wasn't feeling well. However, she loaned him her car. He drove first to the Bosun's Locker, a bar nearby, cashed the $75 check he had received for his talk, had a few drinks, briefly spoke with Don Hopkins and several others and then, at about 10:30, he drove to the Congregational Church on Forty-second and Grove Street, where he attended weekend social functions regularly.

Huey stayed at the church until past one, spending most of his time talking to people, because, as he explained, "I don't know how to dance." He spoke to many people that evening, including Gene McKinney, an old friend.

At about one-thirty Huey suggested to McKinney that they go to a party on Thirty-seventh Street, a short distance away. He had invited a number of people to this party, saying it was being given to celebrate the end of his probation.

"Really, I was just joking with them. I told them I was getting off probation and there was a celebration for me, but it was just to lure them to the party."

They gave two other young men neither of them knew a ride to the party from the church, arriving there shortly before two, and they stayed until the party broke up after four. McKinney asked Newton to drive him to Seventh Street to get something to eat. He sat in the VW while Huey had a lengthy conversation with the host and hostess. Then they headed for Seventh Street, where the all-night soul-food restaurants were still open.

After pausing at the stop sign at Seventh and Willow, Huey made a left turn onto Seventh. As he made the turn, he noticed the flashing red light of a police car in his rear-view mirror.

"I pulled over to the curb and came to a stop. The police officer got out of his car, walked over to mine, and said, 'Well, well, well, what do we have here? The great Huey P. Newton.' He had had his head almost in my window, maybe six inches to a foot away from my face. He asked me for my driver's license which I gave him. Then he asked me who the car belonged to, and I said it belonged to LaVerne Williams. As I said this, I took the registration from the window [visor] and handed it to him. He gave me my driver's license back and went to his car with the registration."

Under my questioning, Huey said he put his license back in his wallet and they waited. A second police car arrived. The second officer consulted with the first, then walked to the car and said, "Mr. Williams, do you have any further identification?" Huey corrected him, saying, "What do you mean Mr. Williams? My name is Huey P. Newton, and I've already shown my license to the first officer." Heanes looked at him and said, "Yes, I know who you are."

Though Huey had not seen either officer before, he said it was a common thing for him to be stopped, that it was unusual for him to drive and not be stopped. Even so, in more than fifty previous stops he had not been given any tickets. We introduced his driving license into evidence.

The second officer stood alongside the VW for four or five minutes, Huey stated, while the first officer remained in his patrol car. Huey estimated that he had been stopped for ten minutes when the first officer returned and ordered him out of the VW.

As he got out he picked up a law book from between the front seats, just behind the handbrake. The second officer walked around the front of the car and escorted McKinney to the driver's side, the one closer to the street than the sidewalk.

"I thought I had picked up my criminal evidence book, which covers search and seizure and reasonable cause to arrest."

What he actually had picked up was another similar-looking volume.

"I got out of the car with the book in my right hand. I asked him [Frey] if I was under arrest. He said I wasn't under arrest, but 'just lean on the car.' So I had the book in my hand and I leaned on the car. The officer made a frisk in a very degrading fashion. He took my shirttail out and made a complete search of my body.

"At this time, the four of us are in the street. The second officer has come around to the street side with the passenger, Gene McKinney. Right after I was searched, the first officer told me to go back to his car. He wanted to talk to me.

"So I took a couple of steps going back, and he got on the side of me and took my left arm with his right, and we started to walk back to the car.

"Actually, he was kind of pushing me, because he was walking at a pretty rapid rate. I started to walk at a normal rate, but we passed the first car and approached the second, but he kept going. We stopped at the back door.

"I took my book and opened it and said, 'You have no reasonable cause to arrest me.' He said, 'You can take that book and stick it up your ass, nigger,' and as he says this, he gives me a straight-arm in the face with his right—it would be his left, I guess, because he still had a hold of my arm with the other hand—and he hooks me in the face and kind of dazed me.

"I stumbled backwards in an easterly direction for maybe four or five feet. I was dazed and went down on one knee. I think I still had my book in my hand, and, as I was getting up, I saw the officer draw a service revolver, and then I felt like—a sensation like boiling hot soup had been spilled on my stomach. Then I remember hearing a sound, a loud sound or volley of shots. It was like an explosion to me.

"I didn't know what it was. It seemed as if it was coming all around me. I can vaguely remember crawling on the ground or moving, or being moved. I vaguely remember being on my hands and knees and things were spinning. I don't know if someone was carrying me or something, but I had a moving sensation—a feeling of being propelled.

"After this, I don't know what happened. The next thing I remember is that I'm at the entrance of Kaiser Hospital."

He remembered being in excruciating pain and delirium and having to wait a long time to receive medical attention. Shortly after he was placed on the gurney, the police stormed in and handcuffed him.

"They started to make statements like, 'You killed a policeman and maybe two, and you're going to die for this. If you don't die in the gas chamber, then we'll have you killed in prison; and if you're acquitted, we'll kill you in the streets."

The entire courtroom was transfixed by Huey's account. I could see the reporters furiously taking notes. Jensen also was scribbling away, preparing for cross-examination. Judge Friedman had turned his swivel chair toward the witness stand and was listening with rapt attention. I could feel the hushed stillness of the spectator section behind me.

"I regained consciousness at Highland Hospital. The police woke me up. One officer held a sawed-off shotgun about three inches from my face. Everytime I passed out, the police would wake me again by shaking or kicking the bed. They said they had a razor blade and were going to cut the tubes going into my nose, saying that I was going to 'commit suicide.' "

I then asked him to show the jury the scars the bullet wound had left on his body. He pulled his sweater up to his chest and showed a spot above the waist. This was the entry wound. Then he turned around, and I showed the jury the exit wound in his back, some distance below the point of entry. That meant that the bullet which nearly killed him had to have been fired by someone taller than he.

Heanes had testified that Huey was facing him when he fired, but he also had been down on one knee. It would be impossible for a bullet fired from that angle to enter in a downward trajectory. Such a bullet would take an upward trajectory. The bullet which killed Frey moved with such a trajectory. Our conclusion was that Newton had been shot by the much taller Frey and that Frey was shot by Heanes.

Only a few questions remained, primarily about the marijuana, since the prosecution was trying to make it a motive for the shooting. He said it was against party rules to use narcotics, and, beyond that, it just wasn't very wise to carry them around because Panthers were being stopped almost daily by the police. He said he had no idea how the marijuana had come to be in the car, that he had not seen anyone bring a paper bag into the VW.

That finished my direct examination. I nodded to Jensen and said, "You may inquire." I was confident that Huey's sincerity, knowledge-ability, and articulate presentation of the evidence had impressed the jury. I was certain that our version of the shooting was far more plausible than the prosecution's garbled and contradictory account. Still, we would now have to watch Jensen try to discredit Huey as best he knew how.

CROSS-EXAMINATION OF NEWTON

Jensen began to cross-examine in his characteristically methodical way, slowly and carefully going over the events leading up to the shooting. Each time he approached a point at which the witness would be expected to describe the events just prior to the shooting, Jensen either backed off or changed the subject. After establishing that Newton was unarmed but did not know if McKinney was carrying a weapon, Jensen raised the issue of the felony conviction.

Huey told the jury this story. While at a party he had an argument. He had been cutting into a steak when a man pushed him and appeared to be reaching into his pocket for a knife or gun. As the man moved again toward him, he stabbed out with the steak knife to protect himself, wounding the man. The scuffle was broken up quickly and after learning that the man wasn't badly hurt, Huey and his brother Melvin left the party. A few weeks later, charges were filed against him.

During Huey's second day on the stand, Jensen brought up the shooting. He had Huey go through it all, step by step, questioning every detail minutely. Jensen had him act out several sequences much in the same way I had asked Heanes to act out his role. Jensen asked if he had felt the boiling hot sensation in his gut at the same time as he heard the gunfire. Huey said he felt it first. Jensen asked if he saw a flash from the gun; he said he didn't remember seeing one. Jensen asked how he had got to the hospital; he said he was blacking out and simply didn't remember.

So it went, Jensen trying to trip him up on details and Huey patiently recounting everything that had happened. Not getting very far, Jensen then brought in tangential information to discredit Huey.

First there was a scuffle several years before with a Berkeley policeman, but Huey put Jensen on the defensive by saying that the off-duty officer had admitted in court that he'd been drinking heavily just before the melee.

Jensen used what Newton had written or said the previous summer to convince the jury that the Panthers advocated the indiscriminate murder of policemen.

On July 20, 1967, the Black Panther newspaper had published an article, "The Correct Handling of Revolution," by Huey Newton. Actually a long theoretical essay, it had been written in response to the riots in Newark and Detroit earlier that year. The article contained the following two paragraphs, which Jensen asked Huey to read from the witness stand:

When the vanguard party destroys the machinery of the oppressor by dealing with him in small groups of threes and fours and then escaping the might of the oppressor, the masses will be overjoyed and will adhere to the correct strategy.

When the masses hear that a gestapo policeman has been executed while sipping coffee at a counter, and the revolutionary executioners fled without being traced, the masses will see the validity of this type of approach to resistance.*

Taken out of context, those two paragraphs could have provided Jensen with the motive he so badly needed.

"In the article you were talking about killing policemen as they sat sipping coffee and then escaping, isn't that right?" Jensen asked.

"In the full context of the article, I show that these things will probably occur. But I feel the subjective conditions do not exist now," Huey replied.

"What did you mean when you wrote, 'When the masses hear that a gestapo policeman has been executed while sipping coffee,' etc.?"

"That is presuming a revolution is in existence. The people feel that peaceful means have not been thoroughly exhausted, so, therefore, the time for revolution is not now. First they must exhaust all peaceful means, and if they don't get their freedom after that, then we not only predict, but we would encourage revolution."

"Would you encourage it by having small groups of three and four go around and find people sipping coffee and execute them?"

"We would encourage it just as this country did in 1776 when they broke with the English because of taxes on tea."

"No. Just answer whether you would or would not," Judge Friedman interjected, "and then explain your answer."

"In the height of revolution we would, but we would not encourage it when there are peaceful ways to achieve our goals and our freedom."

*What Jensen avoided was that Huey had also written, in the same article, that such things would happen only after it was "no longer advantageous for them to resist by going into the streets." Just before the article was printed, Newton had sought to clarify his statements, to point out that he was talking about the future. He wrote, "Where the government has come to power through some form of popular vote, fraudulent or not, and maintains at least an appearance of constitutional legality, the guerrilla outbreak cannot be promoted since the possibility of peaceful struggle has not been exhausted." But his addition, directed to the young revolutionaries calling for instant change, had arrived too late and the article had been printed without it.

A few weeks before this essay appeared, the Panther newspaper had published a poem Huey had written. It went like this:

Guns Baby Guns!

Army .45 will stop all jive
Buckshots will down the cops
P-38 will open prison gates
The carbine will stop the war machine
A .357 will win us heaven.
And if you don't believe in playing
You are already dead.

Huey read it from the witness stand, admitting that it wasn't very good poetry, but there it was, in black and white, with him listed as the author. On the same page there was the usual list of weapons the Panthers recommended for self-defense which appeared in every issue of their newspaper and included an Army .45 caliber pistol, a 12-gauge shotgun, an M-1 carbine, a .357 Magnum pistol, and a .38 caliber police revolver, or P-38.

Jensen implied with the poem and list of weapons that Huey advocated indiscriminate murder of cops but made very little headway with it. After almost an entire day of cross-examination, he gave up. He had used everything he had, but he couldn't crack Newton's story or successfully use his writings against him. Nor could he make him lose composure.

I felt Huey had been a superb witness—the best I had ever seen. The jury had seen the intelligent, idealistic, magnetic person I knew he was—not the cold-blooded cop killer that Jensen was trying to portray. He had answered every question, never raised his voice, never lost his temper; at the same time he had given a lucid explication of the aims and ideals of the black liberation movement.

A SPECIAL LANGUAGE

Earlier in the trial I had tried to present the expert testimony of Dr. Herman Blake, a black professor of sociology at the University of California (Berkeley), an expert on the language and customs of the black community. We had called Dr. Blake to show that black rhetoric had a different meaning than it did for whites. This type of testimony was innovative, and Judge Friedman at first refused to let him testify.

I was sufficiently concerned about the effects on the jury of the article and the poem to again attempt to have Dr. Blake's testimony admitted. Judge Friedman granted us another hearing, and this time I was able to convince him of the importance of showing the jury that the special language of the black community, in which much of the Panther newspaper was written, did not mean to them what it meant elsewhere. Friedman had been aware of Jensen's effort to build from this language the specific intent he needed to show that Newton had acted with malice aforethought.

We wanted to prove that the language itself should not be used against Huey because it simply did not mean to him or to his people what it would mean to a white person. After a lengthy hearing, Friedman ruled that Dr. Blake could testify before the jury.

When Dr. Blake took the stand he explained the special language of the black community. He talked about *signifyin'* where "black people are talking, using one language, when they have completely different ideas in mind. It's a way of expressing one's self in one language about completely different phenomena.

"A group of youths see a pretty girl walk by. They want to comment on her appearance, but don't do it directly. They might talk about the weather and say, 'It's a fine day today,' or 'Things are sure lookin' good today.' "

He explained other verbal concepts such as the one called, "take care of business," on which Jensen had harped considerably during cross-examination, saying that it had literally dozens of different meanings according to the context in which it was used—food, sex, politics, anything, depending on who said it and to what it referred.

Dr. Blake explained black slang, the wording of Huey's poem, the rhetoric of the movement, including the word *pig*—and when his testimony was finished we felt that it had been immensely valuable in counteracting the impression that the jury may have gained by Jensen's attempt to turn Huey's words into swords against him.

DR. DIAMOND TESTIFIES AGAIN

Our final witness was Bernard Diamond. Diamond had worked in an Army hospital during World War II treating the psychiatric problems of soldiers suffering from bullet wounds. Because he had not personally examined Newton, my specific question about Huey's wound was not allowed. However, I was allowed to ask the question hypothetically, and Dr. Diamond said the "hypothetical symptoms," the lapsing into and out of consciousness with vague memories, were fully compatible symptomatic behavior for someone with a penetrating abdominal wound. My next hypothetical question was:

"Is a person's memory better immediately after an event, or does it become better ten months thereafter?"

"An individual's memory is almost always better closer to the event. The earlier recollection is likely to be more faithful than a later one."

Diamond's testimony lent credibility to Huey's story about blacking out after the shooting, the testimony further reduced the veracity of Grier's. Jensen attempted sarcasm on cross-examination but ran into a problem.

"Does everybody who gets shot in the abdomen black out for half an hour and travel across the city to get to a hospital?"

"Not everybody, but it's quite common to do so. A gunshot wound which penetrates a body cavity is very likely to produce a profound reflex shock reaction, and it is not at all uncommon for a person shot in the abdomen to lose consciousness and go into this reflex shock reaction for short periods of time."

Sometimes it's better not to ask a question if you don't know the answer you're going to get.

We rested our case after Diamond's testimony. Jensen put on several rebuttal witnesses, but they had little effect. It was now the end of August, and the Democratic convention had just ended in Chicago. Antiwar demonstrators had recently received a taste of the kind of police violence that poor blacks experience almost daily.

Final arguments were to be put off until after the Labor Day weekend. We were quite confident, feeling the prosecution had not presented much of a case. There was no murder weapon, one eyewitness said he never saw a gun in Huey's hand, and Henry Grier had been thoroughly discredited—it would be hard for the jury to believe a thing he said. Jensen had not established a clear motive for the alleged killing. While establishing a motive isn't legally necessary, most jurors are inclined to look for one in a murder case where the question of premeditation is important. The initially hostile press had become friendlier.

THE FINAL ARGUMENTS

Jensen's lengthy summation revolved around several points. "Who did it?" he asked the jury. "Who is it that was a foot away, eighteen inches away, six inches away? Who fired a weapon?"

His argument was, that since Huey was at the scene and Grier, Heanes, and Huey himself had all said he was close to Frey when the shooting occurred, only Huey could have fired the fatal shot. The prosecutor said that if they didn't want to take the word of Officer Heanes, they had to believe the testimony of Henry Grier. He referred sarcastically to Gene McKinney's presence on the murder scene.

"If you think he [McKinney] had something to do with the murder of Officer Frey, you're not going to find him on the witness stand, with his lawyer standing there, saying, 'Oh, yes. I was there.' You're not going to find Mr. McKinney making any admission that puts him there if he thinks he's going to get into trouble."

McKinney, in spite of his refusal to testify, had been the next most important defense witness to Huey himself, as the defense's whole contention was that if Newton did not shoot Frey then someone else did. Who else was at the scene? Newton, Frey, Heanes, and McKinney. There were also people across the street. Therefore, the defense had shown that Heanes possibly could have shot Frey and that McKinney was present while the shooting was taking place. McKinney's refusal to answer on the grounds that it might incriminate him, when asked if he shot Frey, produced the implication that McKinney might have shot Frey. That is why Jensen went berserk when McKinney "took the Fifth"—McKinney created an enormous amount of reasonable doubt.

In my summation I concentrated heavily on Grier's testimony. We had prepared a series of charts outlining the glaring inconsistencies and direct changes in testimony between Grier's original statement to the police and what he said on the witness stand.

Then I took up the jacket that Newton had been wearing on October 28, 1967. I picked up Officer Heanes's .38 caliber revolver. The undisputed testimony of the pathologist was that Frey was killed by a .38 caliber bullet. I placed the .38 caliber pistol into the left pocket of Huey's coat. The pistol crashed to the floor. I tried the same thing with the right pocket. The revolver fell out again. The pockets in the coat were only two or three inches deep. It was impossible for either pocket to hold a gun of that size, or any gun for that matter.

I pointed out that Grier stated originally that the man he saw shoot Frey had reached into his *jacket* pocket and pulled out the gun. At the trial, however, he maintained that the man had reached into his *shirt* for the gun. "The reason that had to be changed is obvious," I said. "You can't put this gun in this pocket and make it stay there."

I emphasized that Newton's law book had been found at the rear of the police cars, indicating that he was carrying it in at least one hand, and I stressed Officer Heanes's testimony that he had seen no gun in Newton's hand. I knew the jury had been impressed when Heanes had admitted that he had never seen a gun in Huey's hand. I noted how strange it was for the Oakland police to stop a known Panther vehicle, place one of its occupants under arrest, but neither frisk nor handcuff him. These were the hard facts, the contradictions in the prosecution's case.

I asked why the blood on the law book had not been analyzed, why the paper bag containing the marijuana wasn't dusted for finger-prints, and why the taller, heavier Frey took Newton beyond his own patrol car.

"What was he going to do back there?"

I reminded the jury that the bullet that wounded Newton passed through his body on a downward trajectory, while the bullet that killed Frey passed through his on an upward trajectory.

After thus analyzing the evidence, I spoke about Huey, about the kind of person he was, the forthrightness of his testimony. I talked about racism, about how I had learned about black America by entering the case, about John Frey and the sort of person he was, and how Mayor Daley had just used the police in Chicago. Then I came to the Kerner Report.

"The Kerner Report lays down the hypothesis and the problems of black America today. White America listen: the answer is not to put Huey Newton in the gas chamber. The answer is not to put Huey and his organization in jail. The answer is not more police. The answer is to wipe out the miserable conditions in the ghetto so that black brothers and sisters can live with dignity, so they can walk down the street with pride."

I concluded with these words, "I personally know what discrimination is. I hate it. This case is an outgrowth of discrimination. This case is a diabolical attempt to put an innocent man into the gas chamber, and my government should not be party to that kind of scheme."

The judge then gave his instructions to the jury. These are guide-lines on legal points, which they must follow in their evaluation of the evidence. Prior to the trial's end each side submits to the judge the instructions it wants given and he decides which he will give. Attorneys have the right to argue if they disagree with the judge's decisions. In this case, I had submitted an instruction on unconsciousness, which would tell the jury that a lack of consciousness was a valid defense to the charges completely. Newton had testified that he had lost consciousness for periods of time after being shot and Dr. Diamond had testified that this was entirely compatible with the type of wound he had received. Nonetheless, Judge Friedman refused to give this instruction, though we considered it essential to our case. Perhaps he felt that it would tip the scales in our favor, maybe even gain us an outright acquittal. I argued long and vigorously, but the judge still refused to instruct the jury about unconsciousness.

CRISIS WHILE THE JURY DELIBERATES

On Thursday morning, September 5, 1968, 149 days after the trial began, the jury retired to begin its deliberations.

Usually there is little to do but wait. Jurors sometimes request testimony be re-read, or question the instructions, and the lawyers must be available. Though some attorneys return to work while awaiting a verdict, I can't. Generally I wait in or near the courtroom, speculating with friends, lawyers, media people. It occasionally seems to me as if I've spent my entire life waiting for juries to return with verdicts.

The Newton case still stands out as the most complex, emotional, fascinating case I've ever tried. It had almost every conceivable element—the whodunnit factor, political and racial overtones, the black liberation movement, the spectacle of police and prosecution suppressing and fabricating evidence, the bias of the trial judge, who did not grant a single defense motion. We also had challenged the grand jury and raised important social issues. Both sides had introduced sophisticated scientific evidence.

Nonetheless, I was not prepared for what happened next. The jury had been out only a short time when the foreman sent in a note saying they wanted to see Grier's original statement to the police made the morning of the shooting. Ordinarily it would have been routinely sent up to the jury room.

However, the court clerk did not have a copy. The judge called Jensen and me into his chambers to ask if either had a copy. Mine had notes scrawled all over it and wasn't usable. Jensen didn't have a copy either. He went to his office and later returned with the original working draft, the transcription as it had come off the tape.

At once Keating and I could see a change had been made from the copy submitted to us, the one from which I had cross-examined Grier. In the altered passage, McConnell had asked Grier how old the man who shot Frey appeared to be. Grier had answered, "I couldn't say because I only had my lights on. I couldn't—I did get a clear picture, clear view of his face, because he had his head kind of down, facing the headlights of the coach and I couldn't get a good look." On the original transcript, the word *did* had been amended in red ink to *didn't*. On our copy, however, the *did* was unaltered. Now this sentence had given us some trouble in the trial because it makes Grier's statement ambiguous. In the charts we prepared for the final argument we had omitted this sentence, filling in the space with Xs. Jensen had made much of this in his rebuttal, implying that I was deliberately trying to mislead the jury. Of course, when the whole paragraph was considered it was obvious that the thrust of it was that he did not, could not see the man's face.

At this point Jensen and I got into a heated argument. I would not agree to the statement going upstairs with the *did* left in; he would not agree to sending it marked *didn't*. Though I had repeatedly asked Jensen to let us hear the original tape, he had always managed to stall us off until we had finally accepted the version given to us as completely accurate. In the impasse the jury was told that the transcript was not immediately available.

To us, this alteration assumed major importance: if we could show the jury the prosecution had changed the evidence our whole theory of a police-prosecution conspiracy to convict Newton would hold up. We now pressed for the original tape, but Jensen stalled us again by saying he did not have the right machine to play the tape. Later that night he played a "dub" for Keating who couldn't tell from the dub what the disputed word was. We were promised the tape for the following morning, but when we arrived at Jensen's office he claimed he still did not have a machine. Now, however, the jurors had asked for a re-reading of some testimony, so Jensen, Fay Stender, and I had to return to the courtroom, leaving Keating with police inspector Robert Bernard to listen to the original. Keating had provided himself with a tape recorder and took a copy off the tape which showed clearly that Grier had indeed said *didn't*. I had hoped to have the judge hear the tape, change the transcript, and send it to the jury in the morning, but most of the day was taken up with the re-reading of testimony.

We knew all along it was not going to be easy to get Friedman to listen to the tape and change the transcript; for a judge to hear new evidence while the jury is deliberating is almost without precedent. It was late Friday afternoon, and the jury had been out for more than a day, when Jensen finally brought the tape and the machine down to the courtroom. We then listened to the tape, marked it, and gave it to the court clerk. While Stender was drawing up the legal papers to get it to the judge, Keating took his copy of the tape to the media. That evening almost every radio and TV station in the Bay Area played the crucial segment. Grier had said *didn't,* no doubt about it. Thousands of people heard it that night. I hoped this would provide pressure on Judge Friedman to hear the motion, and I jokingly said to Keating, "I bet the old bastard will grant it. Do you know why? Because his wife probably saw you play the tape on TV and she heard it as *didn't* and told Monroe what she thought of this funny stuff." Keating laughed, but I was only half kidding.

As we were working to prepare the motion, we worried desperately that the jury might bring in its verdict before we could be heard, but by Saturday afternoon Friedman agreed to hold a hearing. Then, just as the tape reached the disputed passage the volume suddenly dipped and Grier's voice was barely audible. Instead there was a soft, scratchy noise. The judge, seeming bewildered, looked at me. I could barely contain my anger as I said,

"If your honor please, at ten-thirty yesterday morning we transcribed that same thing. It was a lot clearer."

"Why was it clearer yesterday than it is today?"

"Because—" I leaped to my feet and shouted, "it's been played over and over again before the matter got into court here today!"

"When they played it to transcribe it they played it over and over," Jensen said. "That is why we take transcriptions. Your honor has listened to it and I think that takes care of that."

"It may take care of it as far as you are concerned," I said, "but when at ten-thirty we recorded that identical section it was clear as a bell."

I then offered to play our tape. Friedman accepted, heard *didn't,* and ruled that he would send the transcript to the jury with *n't* inserted but without judicial comment. It was better than nothing, but we felt that in the light of Jensen's making so much of our omission of the passage in his rebuttal, he should have pointed out the change.

Keating spoke to the press saying:

"The evidence speaks for itself. All I know is that the defense was given a false document. You gentlemen have been in court. You've heard Mr. Garry speak about tampered witnesses. Well, this is part of the prosecution effort to frame Huey Newton for something he didn't do."

THE VERDICT

The jury remained out all Saturday afternoon. The defense team and Newton's relatives were the only people permitted in the courthouse on the weekend. We waited all Saturday night, all day Sunday. The jury had been deliberating for four days and our nerves were frazzled: waiting in a capital case is almost unbearable.

Huey was upstairs in the county jail, the calmest of us all. The defense team, his family, and I took turns going to see him. Through it all, he remained confident that he would be acquitted.

Finally, late Sunday evening the bailiff brought word that the jury had reached a verdict. We rushed to the courtroom—family, attorneys, media representatives, and the few weekend spectators allowed inside the courthouse. Newton walked in and strode casually to his seat beside me. In the total silence around us Judge Friedman took the bench, ordered the courtroom locked, and asked that the jury be brought down.

Usually you can tell the verdict by the jurors' faces. If they smile and look at you or your client, you know you've got an acquittal. But when they look drawn, or avert their eyes, you know you're in trouble.

As the Newton jury filed in, I couldn't tell a thing. I looked at David Harper, who had been selected foreman, but his face showed no emotion. Some jurors looked bored, others merely tired. Harper was asked if the jury had reached a verdict.

"Yes, we have, your honor."

The bailiff took the slips of paper with the verdicts on them and handed them to the clerk. In a flat monotone she read the verdict.

"We the jury find the above named defendant, Huey P. Newton, guilty of a felony, to wit, voluntary manslaughter." On the second count, assault with a deadly weapon on Officer Heanes, Huey was acquitted. Though we won on two of the three original counts, still we were disappointed. We had hoped for an outright acquittal.

What the jury had done was obvious. It was a compromise verdict.

A person charged with murder can be found guilty or innocent of first-degree murder. However, the jury has the option to bring in a guilty verdict on a lesser included offense—in the case of murder, second-degree murder and manslaughter are both in this category.

We felt the verdict was inconsistent and not based on the evidence. In denouncing the verdict to the press as "chickenshit" and "racist," I said, "Either Newton had the gun or he didn't have the gun."

We wondered how the jury could reach such a verdict on the flimsy, doctored evidence presented to it by the prosecution. We had to attribute it to the climate of fear built up around the case.

We were able to talk to David Harper later. He told us that from the first day he had worked to get himself elected foreman. We had seen during the trial that he was easily the most dominant jury member, but we hadn't known if he would identify with Newton's plight or his own successful position in the predominately white world of banking.

Harper may have lived in one of Oakland's exclusive areas, but he hadn't started out there. He understood Huey perfectly. He said that never in his life had he been prouder to be a black man than when he heard Huey on the witness stand. From the beginning, after he was elected foreman, he had spent an hour telling the jurors about his background, his experiences, his struggle to get ahead, supplementing what Huey was saying on the stand.

In spite of his efforts, the jury was divided three ways after nearly four full days of deliberation. Four jurors were for an acquittal, four for a second-degree murder verdict,* and four were undecided. Early Sunday evening Harper sat down and began writing a note to Judge Friedman.

"What are you doing?" a juror asked.

"I'm writing to the judge to tell him that, because of our prejudices, we can't reach a verdict."

"Don't do that. Let's see if we can get together."

What Harper really wanted was a compromise, because, if there were no verdict, Newton could be tried again for murder, and in a second trial there might not be any blacks on the jury. Shortly afterward the jurors agreed to acquit Newton of assault with a deadly weapon. As the kidnapping charge had already been dismissed, they

*Murder without premeditation, which doesn't carry the death penalty.

were left with murder. Eleven to one they agreed on the compromise verdict of voluntary manslaughter.

One woman held out against the compromise, demanding a conviction on a more serious charge. She remained adamant for several hours, but at about ten P.M. she went to the bathroom. When she came back she agreed to go along with the compromise.

After the jury filed out Huey stood up, turned toward the spectators, threw his left fist in the air, and with a big smile said proudly: *Power to the people!*

Three weeks later Judge Friedman sentenced him to from two to fifteen years under California's indeterminate sentence procedure. The judge would not set appeal bond nor would he allow Huey to say goodbye to anyone. He was whisked off to prison in San Luis Obispo, 300 miles south of Oakland, making it extremely difficult for friends, relatives, and lawyers to visit him. After informing prison officials that he wouldn't work for anything less than the minimum wage he was kept in solitary. Prisoners who tried to associate with him in any way were disciplined.*

THE APPEAL

On May 29, 1970, the District Court of Appeals reversed the manslaughter conviction and ordered Newton released from prison pending a new trial. On August 5, 1970, he walked out of the Alameda County Courthouse into the bright summer sun and was almost mobbed by five thousand jubilant supporters. The demand, "Free Huey," had become a reality.

He was not completely free however. He would have to stand trial again on the manslaughter charge, though because of the jury's verdict he could not be tried again either for murder or for assault with a deadly weapon.

The appeals court had many grounds upon which it could have reversed the conviction. Fay Stender wrote an impressive brief outlining the numerous prejudicial aspects of the trial, but the court

*A few days after Huey was sentenced, the district court of appeals overturned Judge Sherwin's courageous decision to defy the Adult Authority and ordered Eldridge Cleaver back to prison within sixty days. We appealed this ruling up to the Supreme Court, with no success. Toward the end of November 1968, Cleaver disappeared, turning up first in Cuba, then in Algeria.

chose to act on more narrow grounds. It ruled that Judge Friedman should have given the jury the instruction on unconsciousness that I had argued for. The court held that this instruction would have allowed the jury to conclude that, if Huey was unconscious after being shot, then he had a completely valid defense.

The court also said that the ploy of reading Dell Ross's grand jury testimony in front of the jury—after it became clear he would not testify—was highly prejudicial. It ruled that this had allowed the prosecution to bring in testimony without giving the defense the right to cross-examine, which is precisely what I had told Judge Friedman during the trial. The appeals court warned that this tactic was not to be permitted in any future trial.

So Huey was free on bail, ready to resume leadership of the Black Panther party. In the eyes of many people he had been vindicated, but he was tried for manslaughter in July 1971. During that trial the bloody law book mysteriously disappeared and we were never able to place it in evidence. The trial ended with the jury unable to reach a verdict.

Jensen took the case to trial a third time at the end of 1971 and got another hung jury. But, during that trial Judge Lyle Cook, whom we had tried to challenge on charges of racism, voided the 1964 felony conviction on the grounds that it had been illegally obtained.

At the begining of 1972, Huey had no felony convictions on his record. Jensen announced that he was dropping the manslaughter charge because two trials had ended in hung juries. He promised to reopen the case if any new evidence emerged, but none ever did.

6.

Conspiracy

In January 1969, just four months after the Newton case came to a close, I began the trial of "The Oakland Seven," a group of young political activists charged with conspiracy as a result of leading a week of anti-draft demonstrations. They were: Bob Mandel, 23; Mike Smith, 27; Steve Hamilton, 23; Frank Bardacke, 26; Reese Erlich, 21; Jeff Segal, 26; and Terry Cannon, 28.

All had been active during the sixties. Mandel had left graduate school to organize against the Vietnam war; Smith was an organizer of the Free Speech Movement and the Vietnam Day Committee; Hamilton, a ministerial student, had been expelled from Berkeley for participating in an antiwar sit-in; Bardacke was a popular student leader; Erlich was a member of SDS and an organizer for the Peace and Freedom party; Segal, a former student body president at Roosevelt University in Chicago, had been the national antidraft coordinator for SDS*; Cannon, a former SNCC and SDS member, edited the monthly paper, *The Movement.*

In the second half of the 1960s, an era of political protest and massive demonstrations—civil rights, nuclear testing, Vietnam— many of the most important demonstrations against the Vietnam war were led by students and young activists. Berkeley, a center of militant antiwar activity, had already gained a nationwide reputation for its demonstrations against HUAC and discrimination in employ-

*In addition, Segal already had been convicted of refusing induction and soon after the Oakland demonstrations his bail was revoked and he began a four-year jail term. During the entire trial he was confined to the county jail atop the courthouse.

ment, and made front-page news with the Free Speech Movement. In 1965 Berkeley activists initiated a continuous series of antiwar protests—marches, teach-ins, sit-ins, vigils at a nearby weapons depot, and four attempts to prevent troop trains from entering the Oakland Army Terminal.

They then proclaimed October 16–20, 1967, as Stop the Draft Week, setting up a committee to coordinate the plan to close down the Oakland Induction Center, one of the largest on the West Coast. At the appointed time, thousands of demonstrators converged on the center. On Monday, October 16, when a large group of pacifists led by folk-singer Joan Baez sat in the doorway of the center, over a hundred were quietly arrested.

The next morning six thousand people turned out at dawn for the first "militant" demonstration. They soon clogged the street in front of the center. Suddenly, club-swinging police charged into the crowd, dispersing it in a few minutes. Scores of students, bystanders, and newsmen were injured.

The following two days, Wednesday and Thursday, the center was picketed quietly, but the last day, Friday, ten thousand demonstrators returned to downtown Oakland, still bitter about the beatings. Only this time they were better organized: many wore helmets and protective clothing. They ringed the area round the center, building barricades in the streets, stopping traffic in central Oakland, and keeping busloads of draftees away.

This demonstration, which took place one day before the march on the Pentagon, did not endear the activists to the powerful businessmen who ran Oakland, most of them ardent supporters of the Vietnam war, some of whom had been targets of demonstrations against racial discrimination in employment. In addition, Stop the Draft Week had cost the city of Oakland several hundred thousand dollars in police overtime. Despite the public uproar, the police made few arrests after Monday partly because the demonstrators avoided being arrested, partly because the police seemed more interested in beating the demonstrators than in arresting them.

District Attorney J. Frank Coakley came under pressure to prosecute those responsible for Stop the Draft Week, but there did not seem to be any grounds for a major prosecution, and by the end of 1967 no charges had been filed. Official Oakland had been trying for years to stop the Berkeley protests but they had always run up against the First Amendment guarantees of free speech and freedom of political expression. The right-wing element persisted and, through a local radio commentator, Pat Michaels, launched a campaign to indict the Berkeley activists under California's criminal conspiracy law.

Conspiracy laws are a prosecutor's dream because it isn't necessary to prove that the accused ever *did* anything. All he must prove is that one or more people "conspired, combined, confederated, and agreed" to carry out an illegal act. Clarence Darrow wrote, "If a boy steals candy, it is a misdemeanor; but if two boys agree to steal some candy and don't do it, then they are felons." Another factor is that in a conspiracy case the prosecution can bring in prejudicial information against the defendants that normally would be inadmissible— speeches, public statements, off-hand remarks, all perfectly legal in themselves—and use them to try to prove conspiracy.

Coakley convened the Alameda County grand jury in January 1968; it dutifully returned conspiracy indictments against the young men. Subsequently, they were charged with conspiring to trespass and resist arrest during the draft week demonstrations.* Clearly the seven with their history of political involvement had been singled out. Coakley told reporters, "Technically, a hundred, or even a thousand demonstrators could have been indicted, but we simply don't have enough courts so we have to take the most militant leaders."

A few days after the indictment, the federal government brought conspiracy charges against Dr. Benjamin Spock and four associates in Boston, also for antidraft activity. However, we raised so many challenges to the California conspiracy that Spock came to trial first and in July 1968 he and three of his co-defendants were convicted of conspiring to undermine the Selective Service System.

The Oakland indictment seemed to strike at the heart of the First Amendment and it was on that basis that we challenged it. We were being closely watched by activists and prosecutors alike, for another government victory would encourage more prosecution. We therefore argued that both the right to protest governmental action and agreement to engage in political activity were protected by the First Amendment, that the sole purpose of the indictment was to deter and inhibit free association and free speech. In our argument we cited two higher court decisions.

In the first, a group of American Nazi party members wearing

---

*Trespass and resisting arrest are misdemeanors, seldom punishable by a jail term, but conspiracy is a felony which carries up to a three-year prison term.

brown uniforms and swastika armbands picketed a meeting celebrating the fifteenth anniversary of the state of Israel in New York. Public disorder resulted, and five Nazis were convicted of conspiracy to create the disorder. The United States Court of Appeals reversed the conviction on the grounds that the judge's instructions to the jury had implied that a conspiracy could exist merely because the Nazis had used slogans, signs, and symbols which they knew would inflame the crowd. The court held that although such might be inflammatory the instigators were nonetheless protected by the First Amendment.

The second was the Terminello case which the Supreme Court had decided in 1949 and which decision in part read:

> A function of free speech under our system of government is to invite disputes. It may indeed serve its high purpose when it induces a condition of unrest, creates dissatisfaction with conditions as they are, or even stirs people to anger.

In another motion, we cited Robert Jackson, a former justice of the Supreme Court, who said, "the modern crime of conspiracy is so vague, it almost defies definition."

We did not succeed in getting the indictments dismissed on constitutional grounds, and the case finally came to trial in January 1969. Mal Burnstein, a criminal lawyer from Oakland with a wealth of political trial experience, joined me, along with Dick Hodge, a young San Francisco attorney who had once been a deputy district attorney.

Our firm represented Mandel, Smith, Hamilton, Bardacke, and Erlich, with Burstein and Hodge representing Segal and Cannon, respectively.

The assigning of certain attorneys to certain clients was a technicality, for we had decided upon a united defense. Though the attorneys as a group were actually representing the defendants as a group, the technicality gave us the advantage of three chances to cross-examine witnesses, argue on behalf of our clients, and respond to anything the prosecution said. This way we also avoided the situation, which sometimes happens when there are multiple defendants and more than one lawyer, of any attempt to get some off at the expense of the others. Though the seven disagreed on many things, they were united in their determination that the Vietnam war be a major issue in the trial. We lawyers were committed to the ideas of our clients though we knew that Lowell Jensen would contend that the trial had nothing to do with the war, that the boys had been indicted only because of some disturbances in downtown Oakland.

We moved to be allowed to present evidence about the Nuremburg Principles* to the jury, but we were turned down. We did receive permission to question jurors about them during the voirdire. This premise was to be the cornerstone of our defense: we had to give the jurors an alternative. We wanted them to understand that stopping the war was important, that the seven accused had a duty and a responsibility to do what they could to stop an illegal war. Having provided this foundation in the minds of the jurors, we could then go on to prove that many people joined the demonstrations voluntarily and not at the urging of our clients. We would also point out because they wanted to do something about the war, that while hundreds helped organize Stop the Draft Week only these seven had been singled out for prosecution.

THE TRIAL BEGINS

The judge assigned to the case was George W. Phillips, the same judge who earlier had declared a mistrial when the district attorney had excluded blacks from the jury. However, as the trial opened Phillips was decidedly unfriendly toward us. He was upset when he learned that I, not Barney Dreyfus, was to handle the trial; he had expected to be dealing with the suave, scholarly Dreyfus, an outstanding constitutional lawyer, in this very important First Amendment case—not the loudmouthed Garry with his propensity for asking difficult questions.

Jury selection would be crucial, as in the Newton case, except the prejudice we must weed out would be bias against young people, demonstrations, beards, long hair. Furthermore, many potential jurors worked at military-related facilities, and in the wake of the 1968

*The Nuremburg Principles, now a recognized precept of international law, were developed after World War II when the Allies prosecuted war criminals. The Principles hold that every citizen of every nation has a duty and a responsibility to see that a nation's leaders do not carry out crimes against humanity. Lower-echelon Nazis tried to claim innocence on the grounds that they were only carrying out orders, that it was not their responsibility to try to stop the mass exterminations. The Tribunal ruled otherwise.

presidential campaign of Richard M. Nixon there was a lot of law-and-order rhetoric in the air.

To aid us in making sure the jury understood our case, we drew up a list of fifty questions, among them:

Are you in favor of, and do you support the war in Vietnam?

Do you believe in the right of a person to exercise "civil disobedience" against a law he believes to be illegal, inhumane, and a crime against humanity?

Do you believe in the principle, as expressed in the Nuremburg judgments, that "individuals have international duties which transcend the national obligations imposed by the individual state"?

Would you give as much credibility to the testimony of an ordinary citizen as you would to the testimony of a police officer?

To what extent would you protest a government policy you considered criminal, immoral, and unjust?

Could you support any form of physical defense to a Nazi or fascist takeover of the U.S.?

During the first week we examined a retired Marine colonel. We asked the ex-combat officer if the fact that some of the demonstrators used their bodies to prevent busloads of draftees from reaching the induction center created a prejudgment on his part.

"Certainly not," he answered. "That was a different war."

From that slight emphasis, I deduced that he regarded World War II as justifiable but did not feel the same about Vietnam, so we left him on the jury.

The aim was, in addition to getting the jurors to understand they were of a different generation and cultural background from our clients, to see that the actions of the Oakland Seven were in the finest American tradition, protected by the First Amendment. We wanted to show that no conspiracy existed, that the police themselves had initiated the violence.

Our posture was not defensive. We felt that the government and the police ought to be on trial, not our clients. As I had said many times in speeches before the trial, "They shouldn't have indicted the Oakland Seven. They should have pinned medals on them." Our job was to convince a jury of this.

In early February, when the jury was sworn in, the bitter student strike at San Francisco State College was in its third month. There were frequent police-student clashes there, and, in Berkeley, where

Third World students had gone on strike, the newspapers and television screens were filled with stories of demonstrations far more disruptive than those at the Oakland Induction Center had been. Because a fair trial in such atmosphere was impossible, we moved for a dismissal of the charges, but we were turned down.

Judge Phillips ordered the clerk to read the indictment. I had read it myself many times before, but, listening to it in court, I was struck by the total absurdity of the conspiracy law. The seven defendants, it said, "did conspire, combine, confederate, and agree," to get others to trespass and resist arrest. None had been arrested on either misdemeanor.

California law requires that the indictment cite the overt acts carried out in furtherance of the conspiracy. The grand jury had listed the overt acts. The first read:

> Pursuant to the above said combination, confederation, agreement, or conspiracy, defendant Reese Erlich did on or about October 5, 1967, in the city of Berkeley, arrange for a meeting of, did meet with, and did direct a meeting of, several other persons at the Wesley Foundation.

In plain English, Erlich arranged a sinister public meeting in a church foundation building. The other overt acts, stripped of the legal verbiage, charged that Segal had distributed leaflets outside the Oakland Induction Center; Smith had met with a group of people in a park and taught them how to use clubs; Smith and Mandel opened a bank account for the Stop the Draft Week Committee; Segal and Hamilton met people prior to the demonstrations and walked with them to the induction center; Cannon met people in a park and distributed or displayed clubs to them; Bardacke met people on a street corner and walked with them to the induction center; Mandel paid for buses and brought loudspeaker equipment on to the Berkeley campus; and Smith encouraged people to go from Sproul Plaza to the induction center.

None of those acts were illegal, yet the prosecution would argue that, combined with an agreement between our clients and the demonstrations that resulted, they constituted the crime of conspiracy to trespass and resist arrest. That's why antiwar activists were so concerned about the use of conspiracy laws—almost any legal activity can be seen as part of a criminal conspiracy by an ambitious or vindictive prosecutor.

Jensen did not mention the war in his opening statement. He said our clients had planned a demonstration, "which had as its specific purpose the commission of a crime." Listening to him, one would have thought that seven hardened criminals had got together, and, for no reason at all, plotted to close down the induction center. The entire case, he told the jury, came down to whether or not the defendants had conspired to violate the two misdemeanor ordinances.

Evidence of this conspiracy, he said, was the fact that the defendants held meetings, planned strategy, held rallies, and taught people to use clubs against the police. He went on to say that the plan was so sophisticated that monitors carrying walkie-talkies were employed to achieve the goal of shutting down the induction center. He neglected to say that police undercover agents had supplied the demonstrators with the communications equipment and at times had taken part in the planning process.

When Jensen finished, I rose to make the opening statement for the defense, but Judge Phillips told me to sit down. He said we could make our statement when we opened the defense case. The judge has this option, but the California custom has always been to allow the defense to reply to the prosecution right away, unless the defense side wants to wait. I was sure Phillips was still unhappy that I was trying the case, and not Dreyfus. I had felt an undercurrent of hostility from him all during jury selection so I went in and spoke with him during a recess, and after that he was more evenhanded.

Jensen's first witness was Raymond Brown, deputy chief of the Oakland police department. A large, soft-spoken man, Brown had been field commander on Tuesday morning when the police had charged into the crowd at the induction center. He also had been in charge during the pacifist sit-in the day before.

Brown told the court that, on Monday, he hadn't declared an illegal assembly because fewer than two thousand people had gathered and the streets weren't entirely blocked. On Tuesday, however, about six thousand were in the streets by six A.M., with more arriving all the time. Twice he warned the demonstrators over a police loudspeaker to get back on the sidewalks, but his warnings weren't heeded. Then he declared an illegal assembly, twice reading a formal dispersal order that had been prepared weeks in advance.

According to his testimony, the Tuesday crowd was hostile and completely blocked the street, whereas the Monday gathering had been passive. He ordered some of the seven hundred cops under his command to form a wedge. When the second dispersal order was greeted by shouts of derision, he ordered the wedge into the crowd. It took less than six minutes to clear the street.

My first question on cross-examination was: "How many stoolpigeons did you have in that crowd?"

Jensen objected, Brown pretended not to understand, the judge looked shocked, and the spectators laughed. I asked the question again, but got no response. I had used stoolpigeon deliberately because union members on the jury would understand its pejorative connotations.

"All right, tell me how many undercover agents you had in that crowd."

"About twenty."

"And how many of your agents attended Stop the Draft Week planning committee meetings?"

"I believe six."

"Did you give your men orders to beat up newsmen?"

"No," Brown replied indignantly, but dozens of press people had been beaten during Tuesday's rout, and several had filed formal complaints. Brown admitted receiving these, and, after lengthy sparring, conceded that he did see policemen club demonstrators and newsman when the street was cleared.

Then I showed him a leaflet that had been passed out by the pacifists who sat in the previous morning. Their literature had exhorted people to sit-in (trespass) and go limp (resist arrest).

"Did you arrest any of these people for conspiracy?"

"No."

"Didn't they notify you three weeks in advance that they intended to sit in the induction center doorways?"

"Yes."

"Then why weren't they arrested for conspiracy?"

Brown had no answer. It was illogical to arrest one group for conspiracy and not the other, because both had done the same things. Our clients' rhetoric had been more militant, and the Friday demonstration much more disruptive, but that had nothing to do with conspiracy. It was obvious that the district attorney and others were out to get the Oakland Seven because they were radical political activists.

Hodge pointed out that Brown had told the grand jury that he gave a code 200 to the plainclothesmen in the crowd, just before he sent the wedge charging in.

"What is a code 200?" Hodge asked.

"It's a signal for an officer to get out of the area,"

"Why did you give it?"

"There was a possibility they could get hurt."

Brown was followed by the manager of the building in which the induction center was located. Despite Jensen's repeated entreaties, the man simply couldn't recall any acts of real violence by the demonstrators.

AN INFORMER

Early in the trial Jensen produced his first star witness, James Bruce Coleman, 22. Coleman had been a cop only a short time when he was told to attend Stop the Draft Week meetings, make notes, and report back to his superiors. His testimony was that, in order to join the committee, all he had to do was walk into a meeting and sit down. He used phony identification to make it difficult to trace him to the Oakland police in case he was challenged. Coleman attended numerous planning sessions, went on reconaissance trips to the induction center, made suggestions, represented the committee at meetings of other groups, and offered to supply a large number of firecrackers so the protesters could harass the police. The Stop the Draft Week leaders, however, were not fooled by Coleman and his cohort Robert Wheeler, but, since their cars were useful, they saw no need to kick them out. But Lee Felsenstein, in charge of communications equipment, gave them a set of phony radio codes in sealed envelopes to deliver to the Stanford organizers, telling the Stanford people to return the envelopes unopened. He got them back to find both had been steamed open; one contained an altered code. At the pre-demonstration rally, Felsenstein took the two to the office (Mandel's apartment) where he produced the envelopes and tampered codes. He told them they were "ratfinks," that everyone knew they were police spies, and to stay away from the demonstrations. They departed, not to be seen again until they appeared in court.

Coleman seemed nervous even when Jensen questioned him and couldn't recall very much without referring to his notes. He gave his answers in a stilted, formal way, such as, "At this time, I observed Mr. Smith in conversation with persons unknown to me." If he didn't know something, he would reply, "I do not know, sir," in a little sing-song way, like a British public school student.

He seemed unsure of everything, often beginning his answers with, "I have indicated here that . . . ," meaning he was relying on his notes, not his memory. He was dressed in a narrow dark-green suit, and his short hair was plastered down on his head. He presented a sharp contrast to the defendants who usually wore jeans, T-shirts, leather or corduroy jackets. Segal, who was in jail, wore a suit and tie but his hair was bushy and he had a large mustache. Our clients presented themselves as they really were, from their long hair to their leather boots.

Coleman tried to avoid looking our way as he attempted to link each defendant with an overt act: Erlich had told a group that the Oakland protests would require a new breed of demonstrator; Mandel had said that trained monitors would picket and create havoc; Cannon told a rally that the demonstrators' aim was to "shut the mother down"; Bardacke suggested that confetti, marbles, lettuce, and shaving cream be used to slow down the police. He couldn't say if Bardacke had been serious or not.

While Coleman testified, Jensen introduced photos taken by other agents of various planning meetings, some held in parks, near the induction center, or along escape routes. The pictures showed numerous people, but Coleman was asked only to point out the seven defendants. Only two of the many photos showed two or more of the defendants together.

Coleman's testimony had Cannon with a group of eight, Segal with another group, Hamilton and Mandel talking separately with others, but the conspirators never seemed to talk to each other. Some of their paths crossed only once during Coleman's entire tale. He mentioned Lee Felsenstein, Morgan Spector, Bob Avakian, and Jack Weinberg repeatedly—but none of these had been indicted.

Coleman couldn't testify to what happened at the demonstrations because he wasn't there, but he mentioned almost any idea that was tossed out at a meeting, whether it was used or not.*

Much was made of the demonstration Smith gave on the use of

---

*This is why conspiracy laws are so dangerous. A suggestion, not acted upon, can be used as evidence of a conspiracy, or an intent to conspire, years after the suggestion has been made. If conspiracy laws were widely used and the First Amendment disregarded, people would be afraid to talk to their neighbors about forming a block association. It could be construed as a conspiracy to disrupt local government if the neighbors organized a sit-in to demand a new traffic light or stop sign and public disorder resulted.

clubs, and the fact that Cannon once brought heavy wooden sticks to a meeting. (The draft committee had considered using heavy picket signs or equipping monitors with sticks but had decided against it because they feared the sticks would provoke a police attack. Yet, the sticks, the walkie-talkies, and the communications command post were all pointed to as part of a military operation. The fact that police agents supplied some of the radio equipment was never mentioned.)

Obviously, Coleman was one of the keys to the prosecution's case. I could see that he was nervous and almost totally dependent on his notes. I knew that his story contained numerous discrepancies. Therefore I went after him.

"Mr. Coleman," I began, moving toward the witness stand. "Do you know what a ratfink is?"

There was laughter from the spectators and a heated objection from Jensen, which Judge Phillips angrily sustained.

"I won't tolerate that kind of conduct, Mr. Garry."

"I'll connect it up later, judge." I then turned back to Coleman, who was sitting with his hands folded on his lap like a choir boy.

"Well, have you ever been called a ratfink?"

"Possibly."

"Didn't a member of the committee tell you he knew who you were and didn't want you or any other fink around?"

"That's correct."

"He called you a ratfink, isn't that right?"

"Possibly."

"And that was the truth, wasn't it?"

The entire courtroom burst into laughter.

Judge Phillips sternly warned against further outbursts and cautioned me against making speeches. I wasn't just grandstanding, however. I wanted the jury—and especially the union members, who also called spies "rats" and "finks"—to understand what Coleman's function had been.

"Didn't they tell you they didn't want you creating incidents at the demonstration?"

"Yes."

"Weren't the defendants constantly talking about the danger of police agents creating incidents that would give the police a chance to beat up demonstrators?"

"That's true."

"Wasn't the constant theme of the meetings you attended the illegal, immoral, and aggressive nature of the Vietnam war?"

Coleman grudgingly conceded that this had been true.

"Didn't Mr. Cannon repeatedly say that the draftees were not the enemies of the demonstrators?"

"That's correct."

It struck me as odd that before responding Coleman always consulted his notes. Then I noticed that they were Xeroxes. Coleman had quoted Mandel as saying, "A cop will get you for assault if you breathe on him," and though this would tend to show the leaders counseled people to avoid the police rather than do battle with them, Mandel told me he had never made that statement. We demanded to see Coleman's original notes. I instructed him to read the statement he had attributed to Mandel. Reluctantly, he admitted that his notes indicated that Morgan Spector made the statement. We then sought to show that Coleman's notes had been doctored, so that statements and actions taken by others would be attributed to our clients at the trial. Hodge read off the names of people Coleman had mentioned repeatedly, but who hadn't been indicted.

"Were they leaders?"

"I would say they were most active."

"You took your notes pretty selectively, didn't you? You left out a number of statements."

"That's correct."

"If a person talked for say, forty minutes, you'd just take down the information that was most damaging, isn't that right?"

"Well, I would say just that which was most useful."

MORE WITNESSES

Lt. Ernest Smith took more than seven hundred pictures at the demonstrations, but in only two of these police photos did any of the defendants appear. One picture showed Smith and Mandel talking to a group of people, another showed Smith talking and gesticulating. Burnstein cross-questioned Lt. Smith, whose photos showed policemen clubbing demonstrators. Smith said he'd seen a scuffle at the point of the wedge but maintained he saw no police violence.

"Didn't you see any policemen hit anyone?"

"I believe I saw some clubs raised in the air."

"Did you see any of them landing?"

"No, sir!"

Smith's emphatic response touched off another round of laughter among the spectators.

When Jensen called Jan Blais, an assistant dean at Berkeley, to testify that Erlich had set up a series of Stop the Draft Week meetings on the campus, we made no effort to challenge him. What he said was true. But we used the cross-examination as an opportunity to launch our attack on the district attorney, Frank Coakley, and his selective prosecution of our clients.

I attempted to question Blais about the pressures the Alameda County Board of Supervisors and Coakley's office had placed upon the university in an attempt to impede the demonstrations, but I was cut off by an objection. We then moved to bring in Coakley himself to testify, contending that the district attorney had focused on the Seven and were out to get them from the start. We maintained that they were indicted not for anything they did, but for what they had been saying about the war. Jensen replied that it was an illogical fallacy to think that our clients were being prosecuted for their political beliefs.

I itched to get Coakley on the witness stand. I had cross-examined him in federal court just before the Newton trial and he'd made a damned fool of himself. He was so crotchety and so cantankerous that I was sure he'd blurt out the truth in a fit of pique. Unfortunately, Judge Phillips would not let us call him.

On days when court wasn't in session, or when there were lengthy legal arguments, our clients were out demonstrating. They led one protest outside the gates of San Francisco's Presidio, where twenty-seven young soldiers were being tried for mutiny. At other times, they went over to San Francisco State or to Berkeley. When the Third World student strike erupted, they virtually commuted between the courtroom and the campus, often driving back to Berkeley for a rally during the court's lunch recess. All felt they had been indicted partly to limit their political activity, and they were determined not to let that happen. We lawyers made no attempt to discourage them, for, in our view, that was what the trial was all about —the right to engage in political activity without undercover agents and police spies snooping about. If we lost, and the government was successful with conspiracy prosecutions elsewhere, it could mean that the police might be able to stop protests before they got started. In order to get a court injunction or a conspiracy indictment the state would only have to show that the demonstrators were planning actions that might be illegal. By giving the police and prosecutors great leeway this would seriously erode the First Amendment rights to free speech and free association.

Captain James McCarthy was in charge of the tactical unit that cleared the street. He said police intelligence informed him that the demonstrators on Monday and Wednesday were willing to be arrested, but there would be confrontations on Tuesday and Friday. His orders for Tuesday were to move the protesters out at all costs, and not to make arrests. Therefore, when his men came to the people sitting in the induction center doorway, they were moved out too.

Those who sat in passively on Tuesday suffered the worst beatings. They had expected to be peaceably arrested, as had the sit-ins the day before, but the police were all geared up for a militant demonstration, and clubbed and maced anyone in their path.

All the prosecution's photos showed the demonstrators either standing quietly or milling about and chanting—until the police charge. McCarthy acknowledged that he saw a TV cameraman go down. "He was in the way, I presume," he explained. However, he couldn't explain why his men had maced a young girl who had fallen beneath the charging policemen.

We doubted McCarthy's claims about police intelligence. I handed him a demonstration leaflet which the police saw weeks in advance and asked him to read one particular line aloud. "There will be no aggressive violence against the cops," McCarthy read. He admitted he heard demonstration leaders say they intended to remain in the street until they were arrested, but the police still went ahead with the charge. It all added up to an Oakland vendetta against the radical students from Berkeley.

It seemed clear that nothing illegal took place before the police charge. The demonstrators, hearing about what had happened the previous day, assumed they would be arrested if they remained in the street. Even if blocking the street was deemed illegal, the courts have long held that political expression takes priority over the flow of traffic. It would have been simple for a handful of policemen to reroute the early morning traffic. Had they been in sympathy with the demonstrators, they probably would have done so.

Two years before, a federal court had ordered the Oakland police to divert traffic to accommodate a march from Berkeley to the Oakland Army Terminal. They could easily have done the same near the induction center. In our view, their real purpose was not to maintain order but to suppress dissent. They tried to do this by beating up as many demonstrators as possible, hoping to discourage them from ever coming back to Oakland.

A SECOND SPY

Undercover agent Robert Wheeler followed Captain McCarthy to the stand. Wheeler had infiltrated Stop the Draft Week by claiming he was an SDS member from Rochester, N.Y. He, too, had been given phony identity papers by the Oakland police, but they weren't necessary. Like most antiwar groups, the committee was completely open. Names and credentials were rarely checked, and everyone was encouraged to participate.

Wheeler also testified from notes, but he was much surer of himself than Coleman. However, he displayed a certain cockiness and arrogance. Like Coleman, he tried, on direct examination, to link each defendant with the overt act listed in the indictment, to cite meetings they had attended, or report remarks they had made. He tried to picture Segal as an outside agitator because he was an SDS national officer from Chicago, but all he could say was that Segal had made a few speeches. Jensen spent some time on Wheeler's description of Smith's demonstration of police club techniques (Smith had gained his knowledge during a brief stint as a San Quentin prison guard), and I began cross-examining Wheeler on this point.

After several probing questions, Wheeler admitted that the bulk of Smith's demonstration was devoted to showing people how to defend themselves against police club blows. He also described how he gave the committee a citizen's band radio and other communications equipment (which the police easily jammed the day of the demonstration). In addition, he had passed out leaflets urging others to attend the demonstration. We pointed out that Segal had been indicted for doing the very same thing.

With the help of voluminous notes Wheeler talked for several hours, describing many meetings, quoting more than a dozen different people. He revealed that he had been shown pictures of Cannon, Mandel, and Hamilton before he began his assignment, and was told they were leaders. Just before I finished questioning him, I asked, "Did you ever see all seven defendants together at one meeting?" Wheeler thought for a moment, thumbed furiously through his notes, then said reluctantly, "No, I didn't."

"So you never saw them together?" I repeated, looking over at the jury to emphasize the point.

"No, I didn't." Wheeler repeated.

Hodge asked Wheeler how he had compiled such an impressive set of notes. Wheeler claimed he would attend a three- or four-hour meeting and then go home and accurately transcribe exactly what each person had said. He insisted that the statements he had attributed to the defendants were verbatim quotes. He said he had almost total recall.

Hodge was skeptical and challenged him. The questions and answers flew back and forth at a rapid pace, with the ever confident Wheeler fending off Hodge's questions and exuding smugness. The exchange continued at a hectic pace until the court reporter, unable to keep up, asked Wheeler to repeat his last statement. After a long pause he said, "I can't remember what I just said." On that note we let the memory expert off the witness stand.

As the trial rolled on our confidence rose. We noted, as did the media, that Jensen still had not managed to put the seven defendants in one place at one time, despite the two undercover agents who had roamed through planning meetings at will. This isn't a requirement under the conspiracy law, but, as a practical matter, it's harder to convince a jury that a conspiracy existed if the conspirators were never all together in one place.

THE STUDENTS ON TAPE

We also noted, but kept to ourselves, that there had been no evidence yet presented about the Friday demonstration that had successfully closed the induction center. On Tuesday the demonstrators were quickly routed by the police, but on Friday they were better prepared and more organized. Besides helmets and padded clothing, many demonstrators carried plywood shields to ward off police clubs. Some of these shields bore a large picture of Che Guevara, the Cuban revolutionary who had been killed in Bolivia earlier that week.

When the police converged on Friday's demonstration, the protestors broke into small groups and retreated. They used benches, trashcans, and parked cars to build barricades. The police were unable to make many arrests because the demonstrators kept retreating and regrouping, continually widening the perimeter of barricades. A thousand extra policemen had to be called in from all over the Bay Area before buses filled with draftees could get through. That demonstration had tied up most of downtown Oakland. We were extremely worried about it, but the jurors hadn't heard a word of it.

When Jensen asked to play a tape of the speeches several defendants had made to an outdoor rally on the Berkeley campus the night before the Tuesday demonstration, we invoked the legal principle that speeches and statements cannot be taken out of context. We insisted that the entire tape be played so the jury could hear everything that was said that night, instead of getting only those parts the prosecutor wanted them to hear.

Smith had chaired the teach-in and was constantly admonishing the demonstrators to remain calm, not to panic, to try and maintain a sense of humor. The microphone was thrown open for most of the evening and scores of people got up and talked about why they were going to the induction center to demonstrate, despite strong opposition from the notoriously heavy-handed Oakland police.

What emerged was an emotional and anguished discussion of the effects of the Vietnam war on a generation of young people. Young men spoke of their unwillingness to kill, or to die, for a corrupt dictatorship eight thousand miles away. There were pleas for unity and descriptions of how their commitment to protest the war had brought them closer together. Through it all ran the theme that no matter what the law said, no matter what the police or the government tried to do, they were morally right.

There were moments of humor, exhilaration, frenzy—even statements opposing the protest. The microphone was open to anyone, and Segal served as an informal chairman along with Smith. At one point on the tape Smith said, "One of our major purposes is not to have a confrontation with the police," and, later on, "We've got to stick together. They have the billyclubs, but we have the people of the world behind us."

"Feel responsibility for the brothers and sisters who are with you," Segal advised, "and help them when you can."

A legal advisor distributed a phone number to call if there were arrests. The stream of personal and political statements went on for hours. At another point Smith said, "Will everybody please wake up. I hope we have some people who want to play some songs." The tape revealed that the demonstrators were not highly organized, that their organization was more haphazard than military.

While the speeches had gone on, thousands had huddled in the Sproul Plaza darkness and discussed what they might face the next morning. Many were scared and said so over the microphone. The tape went on for over five hours. As we sat listening to it in the courtroom, watching the jurors' faces, our confidence grew. We were sure it was the first time they had ever heard radicals or antiwar activists talk directly to them, without having it first edited down and molded by the media.

When the tape ended, Jensen rested his case. This confirmed what we had begun to suspect. There was no evidence of a possible conspiracy to plan the more disruptive Friday demonstration because Coleman and Wheeler had been dismissed on Monday evening, and the planning for Friday had taken place between Tuesday and Thursday. That's why Jensen had tried to magnify the Tuesday demonstration out of all proportion. He had no other evidence. Had Coleman and Wheeler not been kicked out Monday, Jensen probably would have focused on the more successful Friday demonstration and had a stronger case.

THE MOVE TO DISMISS

When the prosecution rests, the defense customarily moves to dismiss the charges for lack of proof. Too often these motions are mere ritual. However, when we moved for a dismissal Burnstein brought in a stack of legal precedents and five different motions. Some attorneys let minor things slide, or make their motions as if they don't really expect them to be granted, but I believe in arguing every point, no matter how small, and in covering all the fine points and technicalities. Appeals courts sometimes feel more comfortable reversing a conviction on a minor technicality rather than on a major issue, so you have to give them a lot of points to choose from. If you don't raise these points during the trial, you can't use them in an appeal.

We argued that the prosecution had not proved that a conspiracy existed, that its case was based almost entirely on circumstantial evidence. Judge Phillips conceded that Jensen's case was "mushy," but said, "the law of conspiracy is so broad and so vague." It was obvious that Phillips had great doubts about the validity of the prosecution. However he was under heavy pressure, especially after declaring the mistrial the year before.

At one point when Burnstein, Hodge, and I were all arguing at the same time, Judge Phillips looked up, shook his head wearily, and said, "You people make it awfully difficult to be a judge."

I said, "Your honor has the power to stop this farce right now." I pointed out that much of the evidence was taken from our clients' public statements and speeches. "People have a right to say what they think and what they believe, and you can't make a conspiracy out of that." We argued until the end of the day with Burnstein citing precedent after precedent, but Phillips decided, very reluctantly I believe, not to dismiss the charges.

THE DEFENSE BEGINS

In our opening statement I talked about the Vietnam war and the Nuremburg judgments, saying we had evidence that the war was illegal, inhumane, immoral, and genocidal. I reminded the jury that the Nuremburg Principles said that citizens had an obligation to do everything in their power to prevent inhumane acts by their government.

"No longer can anyone say, 'I was just a soldier,' or 'I was just obeying orders.'" Then I characterized Frank Coakley as a man without regard for human rights. The real aim of the prosecution, I told the jury, was to make people wary of using their right to free speech.

"This is selective prosecution. Because these seven young men have been leaders among young people in this area, this trial is an attempt to prevent them from continuing their activities."

I said we would show that many people went to the demonstrations for reasons that had nothing to do with our clients.

While we had sought to have the charges dismissed on legal and constitutional grounds, it wasn't as if we didn't have a defense. We had screened over 150 potential witnesses and had selected about fifty of the most articulate, who seemed to be representative of the demonstrators. We also had the seven defendants to call upon.

Our opening witness was Stephen Lindstedt, a former Berkeley policeman who had resigned about a month before Stop the Draft Week. Still in his twenties, Lindstedt went to the pacifist sit-in on Monday, wasn't arrested, and returned with his girl-friend on Tuesday. He said he found the Tuesday scene far too tense and decided not to get involved, to watch from across the street.

He testified that he saw the Oakland police club and mace dozens of demonstrators without provocation. He and his girl-friend left the area, and both were clubbed over the head by Oakland policemen while standing on a sidewalk several blocks from the induction center. Lindstedt said he didn't know any of the defendants. He had gone to the demonstration because he wanted to do something about the war.

Our second witness, the Reverend Claire Nesmith described how he had gone to the Monday and Tuesday demonstrations with his two teenage sons out of a deep conviction that the war was morally and ethically wrong. Nesmith, pastor at San Francisco's Park Presdio Methodist Church, had passed out information about the protest to people he knew, but he had acted on his own and didn't know any of the defendants. He was, however, acquainted with the pacifists who had organized the Monday demonstration.

"Were any of them indicted for conspiracy?"

"Not that I know of."

Whenever one of our witnesses described other people they had gone to the demonstration with, a defense lawyer always asked, "Were any of them indicted for conspiracy?" After a high school student testified that she went to the induction center at the urging of her student body leaders, I asked her:

"How many of them were indicted for conspiracy?"

"None of them were."

As the defense rolled on, the cross-section became broader. We called graduate students, photographers, longshoremen, reporters, professors, a psychiatrist, and several law students, all of whom had been at the Tuesday demonstration. Then we brought on Jerry Jensen, who had covered the Tuesday action for KRON-TV, the NBC affiliate in San Francisco. Jensen had been standing with the demonstrators when he was suddenly clubbed by the onrushing police. He and other newsmen had filed civil suits against the city of Oakland because of the beatings they had received.

Jensen told a story similar to what our previous witnesses had described. He stated that the police had abruptly charged into a passive, milling, chanting crowd. Like the others, he never heard Deputy Chief Brown's dispersal order beyond, "In the name of the people of California. . . ." The rest was drowned out by the demonstrators chanting, "We are the people! We are the people!" His testimony added greatly to the credibility of our other witnesses and gave weight to our theory that the police had initiated the violence.

The turning point came when we called the Reverend Ralph Luther Mollering, pastor of the University Lutheran Chapel in Berkeley. We were trying to show that Berkeley was a center of antiwar activity, that many people had written about and made speeches about the war there, and that any number of individuals had influence over the demonstrators besides our clients.

Mollering had written a pamphlet entitled "Vietnam—An Agonizing Dilemma for the Christian Conscience." By the time he finished writing it, he said, he had become convinced that the United States' position in Vietnam was morally indefensible. By October 1967, he had become an active member of the Faculty Peace Committee.

Jensen objected to Mollering's testimony, so we all went into the judge's chambers for another legal argument. Jensen claimed that the pastor's testimony was circumstantial. "So is your whole case, Lowell," I countered. We maintained that Mollering's testimony would show that faculty members had been making speeches, issuing statements, and going to antiwar demonstrations long before Stop the Draft Week. These not only influenced our clients, we said, but also helped explain their intent in organizing the demonstrations.

Phillips ruled that he would allow Mollering to testify further, but warned us to keep it short.

"If this is going to drag on and take in all his views, I won't permit it. I know ministers. I have five in my family."

Back in court, Mollering said, "Both as an American citizen and a Christian theologian, I am convinced the Vietnam war violates the entire tradition of Western Christianity and Judaism. Therefore I felt conscience bound to oppose it. To do so is the highest form of patriotism because it calls for trying to change government policy, when the government is clearly involved in something detrimental to the interests of its citizens and the people of the world."

Mollering, along with other faculty members, had signed a statement encouraging people to demonstrate at the induction center and to resist the draft. The young minister said he signed the statement because:

"I felt that we who were not of draft age also needed to share, inasmuch as possible, the risk and peril that was involved. If young men were willing to risk arrest, we should be willing to declare our unity with them."

For some reason, Jensen got into a political debate with Mollering, something he had carefully avoided doing before this, maintaining that politics had nothing to do with the case.

"Is it your position that both sides are unjust, illegal, and immoral in carrying out the war, or that just one side is?"

"I wish there were alternatives to the Viet Cong or the South Vietnamese government we support, but my studies and research indicate there is a higher degree of support for the NLF and North

Vietnamese government than for the government we have endorsed and militarily supported."

"Do you equate your concept of justice in terms of popular vote then?"

"No, I wouldn't say that, but we are supporting a government which is obviously the lineal descendant of the French colonial regime. That is, the people who hold power in Saigon are really the beneficiaries of French colonialism and the privileged classes of Vietnam. As a representative of the Christian faith, I would have to cast my lot with those who are seeking liberation from their wretched, miserable state, and who are revolting against the oppressive powers."

The debate went on for ten or fifteen minutes. Jensen asked if the minister's signature on the complicity statement was not a violation of federal law.

"As I understand it, yes, but there is a higher law that says we must obey God rather than man."

The debate ended after that, but Jensen had given us what we had been seeking from the outset—a debate on the merits of the Vietnam war. Furthermore, he had inadvertently provided an important legal opening. He had asked Mollering only a question or two about the legal aspects of the war, but this gave Burnstein an opportunity to use his vast knowledge of international law to bring out points we normally would not have been able to use.

When Burnstein started to question Mollering, Jensen objected because the minister was not a legal expert. However Burnstein said he was cross-examining Mollering on behalf of his client. Since Jensen had raised the legal point in his cross-examination, Burnstein had the right to do so in his. As I had called and questioned Mollering originally, we were cross-examining our own witness, a definite advantage. Jensen's face showed no emotion, but he knew he had made a mistake.

Through Mollering, Burnstein was able to bring out that the Vietnam war violated the U.S. Constitution (Congress had never declared war on Vietnam), the U.N. Charter, and the 1954 Geneva agreements. We had always hoped, but never dreamed, we'd get such information into the trial.

Burnstein later observed with satisfaction, "They gave us a tiny opening, and we drove a truck right through it."

During the recess, an *Oakland Tribune* reporter asked for an explanation of the legal maneuvering. While we talked, two of the defendants, now in very high spirits, came over and asked with broad smiles,

"Hey Charlie, are you as good as Perry Mason?"

"I'm *better* than Perry Mason," I said, winking at the reporter. "*All* of his clients are innocent."

You never saw expressions change so fast. They had spotted the reporter. Their faces dropped and they sprinted for the men's room leaving a trail of laughter in their wake.

When court reconvened, we continued with our stream of witnesses. There was an ophthamologist, a dietitian, a former Air Force captain, and a young assistant track coach at Stanford named Jack Scott. Scott's testimony wasn't much different from our other witnesses, but the Oakland demonstrations were one of his first contacts with radical politics.

Jensen had stopped objecting when our witnesses expounded on their views about Vietnam. A reporter said Jensen didn't seem to have his heart in the case anymore, but he kept cross-examining our people with the meticulous precision that was his trademark. He asked each witness where they had heard about the demonstrations, hoping to link them to the defendants, and in this way show a conspiracy.

One witness heard through Women for Peace, another was informed by the Episcopal Peace Fellowship, and many learned through the newspapers.

"How do you know there's going to be a football game on Saturday?" a teacher asked.

We also called two expert witnesses on Vietnam, Don Duncan, a former Green Beret who had quit the military as a direct result of his Vietnam experiences, and Bob Scheer, the editor of *Ramparts* magazine. Duncan described how he had helped infiltrate CIA teams into Laos, Cambodia, and North Vietnam well before the public was told about any involvement in those countries. He said the South Vietnamese army was totally dependent upon the United States, while the South Vietnamese government lacked popular support. He also described how demoralized American soldiers became once they perceived the true nature of their role in Vietnam. For a few moments, the stark reality of the war came right into the courtroom. We were trying this case in early 1969 remember, when public opinion still favored the war, so most of this information was new and even startling to most jurors.

Our second Vietnam expert, Bob Scheer, testified about the background of the war, and how it really started. In 1965 Scheer had written an important pamphlet documenting this. We had to fight hard to get both witnesses on the stand, because Jensen objected vehemently, but, in each case, we found a technicality upon which we could bring their testimony in.

SURPRISE MOVE

We were now coming to the time when the seven defendants would testify. In all our remarks, both formal and informal, we had stated that all seven would probably take the stand. However, as the trial unfolded, we realized there was little they could add. Everything they could say had already been effectively said by others. Furthermore, the jury had already heard most of them on the Sproul Plaza tape.

By testifying, they would only be opening themselves to a blistering cross-examination by Jensen, not so much about Stop the Draft Week as about their other political activities. Mandel and Erlich were SDS members and Segal was an SDS national officer. Segal and Cannon had written an article about the Friday demonstration which they called "Pop-Art Guerrilla Warfare." If either testified, Jensen could use some of its more exaggerated phraseology against them. Hamilton was a founder of the Revolutionary Union, a Maoist group, and Smith had just joined Segal in the county jail to serve a brief term for sitting in to block Navy recruiters on the Berkeley campus.

Beyond this, all our clients had made statements using the overblown political rhetoric of the 1960s that might sound inflammatory to a jury of older, mainly south-county people. They had all publicly supported the Black Panther party and Huey Newton and held a variety of political views that Jensen was certain to try and make sound sinister. We also noticed that the jury seemed to be getting tired.

We held a short meeting and with very little discussion both lawyers and clients agreed that we couldn't help ourselves by having some or all of the defendants testify. We felt we might do ourselves some harm if they did.

Our final witness was Roland Finston, a Stanford University physicist. He said he had organized meetings and rallies at Stanford for Stop the Draft Week, distributed leaflets, and hired buses to take demonstrators to Oakland.

"Have you been indicted for conspiracy?"

"No, I haven't."

"Are you under investigation for conspiracy or anything else in connection with these demonstrations?"

"Not that I know of."

When Jensen finished his cross-examination, I conferred briefly with Burnstein, Hodge, and our clients. Then I got up and said,

"Your honor, the defense rests."

Jensen's jaw dropped. He looked as if someone had just poured ice water over his head. We knew he'd been looking forward to cross-examining the Seven.

We spent several days in a bitter wrangle over jury instructions, but in the end convinced Judge Phillips to give those we considered most crucial to our case. The judge decided on his own to read several instructions on First Amendment rights.

In his final argument Jensen contended that he had presented overwhelming proof that the defendants had conspired to violate the law. He defined a conspiracy as an unlawful partnership created with the intent of violating the law. Trying to define conspiracy in the broadest possible terms, he said, "Everybody who is a principal is liable, at least for aiding and abetting."

The Vietnam war and the draft, he continued, were not the real issues in the case, and a laudable motive was no excuse to commit an illegal act. "In the eyes of the law," he said, "Robin Hood remains a thief."

Burnstein led off for our side, talking about the First Amendment, how conspiracy laws constantly threatened the right to free speech, and freedom of political action.

"These young men were not acting to violate the law, but to vindicate the law—a higher law," Burnstein began. "Look at the leaflets and statements. There is no agreement there. A whole variety of attitudes and tactics are expressed. Isn't it absurd to say that these defendants who didn't sit in are guilty of a felony, when those who sat in on Monday were guilty of misdemeanors, and those who sat in on Tuesday weren't even arrested?"

Hodge followed with a calm, careful analysis of the evidence. "Even if you believe all the prosecution witnesses, no conspiracy has been proved. The prosecution has not met the burden of proof," he concluded.

I focused on the political aspects of the case. I reminded the jury that there were periods of upheaval when labor unions were struggling to gain their rights. Then I attacked the indictment. "All I can say is that this prosecution was conceived by a senile and demented mind."

Jensen objected, and Judge Phillips said, "I think we have attacked Mr. Coakley enough. There will be no further attacks on him."

"These seven people were singled out to create a threat and put pressure on freedom of speech, the right to assemble, and the right to oppose unlawful acts of this government. Half a million of your own children are in Vietnam. What are they there for? To make American business happy?"

I reminded the jury that we had presented forty-seven witnesses, most of whom had no connection with the defendants, people who demonstrated entirely for their own reasons. I derided the idea that our clients had hypnotic powers that could bring thousands out on the streets before dawn for no reason at all.

"There is no evidence that these seven people are capable of any kind of hypnosis. My experience has been that they're lucky to get to court on time." Then I talked about conspiracy.

"There is a conspiracy in this country. There's a conspiracy to hoodwink the structure of our government so it won't be of the people, by the people, and for the people. There is a conspiracy to impose our military might upon the rest of the world, and there's a conspiracy to create a curtain of fear so we won't open our mouths against tyranny. There is that kind of conspiracy, but these seven young men are not part of it." I closed by reciting from Emma Lazarus's poem which is inscribed on the pedestal of the Statue of Liberty.

> "Keep ancient lands, your storied pomp!" cries she
> With silent lips. "Give me your tired, your poor.
> Your huddled masses yearning to breathe free.
> The wretched refuse of your teeming shore.
> Send these, the homeless, tempest-tost to me,
> I lift my lamp beside the golden door."

"That is America to me. That is the America that was founded. We have gone astray, and it is men like the defendants, and thousands like them, who will make a world we want."

The jury went out and we felt we would not have long to wait. I even boasted to a reporter that it should take no more than seven or eight minutes to reach a verdict, but those minutes stretched to three days and we began to worry. What possibly could have gone wrong? Finally the jury returned with its verdict—*acquittal for all seven!* We were jubilant. The young people who had been attending the tense trial broke into deafening applause and loud cheering. It was a total victory, not only for us and for the Seven, but also for the First Amendment and free speech, for the principles on which this country was founded.

7.

The Government vs. Bobby Seale

At the beginning of 1969, Huey Newton was in prison, Eldridge Cleaver in exile. Several weeks later Los Angeles Panther leaders John Huggins, 22, and Alprentice ("Bunchy") Carter, 23, were shot and killed on the UCLA campus by members of an organization called US, an off-campus black nationalist group headed by Ron Karenga. US was trying to control the black studies program, and Huggins and Carter had rallied black students behind the idea that they themselves should control it. Subsequently, Karenga was booed off the campus. The next day, Huggins and Carter were gunned down. Three US members were later convicted of the murders and sentenced to prison.*

Then, in March, Bobby Seale was indicted in Chicago on charges of conspiracy growing out of the 1968 Democratic convention riots. In April, twenty-one New York Panthers, including most of the leaders of that chapter, were indicted on bomb conspiracy charges. They were held on $100,000 bail each. There was no way the Panthers could ever hope to raise the more than two million dollars required to bail them all out. This indictment revealed that two long-time

*Two years later, Louis Tackwood, a one-time informer for the Los Angeles Police Department revealed that US had been given money, guns, and narcotics by the police and encouraged to wage war upon the Panthers. We also knew, from a *Wall Street Journal* report, that Karenga had met privately with then police chief Tom Redden in 1968. The 1976 report of the Senate Intelligence Committee later confirmed what we had long suspected: the FBI had been active in promoting conflict between the Panthers and US in the late 1960s and early 1970s.

chapter members were in reality New York City policemen. Later that April, a bomb demolished Panther headquarters in Des Moines.

On May 21, 1969, a fisherman discovered the battered body of a young black man—later identified as New York Panther Alex Rackley—in a riverbed some twenty miles north of New Haven, Connecticut. The police determined that he had been shot once through the heart and once through the head with a .45 caliber automatic pistol, that he had been beaten and tortured before being shot.

On May 22, acting on a tip from an informer, fifty heavily armed New Haven police stormed the temporary headquarters of the newly formed Connecticut chapter of the Black Panther party. They arrested eight people in connection with Rackley's murder. These initially were charged with murder, kidnapping, conspiracy, and binding.* They were held without bail. Warrants went out for Panther captains Landon Williams and Rory Hithe, who were arrested in Denver, and for California Panther Lonnie McLucas, who was picked up in Salt Lake City. The authorities also sought George Sams, whom they described as a Panther leader, although party officials said he had been expelled months before.

Sams was known to be aggressive and boastful, had once scored low enough on a reform-school intelligence test to be diagnosed a moron, and had been classified by juvenile authorities as "an alleged dangerous mental defective." Sams also had a long police record. During the spring and summer of 1969 while the FBI searched fruitlessly for him, they raided Panther headquarters in Washington, D.C., Detroit, Indianapolis, Chicago, Des Moines, Salt Lake City, Denver, Sacramento, and San Diego, destroying or confiscating office equipment, literature, money, supplies. Panthers arrested in those raids were mostly released later without charge.

By then it was clear to me and to the Panthers that the search for Sams was only an FBI pretense to cripple or wipe out the party. We also knew that John Mitchell, United States Attorney-General, had established a special "Panther section" in the Justice Department.

GEORGE SAMS'S ACCUSATION

It was August 7 when Sams surfaced in Toronto, more than three months after the New Haven arrests. Technically, he was arrested,

---

*Binding means to tie someone up.

but I believe that he turned himself in for his own protection. He apparently had been informing on draft resisters and other members of the Canadian underground, and, shortly before the arrest, someone had taken a shot at him from a moving car.

Against the advice of his court-appointed Canadian lawyer, Sams talked at length to the FBI, which called in the New Haven police. In a long, rambling interview with New Haven detectives Vincent DeRosa and Edmund Flanagan, Sams claimed that the order to kill Rackley had come direct from Bobby Seale. Seale was supposed to have told Landon Williams to do away with Rackley, Williams to have passed the order on to Sams. Seale had been in New Haven for about twelve hours on the day before the shooting to give a speech at Yale's Battell Chapel.

Sams further related that he had twice been expelled from the Black Panther party—once for a stabbing; once for a beating—both times on the orders of Seale himself. After the first expulsion, he had asked Stokeley Carmichael, then Panther prime minister, to persuade Seale to reinstate him. Although Sams denied bearing a personal grudge against Seale, he said to DeRosa, "I have every intention of destroying the [Black Panther] party." He agreed to waive extradition and to testify for the prosecution in Connecticut. In return, he was allowed to plead guilty to the lesser second-degree murder charge and the other charges of first-degree murder, kidnapping, and binding were dropped.

When Sams was returned to New Haven, Arnold Markle, the state's attorney, convened a grand jury. He charged that Rackley had accompanied Sams from New York to New Haven and, while inside Panther headquarters there, was tied up, beaten, and scalded with boiling water in an attempt to make him admit to being a police informer and to force him to reveal the names of other agents who supposedly had infiltrated the party. The state contended that—in addition to Sams—ten others had taken part in this kangaroo court. The grand jury subsequently indicted: Seale, Ericka Huggins, Warren Kimbro, Lonnie McLucas, Margaret Hudgins, Frances Carter, Rose Smith, Loretta Luckes, George Edwards, Landon Williams, and Rory Hithe, on charges of first-degree murder, kidnapping, conspiracy to murder, and conspiracy to kidnap. Some of the women also were charged with binding.

It was August 1969 when the grand jury indictment came down. Seale was out on bail pending the Chicago trial. The FBI arrested him in Berkeley as he was returning from the wedding of a friend and, since the Connecticut charge was murder, held him without bail. During the next three months, the world watched as Bobby Seale was bound and gagged during the Chicago trial—for repeatedly demanding that Charles R. Garry be allowed to defend him.

Since Seale was one of the defendants and since we had successfully defended conspiracy charges against antiwar activists in Oakland, I was asked to be chief defense counsel for the Chicago trial.

However, in the summer of 1969, while trying a Panther case in Oakland, I was hospitalized with a painful gall bladder condition. The doctors released me on the condition that I return for surgery as soon as the trial ended.

Early in September I flew to Chicago to seek a postponement in the Chicago case, tentatively scheduled to begin at the end of September. Bill Kunstler and I sat in Judge Hoffman's courtroom one morning and watched him grant postponement after postponement to other attorneys.

One lawyer wanted to take his wife to the South seas. "It's a wonderful trip. I'm sure you'll enjoy it," Hoffman said, granting the attorney a three-month delay.

When our turn came, Judge Hoffman would hardly listen to us. I presented documents from my doctors and assured him I would be ready to proceed six weeks after the original trial date. He turned us down cold. Kunstler and Leonard Weinglass had to try the case by themselves.

All the trouble around Seale in Chicago could have been avoided if Hoffman had granted me the postponement, because all Seale wanted was for me to represent him. Six weeks to the day after the Chicago case began, I was in a San Francisco court representing other clients.

After Seale was severed from the Chicago case, having been sentenced to serve four years in prison for contempt—in reality for demanding his constitutional rights—in November 1969 he was returned to the county jail in San Francisco to await extradition to Connecticut. Meanwhile, the government's campaign against the Panthers continued. In November 1969, David Hilliard was indicted for threatening the life of the President—on the basis of one rhetorical line in a speech he made to an antiwar rally in San Francisco while President Nixon was three thousand miles away in Washington, D.C. Hilliard was the last remaining national Panther leader free. Eventually the charge was dropped, but meantime the bail of $30,000 had to be raised.

On December 4, 1969, the Chicago police raided the apartment of Fred Hampton, the popular and competent chairman of the Illinois chapter, killing him in his sleep and also killing Panther Mark Clark. The chief security officer of the Illinois chapter, William O'Neil, turned out to be a paid FBI informant who had drugged Hampton the night before. Later in December, the Los Angeles police attempted to shoot their way into another Panther headquarters but the Panthers shot back and the attempt failed; however, several more Panthers were jailed. Once again, a Panther member in good standing turned out to be an informer—Norris ("Cotton") Smith was being paid by the Los Angeles police.

All of this harassment did not destroy the party; though shaken to its roots, it continued to function and, after the public outcry over the death of Hampton, the government was forced into subtler methods. By early 1970, the Panthers had recovered sufficiently to begin to organize the defense of the party members charged in New Haven.

Before the trial, Markle did some plea bargaining with five of the accused Panthers—Margaret Hudgins, George Edwards, Frances Carter, Rose Smith, and Loretta Luckes. They accepted a deal that if they pleaded guilty to misdemeanor charges in connection with Rackley's death, the other charges would be dropped, but they imposed the condition that they would not, under any circumstances, testify against the others. Markle agreed.

Left in New Haven were Seale, Huggins, McLucas, and Kimbro. Williams and Hithe were in jail in Denver fighting extradition and Sams, of course, had turned state's evidence.

WARREN KIMBRO DEFECTS

Kimbro, 35, was well-liked, well-respected, and a stable New Haven citizen. An Air Force veteran, he was tall and amiable, had been a justice of the peace, and had headed a local antipoverty unit. He had a brother-in-law who was assistant director of community relations at Yale and many friends in both the white and black communities, one of these being Arnold Markle.

Early in 1970, Markle's office took it upon itself to fly Sgt. William Kimbro, Warren Kimbro's brother, a member of the Dade County (Fla.) police force, to New Haven. Without the knowledge of Kimbro's attorney, both Sgt. Kimbro and Detective DeRosa visited Kimbro in his cell, a violation of Kimbro's constitutional rights, but after the fact there was little that his attorney could do. Afterward, Kimbro changed his plea to guilty of second-degree murder and agreed to testify for the prosecution in both the McLucas trial, scheduled for early summer, and the Seale-Huggins trial that was to follow it. Neither Kimbro nor Sams was sentenced, the implication being clear that they would be sentenced according to the value of their testimony to the state.

ERICKA HUGGINS, FEMALE PANTHER

March 1969 was the date the Connecticut chapter was formed, a couple of months after the death of John Huggins, whose hometown was New Haven. Ericka and her infant daughter, Mai, who was only three weeks old when her father was killed, had come East for the funeral. Ericka decided to remain in New Haven and raise her daughter there. She asked for permission to start a Connecticut Panther chapter. In the wake of the FREE HUEY campaign, bogus Panther chapters had sprung up everywhere—young blacks attracted by the militant tone and by the condoning of the use of guns set up headquarters, buying black leather jackets and berets. The central committee had decided to tighten its own internal structure and to weed out unwanted elements. But they made an exception for Ericka, hoping that it would help her to get over John's death. Both the Hugginses had been dedicated and hard-working members; John had been a leader of the L. A. chapter, but Erika had stayed in the background. The committee gave her the go-ahead and she began recruiting members. One of the first was Kimbro, who was fed up with antipoverty politics. By May 1, the new chapter had thirty-five full-time members and was rapidly growing. They were looking forward to Seale's arrival; he had accepted the speech invitation primarily to lend prestige to Ericka's organization. He was also eager to visit the troubled New York chapter, as most of its leadership was in jail, and those manning the operation were new to it.

Then Sams showed up in New York and announced that he had been sent by national headquarters to straighten things out. Since the April indictments, the chapter was accustomed to seeing people from the national headquarters, so the powerfully built Sams's authoritative claim was believed. Clearly, someone should have checked on him, but obviously the party was not at its best. Soon after arriving in New York Sams began slapping Rackley around, but he stopped when the local Panthers protested. Sams had castigated Rackley for sleeping in the office, but they explained that he lived there. He had come to them months before, barefoot, hungry, and destitute, a heroin addict, though he stayed off narcotics afterward and became a hard-working party member. He was grateful for the Panthers' help, trusted them, and had been characterized as a sort of "puppy-dog" who would do anything anyone wanted of him.

Sams wanted Rackley to accompany him to New Haven where, he said, he was going to inspect that chapter. Rackley asked for and got permission to go, and they arrived on May 17. Almost immediately Sams began accusing Rackley of being a police agent. Again, no one bothered to check him out. The Panthers were a "top-down" organization, one in which members are taught to obey the orders of the leaders in the interests of party discipline. Sams spoke with great authority and, besides, he packed a huge .45 caliber automatic pistol which he was given to waving around to emphasize his orders.

Sams initiated the beating and torture of Rackley, ordered that he be tied up in the basement of Kimbro's house on Orchard Street, and himself beat Rackley with a stick. He ordered the women to boil water, carry it down to the basement, and pour it over Rackley, and ordered Ericka to make a tape of the proceedings, which she did, ostensibly to send back to the national headquarters. The interrogation and torture of Rackley went on for three days. It is my opinion that the police were fully aware of the circumstances and deliberately ignored them because they later raided the house without a search warrant. They claimed they didn't need a warrant because they had acted on information provided by a "trusted ten-year informant." We never learned who the informant was, but if they were able to tell the police Rackley had been shot just a few hours after he was killed, they had to know what was going on just prior to that.

A CONNECTICUT LAWYER

Before I could represent Bobby in New Haven, I had to be admitted to the Connecticut bar. Connecticut normally requires that an accused person hire a Connecticut attorney, but they waived that rule for us, probably mindful of what had happened in Chicago when

Judge Hoffman refused to allow me to defend Bobby.* Connecticut had admitted an outside lawyer only once before, when the noted civil rights and criminal attorney Samuel Liebowitz was specially admitted in 1931.

Judge Harold Mulvey, who was to preside over the Seale-Huggins trial and the McLucas case that preceded it, placed two conditions on my admittance. He said we would have to hire a local attorney to help me represent Bobby and apprise me of the local rules, and that I would have to promise that I would maintain order in the courtroom on behalf of my client.

He admitted that no other attorney had ever been forced to make such a promise before, but I guess the hysteria surrounding the Chicago case (even though Bobby had been completely within his rights there, as the appeals courts later ruled) had created the impression that the Panthers made a regular practice of disrupting trials.

The local attorney we hired was David Rosen, a brilliant young graduate of Yale Law School. He did much of the pre-trial work, and was invaluable in preparing the many motions we made. Since David knew the Connecticut rules and I didn't, I often had to rely on him during the trial.

Sometimes, as I tried to make a point, Judge Mulvey would just shake his head from side to side. Then I knew that what I was attempting might be legal in California, but wasn't permitted in Connecticut. "Consult your lawyer," the judge advised me early in the trial, nodding toward David. After that, I referred to David as "my lawyer," often stopping the proceedings and saying, "Pardon me, judge. I have to consult with my lawyer on this."

Huggins was to be represented by Catherine Roraback, one of Connecticut's leading civil liberties attorneys and later to be president of the National Lawyers Guild.

MAY DAY, 1970

McLucas's trial was scheduled for mid-June, and the Panthers began marshaling support for the New Haven defendants. They announced

---

*Theodore Koskoff, former head of the Educational Section of the American Trial Lawyers Association and one of its vice-presidents, had been hired to defend Lonnie McLucas. It was through his persistent effort in my behalf that I was allowed to be admitted to the Connecticut bar.

three days of demonstrations to be held on the New Haven Green, beginning Friday, May 1, 1970. Political activists from all over the country, including Seale's co-defendants from Chicago—Dave Dellinger, Tom Hayden, Abbie Hoffman, Jerry Rubin, and Rennie Davis —were to be speakers, along with Jean Genêt, the French playwright, and Fannie Lou Harmer, a Mississippi civil rights leader.

In response, Governor John Dempsey mobilized the National Guard for the weekend and all police leaves were canceled. Attorney-General John Mitchell had the Pentagon send four thousand Marines and paratroopers to nearby military bases, although the Panthers had stressed that the demonstrations would be peaceful.

Actually, Yale had been in a continuing state of turmoil all that spring. The Yale students had rallied behind the Panthers after the summary jailing of David Hilliard and Emory Douglas for trying to pass a note to Seale at a pre-trial hearing. Mulvey had sentenced them to six months for contempt and released them after one week, but this did not ameliorate the students' feelings, frustrated as they already were by the war in Vietnam. They bombarded Yale president Kingman Brewster with demands that the university contribute to the Panther defense fund. He refused, saying that it would violate their tax-exempt status. But, as a gesture to student sentiment, he issued a public statement saying that he was skeptical that a black revolutionary could get a fair trial anywhere in the United States. He also opened Yale's residential colleges to those arriving for the demonstrations. In spite of the Panthers' repeated intentions of keeping the demonstrations peaceful, the May Day event had all the earmarks of a major confrontation. Some rumors stated that guns were being brought down from Boston. Early in the day businessmen boarded up the windows of downtown New Haven shops, preparing for the worst. The day before—in what looked like another government-inspired provocation—the Baltimore Panther headquarters had been raided. Eleven people were arrested. Then, a few hours later, President Nixon had announced the invasion of Cambodia by United States troops. However, the demonstrations went off peacefully after all, drawing crowds estimated at thirty thousand.

THE MCLUCAS TRIAL

Ted Koskoff defended McLucas. Both Sams and Kimbro testified for the prosecution. The jury deliberated for several days and it was clear they were split. We later learned that the majority had favored an acquittal but the minority had held firm. They finally acquitted McLucas of murder, kidnapping, and conspiracy to kidnap. He was convicted only of conspiracy to murder.

Koskoff had done a brilliant job and he had come extremely close to freeing McLucas, but an acquittal would have been very helpful to our case, so we were disappointed on both counts—McLucas's and our own. And we were deeply embittered when McLucas subsequently was sentenced to twelve years in prison. However, after having served several months in prison, with his case still on appeal, McLucas is at present out on bail.

The McLucas trial ended early in August and at that time I was right in the middle of the Los Siete trial* so I agreed with Judge Mulvey to start the New Haven case as soon as that trial ended. The Los Siete jury brought in its verdict on Saturday evening, November 7, and on Monday morning I boarded a plane at San Francisco airport to begin Bobby's and Ericka's trial. I was met at the airport and driven direct to New Haven where an apartment had been arranged for me at the Yale Law School.

PREPARING THE TRIAL

Soon after arriving in New Haven I learned from David Rosen and Catherine Roraback, much to my chagrin, that the militant supportive atmosphere of the previous May had disappeared almost entirely. There were two reasons for the dissipation of the support: one was that the students were no longer indignant, their momentum had slowed dramatically, the defense committee had dwindled to a few dedicated souls. The other was that, in the light of the McLucas trial, our supporters felt that hard work was no longer necessary; they thought it obvious that the Rackley murder was almost entirely the work of Sams, that Seale—as we had been saying for months—had had nothing to do with it. They felt also that Huggins's role in Rackley's death had been tangential at most. We ourselves believed that she was being prosecuted because of what was perceived as her potential as a Panther leader.

We also faced enormous legal costs—we had almost no money for

*The Los Siete trial involved six Latino youths charged with murdering a San Francisco policeman. I defended three of the youths and three other lawyers represented the remaining three. After a bitter and stormy six months trial all six defendants were acquitted.

the expenses of a trial of this magnitude and, because our firm was trying so many other Panther cases, it was not in financially good shape. Also, we were required to pay $450 daily for a transcript, given free in California, which was essential to our defense effort. And, we had to open an office in New Haven, pay David Rosen and our legal secretary, Pat Gallyot. The Panthers were able to raise some money, but because of other Panthers facing charges elsewhere only a portion could be spared for Connecticut. Therefore, much of the fund-raising burden fell on the shoulders of the defense team.

What people seldom realize is the enormous cost to the defendant of a criminal trial. Few can afford to be as well-represented as they should. The prosecution's costs are paid by the state, which has the complete services of the police and its own investigators as well. Those who claim the courts favor the defendants in criminal cases are either unaware of the facts or don't take into account this inequity in resources. If each side had equal resources, there would be fewer innocent people in jail.

I have maintained for the past ten years that in order for criminal defense to be meaningful the costs of the defense should be borne by the state, for, unless a person is extremely wealthy, it is literally impossible for that person to afford an adequate defense in most criminal cases. The majority of the criminal defense bar associations, in particular the California Attorneys for Criminal Justice, are in agreement with me on this matter.

As with the Newton case, we attacked the composition of the grand jury. In Connecticut the system is even worse than in California. The person solely responsible for the selection of the grand jurors was, in New Haven County, Edward J. Slavin, a friendly, personable man who had been elected so many times that no one bothered to run against him. I tried to question Slavin about his qualifications as the picker of the grand jury, but Judge Mulvey ruled my interrogation irrelevant, noting that the only legal requirement for the office was that the holder be a registered voter. Said Mulvey:

"The duly elected sheriff of the county is the only person who can summon grand jurors. Whether he was a street cleaner, automobile salesman, doctor, or lawyer before becoming the sheriff has nothing to do with it."

I asked Slavin if he had other duties, but Mulvey ruled that question irrelevant also. I was trying to establish that the sheriff had a law-enforcement function.

"I presume the sheriff does some sheriffing, and I want the record to show that we have the head of the major law-enforcement agency in this county picking the grand jury which later indicts our clients."

Slavin said he selected only respectable people as jurors. I asked him to define respectable.

"A person who is considered a nice, decent person. A law-abiding person who lives in the community."

"By whose standards? Yours?"

"Not only mine."

"Who else's?"

"In this case it is my standards because I'm picking the jury."

"In other words, you decide who is respectable and who isn't?"

"Right."

The result of this system was that most of the grand jurors were perpetual grand jurors, being called back time and time again, and Slavin had known almost every person on the grand jury for at least fifteen years, some as long as forty. The indictment against Bobby and Ericka was returned by Slavin's hand-picked grand jury.

We were beginning to feel the prosecution would go to any lengths to gain a conviction, and I had developed a healthy dislike of Arnold Markle. I felt he was using the case to further his political ambitions. In fact, James Ahern, then New Haven chief of police, later wrote a book* in which he said he was astonished that Seale was charged at all. "Despite my personal feelings," he wrote about the case, "it was a fact that there was not sufficient evidence against Seale, and the New Haven Police Department never requested an indictment against him, nor did we expect that Markle would ask for one."

So, partly out of my detestation of Markle and partly for simple advantage, my first pre-trial motion was to switch the positions of the prosecution and the defense tables. As there was more room at the front of the court and we had three lawyers and two defendants whereas Markle had only one assistant, Mulvey granted the motion and ordered the positions reversed. I knew that this would irritate Markle, but also it brought us closer to the jury and the press, giving us a better chance to dominate the courtroom.

Seale had been held in isolation in Montville Prison ninety miles north of New Haven since March 1970. Every time he had to appear in court he would be awakened at four in the morning, manacled, and driven to New Haven. He had to make this 180-mile round trip each day of the trial as well.

Police in Trouble (New York: Hawthorn Books, 1971.)

Ericka Huggins was also being held in isolation, at the Women's Prison in Niantic, and she had to make a similar trip for each court appearance.

The trial had begun November 10, and I had seen Bobby for the first time in months that Tuesday. He looked terrible and was depressed. I asked him to talk about it.

"Charles, I feel so frustrated because I can't fight back in any way. I'm isolated up there, away from everybody. The only time I get a chance to talk with anyone is when you or David [Rosen] visit."

Not only was he isolated, he was forbidden to receive visitors other than lawyers and family (who were, in any case, all on the West Coast); he was denied access to newsmen and even to certain printed material such as the Panther newspaper. Ericka Huggins suffered much the same treatment, to the extent of having her diaries confiscated, though she did have some family in New Haven. Also she was a more self-contained, less outgoing person than Bobby and seemed in a little better spirits than he did. Watching Bobby's deepening depression, I decided just after Thanksgiving to file a suit in federal court challenging the prison's right to keep them in isolation, to censor their reading materials. The NAACP joined our suit. We charged cruel and unusual punishment, saying that although by law they were presumed innocent until judged guilty they were in fact being treated like already convicted inmates. We argued that under these circumstances they would be less able to defend themselves and cooperate with their attorneys. We were heard in Bridgeport by Judge Robert Zampano who took the matter under advisement where he kept it until late April 1971—nearly four months—before he finally decided that Seale's being kept in isolation because he refused to shave his goatee was unconstitutional. It was an important decision, latecoming though it was, because it was the first time a federal court had ever interfered in prison management unless a life or death situation had prevailed. Ericka also was given some limited relief from the isolation treatment.

Meanwhile, there was the jury selection to attend to. I had previously given Judge Mulvey a copy of my book on racism in jury trials,* though, of course, I had no idea if he would read it or not. But I liked the way he handled the first group of prospective jurors. He told them forcefully that our clients were presumed innocent, that they

*Minimizing Racism in Jury Trials (California: National Lawyers Guild, 1969).

were under no obligation to testify, that they did not have to present a defense, that it was the burden of the prosecution to prove them guilty beyond a reasonable doubt. He also instructed the jury panels that the defendants having been indicted by a grand jury in no way implied they were guilty, reminding them that many have been indicted later to be found innocent. And he said that they were to give no greater credence to the testimony of police officers than to that of ordinary citizens, that just because police officers were testifying for the prosecution did not mean automatically that the defendants had been involved in wrongdoing.

After hearing him address the jurors, I felt sure he had read my book.

Another thing different in Connecticut than in California is that jurors are interviewed singly, not in front of the entire panel. That is a benefit, but it is balanced by the fact that once you have accepted a juror you are stuck, whereas in California you can challenge a jury member at any time—even weeks later, which gives time to investigate individual jurors.

I began my questioning of the prospective jurors this way—I'd rise and say, "My name is Charles Garry. I represent Bobby Seale. We're both from the San Francisco Bay Area in California. Have you heard about this case? Do you have an opinion about it? As Bobby Seale sits here now, is he guilty or innocent?"

Most answered yes to questions one and two and rarely did we find one who said Seale was innocent. We established early that most had definite opinions and Judge Mulvey excused them for cause immediately. It got to be a routine: I'd look at the judge, jerk my thumb "out," and he let the person go.

It went on like that for weeks, though sometimes it took a bit more time to uncover the prejudice. We were going through about thirty interviews a day. It was tedious asking the same questions over and over again, day after day—I began to feel like a human tape recording. Our task looked almost impossible. We were using up jurors at an incredible rate.

While the jury selection dragged on, I accepted some speaking engagements. I had dozens of invitations. One reason I took them was to try to counter the bad publicity; the other was that I received a substantial fee and this money was desperately needed for the defense fund. Though Judge Mulvey had issued a gag order that forbade us to speak about the case in public, there was plenty else to talk about. An early speech was to the New London Bar Association.

New London is about a hundred miles from New Haven. The meeting was held in a beautiful old resort that was covered in snow. We arrived to find a big fire going in the old stone fireplace and the banquet room full. The dais was filled with dignitaries from all over Connecticut—judges of every kind and description, including a former chief justice of the Connecticut Supreme Court. After dinner I leaned over to ask the president of the bar association what he wanted me to talk about. He said,

"Well, Garry, I'll tell you this. If you don't tell it like it is, if you don't raise hell with the judicial system, then I personally will be very disappointed. You can talk about anything. But lay it on the line. Don't pull punches. This group has been in need of some straight talk for many years."

I stood up and looked around and began by saying:

"I don't in this entire crowd here tonight see one black face. I guess that tells the story, doesn't it? It says to me that there is not one black lawyer in your group or, if there is, he or she wasn't interested enough to be here. Judging from the people I'm sitting next to, I would have to say that there are hardly any women lawyers amongst you. Perhaps that tells the story of the American judicial system."

I ended up talking about the difficulties of a fair trial under the system.

"A fair trial implies that both sides are equal in strength, equal in the money and resources at their disposal, and equal in their ability to handle themselves in and out of court. When you have the all-powerful state on one side and Joe Blow on the other, Joe Blow is always in trouble."

I got a standing ovation. I had a little trouble understanding this because if this all-white, mostly male body had agreed with me and put its beliefs into practice, I wouldn't have been in New Haven defending Bobby Seale and Ericka Huggins. After I sat down again a superior court judge next to me offered me an explanation. Pointing down the dais, he said:

"The man over there is the former chief justice of our supreme court. He didn't know what the hell you were saying, I'm sure, because he's very hard of hearing. But when everybody else stands up, he stands, too. The reason some of the others stood up was probably to relieve the pressure on their balls."

By Christmastime we had questioned over five hundred people and had found only four jurors acceptable to both sides. The time it was taking was becoming an issue, but the publicity had been so pervasive and the racism so prevalent that it was relatively easy to challenge people for cause. Then, just after the New Year, I was invited on the *David Frost Show*. Ten months before I had been on William F. Buckley's show, *Firing Line,* and I had enjoyed myself and thought I had done pretty well. I was looking forward to another TV encounter, to having an opportunity to talk about the Panthers to a national audience.

Frost had also invited to appear on the same show a writer named Edward Jay Epstein who had just published a long article in *The New Yorker.* He had come to see me early in 1970, claiming to be sympathetic to the Panthers and very interested in seeing the documents concerning the party members who were killed by police. The Panthers, whose records had been lost and destroyed in FBI police raids, had estimated that the number killed was twenty-eight, though we could not fully document it. I had explained this to Epstein who went on to ridicule the press in his article for accepting the Panther contention that twenty-eight of their members had been killed by police. I was angry at Epstein because I felt he had tricked me.

The point I tried to make on the show was that it did not matter what the exact number was—twenty-eight, twenty, ten—or two. Whatever it was, it was too many. But neither Frost nor Epstein would let me make my point. They kept coming back to the number twenty-eight.

"Isn't it true that the figure of twenty-eight is false?"

"I don't know the exact number. That isn't important. What is important is that the government is waging an illegal campaign to wipe out the Black Panther party."

"So you deliberately lied to the press?"

"No, I didn't. I told them the figure was only an approximation, that we weren't sure, that much of the documentation had been destroyed in the FBI raids."

Frost ceased to be a moderator and joined Epstein in attacking me —I lost my temper and called them both racists and a few other choice names.

"How dare you say racism or any other ulterior motive is behind our questions?" said Frost.

It was a very frustrating situation. I knew what I had said to Epstein, but both he and Frost kept distorting it. I was determined not to let them get away with it. I wanted to expose their lies and distortions. I'm afraid my behavior was far from exemplary that night—I didn't intend it to be otherwise. Later my partners and friends told me I was just plain awful and they must have been right because after the show whenever I asked prospective jurors if they had seen me on the show and they said they had, Judge Mulvey immediately excused them for cause. He never mentioned the show to me directly, but his attitude was clear.

By mid-February 1971 we had interviewed almost a thousand jurors but we were still two short of twelve. As we had used up all sixty of our preemptory challenges and as Markle had plenty left, we made a motion to go to trial with a ten-person jury. Markle wouldn't agree, so we took the matter to the state supreme court which deliberated for four days before deciding against us. So we continued the tedious and grueling work of probing the psyches of the jurors with minute questioning to uncover their hidden biases.

However, we had managed to get five black women on the jury and this gave us hope. When the twelfth and final juror was chosen she answered a question in such a way that indicated she was clearly frightened of the Panthers. Seale jumped out of his seat and, grabbing up the attaché case he always carried, started out of the courtroom.

"That lady's a racist. I'm going to the lockup," he said.

Two deputies moved in and shoved him back into his seat.

"I've spent nine months in solitary because that pig Markle recommended it," he shouted angrily—and then, over Judge Mulvey's plea of "Mr. Garry, Mr. Garry," trying to get me to calm Seale down, all the frustrations of the past eighteen months in prison poured out of Seale and he kept on until the judge ordered him removed from the courtroom. After the commotion died down, I moved to exclude the juror who had precipitated the outburst, but the judge turned down the motion. There was nothing else we could do but fight for alternate jurors who were more acceptable to us.

After that, Bobby calmed down and spent the trial as he had the previous months of the jury selection—sitting at the defense table writing, as if he had no business being there in the first place. Bobby felt that he never should have been indicted, and that there was no relationship between anything he had done and the trial. I don't think he and I ever seriously discussed the case.

Markle seemed to take a special pleasure in seeing Bobby roused to anger, as if he were trying to promote himself into the national spotlight via another Chicago-type trial. I despised him and the feeling seemed to be returned in kind. We spoke hardly a civil word during the entire trial. The reporters told me that after the Frost show Markle had put up a framed picture of David Frost in his office. The courthouse joke was that when Markle entered his office in the morning he bowed toward the picture.

Finally, after more than four months and 1,550 people, twelve jurors and two alternates were selected in mid-March. The jury consisted of seven women, five of them black, and five men, all of them white. And on March 18, 1971, the clerk read the formal indictment charging Bobby Seale and Ericka Huggins with four counts each: murder, kidnapping, conspiracy to murder, and conspiracy to kidnap. In addition, Huggins was charged with binding. Unlike most states, Connecticut does not allow opening statements, so as soon as the jury was sworn in and the indictment read to them the prosecution called its first witness.

MARGARET HUDGINS TESTIFIES

To our surprise and dismay, Margaret Hudgins was the first prosecution witness. Though Markle had agreed not to call her to testify against the other Panthers, he had handed her a subpoena as she stood in line waiting for a spectator seat in the courtroom. So much for the trustworthy state's attorney. I was doubly annoyed because, knowing what Markle was like, I had warned the Panthers who had accepted Markle's deal to stay away from the trial. Not that we were worried she would give damaging testimony—but we didn't like the idea of a Panther testifying for the prosecution nor the play that the media would be sure to give it. And that's all Markle got out of it, a few headlines. It didn't add to his case though it gave the state's case an aura of credibility that it didn't deserve and was a hurdle we should not have been made to overcome. Also, since she had been a defense witness in the McLucas trial her appearance now deprived us of using her testimony later when it would have been more advantageous to us.

According to Hudgins's testimony, she had been in Warren Kimbro's house with Huggins, McLucas, Sams, Edwards, and the others while Rackley was being held. Her major recollection was of Sams threatening, bullying, giving orders—all with his gun in his hand. She said the beatings and interrogations were all on his orders.

The state followed Hudgins with a string of technical witnesses—the fisherman who found the body; the policeman who investigated the report; the doctor who conducted the autopsy. We were willing to accept it all. We would concede that Alex Rackley, a party member in good standing, was beaten, tortured, and shot to death. Markle, however, didn't want our concession. He had a series of color slides he wanted to show the jury of Rackley's body, hardly a pretty sight. Certainly Rackley's death was one of the most unfortunate things that ever happened in the history of the Black Panther party. The coroner testified that either shot, the one to the heart, fired first by Kimbro, or the one to the head, fired second by McLucas, could have caused death.

This meant that Kimbro had fired the fatal shot. During the McLucas trial, he had described the scene at the riverbed. There were four people there, Sams, Rackley, Kimbro, and McLucas, but only one gun, Sams's .45 caliber automatic. After the four got out of the car, Sams handed Kimbro the pistol and, nodding toward Rackley, said, "Ice him." Kimbro took the gun and fired it into Rackley's chest, then returned the gun to Sams. The three remaining men started to walk back to the car when, seemingly as an afterthought, Sams now gave the gun to McLucas saying, "Finish him off." McLucas went back and fired a shot through the head of the already dead Rackley.

From the evidence given in the McLucas trial and from our investigations, we had a good idea of the state's case. Sams was not our major worry: we would expose him for what he was. What concerned us was *who* the corroborating witness would be, who Markle would use to supplement Sams's claim that Seale had ordered the killing, for surely, we reasoned, no prosecutor in his right mind would take the case to trial without further evidence, with Sams as the sole accusing witness.

Judging from the prosecution's list of witnesses, Kimbro seemed the most likely candidate. He had already testified against McLucas, he was an upstanding citizen, intelligent, his brother was a cop, Markle was his friend. He had a lot to gain. If he testified the way the prosecution wanted him to it was probable he'd be let off with a minimum jail term.

Therefore, we waited eagerly for him to take the stand to hear what he had to say against Seale.

KIMBRO TAKES THE STAND

Kimbro was a big man, towering over both Sams and McLucas, but Sams was both more powerfully built and more aggressive by nature.

At the time of the shooting, Kimbro was thirty-five and both Sams and McLucas were twenty-three.

Markle led him through the gory details—the beatings, the scalding water torture, the shooting. He said that at one point Sams had stopped the interrogation and ordered Kimbro to give Rackley bus fare back to New York. Rackley left the house, bus fare in his pocket, and for some irrational reason returned for his coat whereupon Sams seized him and ordered him to be taken to the basement, tied up, and beaten again.

I objected repeatedly to this testimony as prejudicial, as none of it related to Seale. Had Bobby been on trial alone it would have been excluded. But in this case, though technically the defendants were separate entities, the prosecutor could take testimony directed at one and use it to prejudice the jurors against the other. Originally the prosecution wanted to try all three together, but McLucas's lawyer made a motion for severance and it was granted.

So far Kimbro had not even mentioned Seale. If anything, he seemed to be going out of his way to implicate Huggins. He said, "Everyone knew Rackley was going to be killed," and he claimed that Huggins had suggested to him not to use his well-known car to drive to the river.

But Roraback brought out on cross-examination that Kimbro had not previously mentioned any such remark by Huggins, not to police investigators nor in previous testimony, that in the McLucas trial he had admitted to telling Sgt. DeRosa that it was Rory Hithe who told him not to use his car. She read that admission from the trial transcript, showing him caught in a flagrant lie. As to the assertion that everyone knew Rackley was to be killed, she again referred to the McLucas trial transcript. During that trial, Koskoff had asked him:

"So when the gun was placed in your hand, it was the first time you knew Rackley was going to be killed and you were going to be the one to pull the trigger?"

"That's correct."

So he was caught again.

I limited my questioning of Kimbro to the one crucial point of whether he would claim seeing Seale inside the Orchard Street house where, Sams would claim, Seale gave the order to kill Rackley. I began by questioning him about all the conversations he had ever had with Bobby. He replied that he had spoken to him just once on the telephone and once at Huggins's apartment on Hurlburt Street just before the speech at Battell Chapel. He could recall no other conversations he had held with Bobby.

Then, to distract him from my main thrust, I began questioning him about David Brothers, a New York Panther who had driven up with Seale. I questioned him closely about what he knew about Brothers, how many times he had seen him, and so forth, but I was not interested in the answers: it was just a device to keep his mind from my main question because I know that when a witness tries to lie on the spur of the moment he usually trips himself up.

"Where was this conversation with Mr. Brothers?"

"I had several conversations with him in May."

"Now you never at any time saw Mr. Seale at 365 Orchard Street, which was your home, and also party headquarters, did you?"

"No, I can't recall."

"And you never had any conversation with him at Orchard Street either, did you?"

"No."

Kimbro's last two answers were crucial to us. We expected Sams to say, as he did at the McLucas trial, that Kimbro had been present when Seale gave the order to kill Rackley. Kimbro's testimony would now refute him directly. In answer to my next question, Kimbro said that the last time he had spoken with Seale that night was at Battell Chapel. Then he testified that he had heard all of Seale's speech there, referring to parts of it.

At that I moved that we be allowed to play the tape of the entire speech, including the question and and answer period. We had been waiting for such an opportunity and had prepared ourselves for its eventuality—we had not only a clear copy of the tape ready to play but also transcripts of the seventy-seven minute oration for each juror, the judge, Markle, and each individual member of the press. Markle could have objected to my playing the tape, but he did not, fairly jumping at the chance for the jurors to hear Bobby talk. Earlier he had implied that the talk had been provocative and I'm sure he felt that the jury's hearing of the speech would work to Bobby's disadvantage. But he hadn't heard the actual tape before, had only seen the police reports on it, not the best way to judge a live performance.

Bobby is a fascinating speaker, though it was never his aim to be one. Before he and Huey founded the Black Panther party he had been a nightclub comedian and he was a born mimic, able to use dozens of voices to make a point or dress up a speech. Once he did an imitation of John Kennedy for me that kept me roaring with laughter all through it. He was persuasive, too, on the subject closest to his heart, the liberation not only of blacks in America but also of people all over the world. His warmth, his humanity, his basic concern, come through in his voice. In the Battell Chapel speech he had been in top form. We knew that speech very well.

Now we hooked up the equipment, passed out the transcripts, and sat back to await the effect. As he talked—about freeing all societies from racism, hunger, and want, and about his idea for doing it which he called "Yankee Doodle Socialism"—the jury seemed to be hanging on his every word, several of them nodding their heads affirmatively as he made his points. In his usual style, he used a dozen different voices and intonations, told stories, and held the audience enthralled.

> The Minister of Defense, Huey P. Newton, went to the streets and he got some niggers off the block that's used to robbing banks; he got some niggers off the block that's used to going for themselves; he got some niggers off the block that deal dope, and he gave them some political perspective, and outlined a program that said, "We want land, we want bread, we want justice, we want some peace, and we want some decent education."
>
> He told these niggers they going to have to work in an organized set; stop that jive-ass, petty-ass, chickenshit robberies and get organized. Huey P. Newton put what Malcolm X said to do on a higher level. Huey P. Newton, brothers and sisters, in case you didn't know it, put this shit into motion.

The tape had an electrifying effect on the courtroom; when it ended the audience stood and cheered. In not objecting, Markle had made a fatal mistake.

With the audience cheering all around him, Bobby rose, before Judge Mulvey could take action:

"This is not Chicago. This is an entirely different scene here, and we don't want those kinds of demonstrations in the courtroom. So please cooperate with us. We're trying to get a fair trial."

The judge made no comment. We then played the question and answer period and again Markle made no objection. It was clear from the tape that by the end of the question period Bobby was exhausted. His voice was hoarse and he says, "I'm really tired now so I'll only take one or two more questions." He had taken a midnight flight from San Francisco which arrived in New York that morning, a three-hour time change. He had spent the day in New York working with the chapter there on its reorganization problems, trying to raise money for the Panther 21 being held on that $100,000 bail each, and then he had been driven to New Haven where he had rested a few hours at Huggins's apartment before going to Battell Chapel to give his speech.

The original plan had been for him to meet with the New Haven Panthers, but no suitable place could be found. The Orchard Street house wouldn't do because people would be working there, counting the money from the rally. The Panthers were also running a search for a lost child from there, and people in a constant stream were going in and out, making it difficult to conduct a serious meeting.

Seale, with Kimbro, Huggins, and Landon, had been driven to Orchard Street but only the other three had gone inside briefly while Seale remained in the car with the driver. Then Huggins and Landon returned to the car and they drove to her apartment, leaving Kimbro at the Orchard Street house from where he later got a ride to Huggins's place.

Kimbro testified that, after a brief stop at Orchard Street, he was given a ride to Ericka's house, arriving there between 11:30 P.M. and midnight and found a group of Panthers gathered in the kitchen. Seale was fast asleep on the couch. Kimbro stayed at Huggins's for a while and then returned to Orchard Street and went to sleep. When Ericka arrived the next morning, she told him that Bobby had already returned to New York. Nothing in Kimbro's testimony indicated that he knew Bobby knew anything about Rackley or even that Sams was in the New Haven area. And he had admitted to being the first one to pull the trigger, with a gun given to him not by Ericka Huggins or Bobby Seale, but by George Sams.

Markle's ace in the hole against Ericka Huggins was the tape she made during the beating of Rackley. She had been called downstairs and told by Sams and Kimbro to make some statements into the recorder. Catherine Roraback argued for two full days against admitting the tape, mostly on the grounds that it had been illegally seized by the FBI, but Mulvey ruled it admissible. The tape established the fact that Huggins had been down in the basement when Rackley was being tortured to reveal the names of agents and informers who had infiltrated the party. Markle had transcripts passed to the jurors, but they could hear her saying:

> So then the brother got some discipline, you know, in the areas of the nose and mouth and the brother began to show cowardly tendencies and began to whimper and moan.

If one listened carefully, one could hear Sams and Kimbro coaching her, telling her what to say. In the background was the sound of her baby girl crying, but of course none of this background sound appeared on Markle's transcript of the tape. At the end, Rackley's voice comes through supplying the names that Sams wanted, real or imagined, of supposed agents.

After Kimbro's testimony was finished, we waited for the surprise corroborative witness, for it was absolutely inconceivable that he would have brought the case to trial without such a person in reserve.

Finally, on April 23, 1971, twenty-three months after the death of Alex Rackley, Arnold Markle put George Sams on the stand. Sams, we now felt, was the key to the case. There had been no mention of charges against Seale when the others were indicted in May 1969. His name wasn't brought into the case until Sams was arrested in Toronto. It was Sams who had to connect Seale with the death of Rackley.

GEORGE SAMS—A CASE HISTORY

We had compiled an impressive dossier on Sams's violent behavior —assaults, a knifing, attempted rapes. He had been in one sort of difficulty or another since the age of fifteen when, after he had beaten a robbery victim in the head, he was sent to a juvenile institution where he was judged below normal in intelligence and "an alleged dangerous mental defective" under Section 134A of the Mental Hygiene Laws of New York State.

In 1963, at the age of twenty-one, Sams had been confined at the Eastern Correctional Institution where the senior psychiatrist, Dr. James Fleming, diagnosed him as an "unstable, inadequate, and immature individual who reacts to his feelings of rejection with incorrigible, hostile, and aggressive behavior." Dr. Fleming recommended close supervision and guidance until Sams gained more control over his "primitive anger and rage."

He was released, moved to Detroit, sustained a head injury while working for an auto firm there, and, in March 1966, while attempting to break into a grocery store next to the house in which he lived, he was shot by police. One bullet struck the base of his skull, requiring major brain surgery. The hospital records showed that after surgery he still had "multiple metallic foreign bodies" scattered through part of his brain with a fairly large piece of metal at the base of his skull.

We knew from interviews with inmates in the Connecticut prison where he had been held since August that he was strong-arming prisoners there, making sexual advances to them, and that even the prison guards were afraid of him. Beyond that, he was a pathological, or compulsive, liar. We moved to have him disqualified as a witness on the grounds of mental incompetency. Such a move had been made for the McLucas case, Mulvey had appointed a psychiatrist to examine him, and the psychiatrist had found him legally sane. Nevertheless, we tried again. We had a Yale psychiatrist ready to examine him, but Mulvey sent him back to the same doctor and, as before, he was found capable of testifying.

Markle led Sams through the same story told to the New Haven police, the FBI, the grand jury, and the McLucas trial jury. In each different recital there had appeared major contradictions. The key testimony concerning us was Sams's assertion that Seale had entered the Orchard Street house after his speech, seen Rackley tied up, and was asked by a Panther what was to be done with Rackley.

According to Sams, Bobby said: "What do you do with a pig? A pig is a pig. Do away with him. Off the motherfucker." Sams alleged that this took place between twelve-thirty and one in the morning, contradicting Kimbro who had placed Bobby at Ericka's apartment between eleven-thirty and midnight.

Sams's testimony mentioned Huggins only tangentially. He said she had been in the house, made the tape, and gone for a car ride, during which time Rackley's fate had been discussed (a point which Kimbro had not mentioned), that she had brought down the first pot of boiling water that was poured on Rackley.*

All during Sams's testimony Roraback and I objected frequently, saying it had no relevance to the case. It is a rule of evidence that testimony must relate in some way to your client. However, Markle claimed that almost everything had relevance even though much of what both Kimbro and Sams testified to took place when neither was present. Mulvey upheld Markle. That is the trouble with conspiracy

*On cross-examination we would show that he had earlier said someone else brought down the first pot of water.

laws—they are so vague that almost any kind of evidence is admissible.

When we got Sams for cross-examination, I led him through the contradictions in his testimony beginning with when he had arrived in New York prior to traveling to New Haven with Rackley. He said it had been April. I showed him the transcript of the McLucas trial where he had put the date at May 12, but he refused to back off.

There followed a whole series of similar questions, contradictions, proofs, as we went back and forth over his testimony tripping him up on point after point. But when I tried to go into his personal background and his propensity for violence I was stopped by Judge Mulvey who said that he had been ruled competent to testify. That effectively cut off all questioning along those lines. Still, by showing the jury the contradictions, we hoped to indicate to them that he was a pathological liar—a person incapable of telling the truth. If his testimony on key minor points could not be believed, how could they believe him on the major contention that Seale had ordered Rackley's death?

"How many people have you killed?" I asked him.

"Mr. Garry," interposed the judge, "are you prepared to substantiate anything of that nature by a charge made against this man?"

"I am going to ask another question. Have you told Warren Kimbro that you killed persons on many occasions?"

"No, sir."

But Kimbro had testified to this already, saying that he, Kimbro, was afraid Sams would kill him if he did not kill Rackley. It had been brought out on cross-examination that Kimbro had told his brother he was afraid for his life if he did not shoot Rackley.

"Would you tell the court what names you have been known by?"

"I have nicknames like Crazy George, Madman, Detroit George, several names. I had the name Dingee Swahoo, which was an African name, and I had the name that Chairman Bobby and David Hilliard gave me, which was Madman Number One."

He admitted telling Sgt. DeRosa that he had "every intention of destroying the [Black Panther] party." He tried to back away from that one, but we had a tape of it.

Even after having Sams on the stand for a day, I was not satisfied that the jury understood what kind of a person he was. We needed some demonstrative evidence about that. We suspected—correctly it turned out—that he was being given tranquilizers, for he had been unnaturally calm, but Mulvey wouldn't let us point that out to the jury, nor would he permit us to show that Sams had assaulted other prisoners, sexually and otherwise. I began probing into his use of drugs and as I pursued the matter I could see him becoming more and more agitated. Suddenly he exploded into a violent tirade, against the Panthers, against me, accusing me of being on the Panther central committee. He rambled and ranted and we made no move to stop him, for here was the proof we needed that he was hysterical and dangerous, capable of saying anything. As Markle did not object either, the tirade went on for a full twelve minutes before Roraback finally objected. Judge Mulvey commented drily, "It's about time someone did or we'd be on this all day."

I questioned Sams about what he had done and where he had gone the day Seale spent in New Haven. His answers were vague and evasive—he couldn't remember where he went, who he was with, what he did, where he slept, or how many people were at the Orchard Street house when Seale was supposed to have been there, nor was he sure who issued what orders on the day of the killing. Evidently he had taken care to stay out of the way when Bobby was around.

Bobby had told me that he never saw Sams in New Haven, never spoke to him there, and if he had seen him at Orchard Street or anywhere else, he would have ordered him to leave and stay away from all Panther offices.

Sams also admitted that during his brief stay in New Haven he had tied up and beaten George Edwards and slugged Loretta Luckes when she put on a record he didn't like. When I finished, I felt that he had been thoroughly discredited, that his outburst would serve to nullify what he had said about Bobby and what he still had to say about Ericka.

Only law-enforcement people remained on Markle's witness list, and the only one of these with relevant testimony was New Haven County detective Nicholas Pastore. Pastore claimed he had followed Seale's car when it left Battell Chapel and drove to Orchard Street. He stopped some distance behind it, he said, and saw Seale enter the house. However, he put the time at 11:20, more than an hour earlier than Sams claimed the climactic meeting took place. Photos and a diagram proved that it would have been impossible for Pastore to see anyone.

In late April, Markle finally sprang his big surprise. As Pastore left the stand, he stood up and said, "The state rests, your honor."

There were gasps of astonishment all over the courtroom. Bobby swung around in his chair and shot Markle an angry look as if to say, *Is this all the evidence you've got to hold me all this time without bail?*

I could hardly believe it myself; I could see that the reporters were stunned, too. We had estimated that more than fifty people had been in the Orchard Street house the night Bobby was in New Haven, yet the state could only produce Pastore and Sams to say he had been there?

THE DEFENSE OPENS

We opened the defense with two witnesses to rebut the testimony of Pastore. Both had parked their cars directly across from the Orchard Street house and gone from there to the chapel in a bus. The position of the two cars would put Pastore some distance from the front of the house.

The first, Craig Gouthier, returned to Orchard Street after Seale's speech and, at Kimbro's request, remained there for about half an hour. He testified that he saw many people going in and out. Roraback questioned him.

"During that time, did you see my client, Mrs. Huggins?"
"No."

"Did you see Mr. Seale?"
"No, I didn't."

The second witness, Valerie White, testified similarly, except that she had been talking with a group of people waiting to meet Bobby. She testified that it had been rainy, a condition that would have further cut down on visibility. I questioned her.

"While you were at the headquarters of the Black Panther party on Orchard Street, during all the time you were there, did you ever see Bobby Seale?"
"No."

"Did you at any time see Mrs. Huggins there?"
"No."

On cross-examination, Markle badgered both witnesses but he did not succeed in unnerving them. They remembered small details that gave greater credibility to their testimony. Gouthier, for example, was sure of the time because the ice cream store on the corner was open, and he remembered how long it took Kimbro to go on an errand because he worried that Kimbro's wife would be upset because he was out so late.

The next two witnesses were used to expose the character of Sams. The first, Linda Young, had lived in the same house with him. She testified that Sams had told her he was very upset over being expelled from the party for stabbing someone, that he hated and resented Seale for having him purged, and that one day he would get even. On cross-examination Markle insinuated that she was cohabiting with Sams, but she denied it emphatically saying she only lived in the same house where he was living and that she stayed out of his way as much as possible. On redirect, I asked her why she avoided Sams. She replied that he had attempted to rape her and had beaten her once.

The second witness against Sams, Shirley Wolterding, knew him in New York after he had returned from the New Haven trip. I questioned her.

"Did you have a conversation with Mr. Sams after he came back from New Haven?"

"He said that he suspected three persons of being pigs. I told him I knew nothing of it. He became very violent and told me he would give me what he had given Alex Rackley, and I had better respect him as a man. Prior to that, he had punched me in my face, and I was crying about my face. He said, 'You should have seen Alex's face.' He told me he offed him because he thought he was a pig and that if he ever suspected me of being a pig he would off me as well."

She also testified she knew Rackley well, that he was very naïve and unsophisticated, like an eager puppy, that nobody in the New York chapter had ever suspected him of being an agent or informer except Sams. I asked her about Sams's use of drugs.

"George sent out for some heroin, and when the heroin came back . . . he asked me . . . to take some. I said no. He pulled me into another room, pulled out a knife, said I was his woman and that I shouldn't embarrass him in front of his friends. He told me I'd better go out and take some of the dope."

This testimony not only served further to discredit Sams, but also it laid the foundation for the defense of Ericka, about whom we were more worried than about Bobby.

A Panther leader, Elaine Brown, flew in from Los Angeles to testify. She said that Ericka had been extremely withdrawn after her husband's death, that she seemed to be in a state of shock. Brown testified that:

"It was difficult for us to have a conversation that didn't eventually lead to her discussing how much she missed John. And that would basically be all she would talk about most of the time."

Meanwhile, I was deciding not to put Bobby on the witness stand. He had not testified well at the McLucas trial and the jury had already heard ninety minutes of him on tape. There was no reason to allow Markle to crosss-examine him. I discussed this with both Huey and Bobby and they agreed. In lieu of putting Bobby on the stand, I called in some character witnesses.

I spoke to Father Eugene Boyle, a Catholic priest in San Francisco's largely black Fillmore District in whose church the Panthers had run one of their first breakfast programs. He agreed to come at once. I asked him to contact Father Earl Neil, a black Episcopal priest with a large church in West Oakland, to ask him to testify. The next morning we picked up both men at the Hartford airport.

We called Father Boyle to the stand first. He spoke warmly of Bobby's reputation for being truthful and peaceful and about the Panther's breakfast program which Seale had handled with him. Bobby had been given a bad conduct discharge from the Air Force for striking his commanding officer, who had insulted him for being black, and he had been convicted of a felony on a mere technicality, for carrying a gun near the city jail. The drawback to a character witness is that the prosecution can legally discuss the entire background of the person for whom the witness is testifying, and Markle brought up both points.

"Well, I certainly am familiar with the fact that Mr. Seale has a background, a police background, and what I am trying to say is that in the black community a man without a police record would not be normal."

Father Neil had been a close friend of Martin Luther King, Jr. He and Bobby had attended the funeral together. He had been active in the civil rights movement, served on several national boards of churchmen, been a member of the Alameda County grand jury, taught at the University of California. He testified to Bobby's excellent reputation in his home community for honesty and peacefulness. Markle said that some of his speeches did not sound too peaceful, and Neil replied that when blacks spoke to each other of arming themselves they were not necessarily referring to firearms but to changing their conditions by arming themselves politically and socially, though they would take up firearms as a last resort.

Both men handled Markle well on the cross-examinations because their testimony was not contrived; they spoke out of their feelings and convictions.

Then Roraback called the mothers of both John and Ericka Huggins as character witnesses for her. Mrs. Huggins spoke of how her son's death had transformed her daughter-in-law's formerly outgoing personality into someone who was withdrawn and quiet. Her own mother testified to her church and youth group activities and work with young children, that she had been a Girl Scout and editor of her high school newspaper.

ERICKA HUGGINS TAKES THE STAND

Now it was time to put Ericka on the witness stand, something we had to do. The tape had proved she was there, but we had to prove that the person on the tape recording was not the real Ericka Huggins. On the stand she was so quiet that the judge had to admonish her several times to raise her voice so that the jury could hear her. Roraback questioned her and she revealed her original desire to work with retarded children. She said that her interest in helping people had caused her to become involved with the Black Panther party. She described Sams's stay at the Orchard Street house with the pistol waving and issuing of orders to all. She had asked Kimbro—in reference to the treatment of Rackley—"Why is all this necessary?" Kimbro, she said, had looked confused and was unable to answer her.

She testified that Bobby and the group of Panthers he was with had gone straight to her apartment upon arrival in New Haven. There— with barely time for him to eat and take a short nap—everyone had clamored for an audience with Bobby. She had tried to tell him about Rackley but hadn't been able to get through the Panther males, most of whom were party officers with party business to discuss.

On cross-examination Markle pressed her on this point—why hadn't she been more persistent to tell Seale about Rackley, then tied up in Kimbro's basement? Hadn't she testified earlier that the sight of Sams pouring boiling water over Rackley had nauseated her?

"Well, you see," she said, her face turning as she looked up out the high courtroom windows, "first of all, it's very hard for a woman to be heard by men."

Markle played the tape of her voice once more; on it she sounded hard-boiled and tough.

"Did you call your in-laws to tell them what horrendous acts had just happened. Did you?" Markle asked insistently.

"No," she said, looking sad, her head down.

"Did you call any clergymen to tell them the horrors that had taken place in that basement?"

"No."

"And no one discussed getting any assistance for Mr. Rackley, is that right?"

"No."

"On Monday morning, did you call anyone to assist Alex Rackley?"

"No," she replied, looking up at Markle.

Her only explanation for her failure to summon outside assistance was that she was not in full control of her faculties at the time. She was doing her party work and taking care of her baby mechanically, without much thought, trying not to think about John. She had tried to confront Kimbro, had made an attempt to get through to Seale, but she was afraid to speak directly to Sams. She disputed Kimbro's contention that everyone knew Rackley was to be killed, saying McLucas had told her they were taking Rackley to the bus station. Kimbro had told her they were just going for a ride.

Markle suggested that she was in charge of the New Haven chapter and was chairperson of the Connecticut chapter. In her soft voice she said this was just not so, but Markle kept on badgering her. She became weary trying to explain and at one point she said she "just couldn't make things any clearer." Her weariness and her anguish were plain—it all came down to whether the jury would believe her or Kimbro.

ONEUPMANSHIP

When she left the stand it was time for Bobby to testify. I had said all along that he would take the stand. The press section was full to overflowing. I stood up and paused for a long moment, then said, "Your honor, the defendant, Bobby Seale, rests his case."

Bobby leaned back in his seat and smiled all around the room. Markle's mouth dropped open and we grinned at him. Both press and public seemed shocked. Then Roraback rested Huggins's case and we waited for Markle to regain himself and be able to speak.

"I'm taken by surprise," he said finally and asked for time to bring in rebuttal witnesses.

"I don't know what right you have to be surprised, Mr. Markle," the judge replied. "Mr. Garry can try his case any way he wants to."

"Well, I've got more evidence to put on."

"Mr. Markle, you've had your chance. You've had months to put on evidence. I'm not going to let you put on any new evidence, and in Mr. Seale's case, you've got nothing to rebut. Mr. Seale has not testified. I'm not going to let you play a game of sandbagging in this courtroom. We don't work that way here."

Markle was stuck. The only rebuttal witness he could produce was a black undercover cop, Carlos Ashwood, who had helped bust the Panther 21 in New York; his testimony was inconsequential.

The prosecution has the right to put on rebuttal witnesses after the defense rests. They cannot testify to anything new but are limited to refuting what defense witnesses have said. Sometimes prosecutors hold back a witness or two for this purpose but I don't think Markle really had anybody. The best rebuttal witness would have been Kimbro's wife. We knew she did not like the use of their house as Panther headquarters, that she wasn't happy about her husband's involvement with the party. Yet she was not called. It was possible that her testimony might not have corroborated her husband's. After several days of legal arguments, we gave summations.

In the final summation, Markle concentrated on Ericka, again bringing out the pictures of Rackley's body.

"This is not a case of police versus Panthers or black against white. This is a murder trial . . . I beg you to remember Alex Rackley's murder."

He scarcely mentioned Seale, but castigated Huggins for what she did not do: she didn't try to stop Sams, she didn't tell Seale, she didn't try to get help from family or friends.

"My client is not charged with the crime of silence," said Roraback in reply. Remember who my client really is, and what she tried to do in this world."

I began angrily and ungrammatically when my turn came.

"The prosecution is a desperate man, and he is using desperate means, but perjury should not be one of them." I pointed out the lies of the prosecution witnesses, and then said, "Not one single person —not one single person has corroborated George Sams! In two years, not one person."

Then, because the jury had to understand why Ericka Huggins had acted as she did, I talked about Warren Kimbro—his past record, his military service, his management of an antipoverty program, his having been a justice of the peace.

"Now if you take a *man* with this kind of background, this kind of strength, a leader in the community here, and can intimidate and scare him to the point where he will kill somebody, then how do you expect people without that background to compete and combat with a crazy fool like George Sams?

"This is the test—if Warren Kimbro couldn't stand up to Sams, how do you expect the rest of them to do it?"

I took them back to the swamp where Sams had handed Kimbro the gun. I said Kimbro had had the gun in his hand, and, from his military experience, he certainly knew how to use it. Yet he was so terrified of Sams that he meekly followed orders. There was no other gun out at the swamp, but according to his testimony Kimbro was afraid he'd be killed if he didn't kill Rackley. I reminded them that Kimbro had been thirty-five at the time of the shooting while Huggins had been only twenty-three.

"If Warren Kimbro couldn't stand the pressures of George Sams, then how could the physically weaker persons in the group do it?"

I went on to talk about Sams.

"George Sams broke down in cross-examination and went into a tirade. I allowed him to go on. I could have stopped him, but I wanted you to see the kind of a man the prosecutor is relying on to put my client into the penitentiary. I feel sorry for George Sams because he is the by-product of 350 years of racism in this country, but I won't permit him, for his own manipulative purposes, to send my client to the gallows on a conviction of any kind, not when I have the type of client that Father Boyle talks about and Father Neil talks about."

That ended the defense. Markle still had one more shot. The prosecution gets the first and the last say, always.

"My reputation doesn't depend on getting Seale. I'm only doing my job. I am the only voice now for Alex Rackley."

And, "A conspiracy is a group. It's like a bunch of grapes squashing together. And if the drippings get on someone, that's their problem."

Well, if juries could believe Markle's view of the conspiracy laws then we would have a lot of innocent bystanders doing time right now!

THE UNEXPECTED OUTCOME

The Seale-Huggins case went to the jury on May 19, 1971, two years to the day since Seale spoke at Battell Chapel. Those in the courtroom had little trouble hearing the jury as it deliberated next door. After an hour and a half, the jury voted unanimously to acquit Seale on all four counts: murder, kidnapping, conspiracy to murder, and conspiracy to kidnap. They spent the next five days arguing about Huggins. Some of the arguments were heated. We heard a male juror say, "If you won't find Ericka Huggins guilty of something then I'm going to change and vote guilty for Bobby Seale."

After five days the jury reported itself hopelessly deadlocked. The votes were frozen at ten to two for acquittal of Ericka on all counts and eleven to one for acquittal of Bobby on all counts—apparently that juror had carried out his threat.

We were devastated. Now it looked as if we would have to go through another grueling trial for which none of us had the time, the stamina, or the money. The next day Rosen and I spent the morning preparing a motion to dismiss the charges. We argued that the jury should have notified the judge as soon as it reached its verdict on Seale during the first day of deliberations. Only then, we held, should they have started deliberating about Ericka.

That afternoon we dragged to court without much enthusiasm. It was now hot, and we had been drained. Rosen argued the motion brilliantly, but I doubted that it would do much good. Mulvey surely knew exactly what we were going to say; it was about the only thing we could do. Markle opposed the motion as strenuously as he could, bordering once again on hysterics.

After warning against any outbursts, Mulvey said, "I will tell counsel very frankly that I anticipated this motion and I thought about it considerably.

"I have been involved in these cases and related cases for something approaching two years. I have, by that happenstance, gained a rather wide knowledge of the factual situation, and, indeed, of the defendants themselves.

"Mrs. Huggins has been confined for more than two years in this state. Mr. Seale has been confined in this state and other states for at least that amount of time.

"I am advised by the clerk of this court that the array of jurors for this court year is practically exhausted, and that the possibility of drawing a panel for these cases is practically nil.

"The state has put its best foot forward in its effort to prove its cases against these defendants. They have failed to convince a jury of their guilt.

"With the massive publicity attendant upon the trial, I find it impossible to believe that an unbiased jury could be selected without superhuman efforts, efforts which this court, the state, and these defendants should not be called upon to make or endure.

"The motion to dismiss is granted in each case, and the prisoners are discharged forthwith."

Despite the judge's admonition, there was pandemonium in the courtroom. Spectators cheered and cried. The reporters almost trampled each other to get to the telephones.

We were stunned. Bobby, Ericka, Catherine, David, and I just sat there for a while. I was amazed that a judge would have the guts to do what Mulvey had done. It was true that the state had spent nearly two million dollars on the case; it was true that we had gone through six months of trial and fifteen hundred prospective jurors; and it was also true that it literally would be impossible to get another jury in the near future, because this trial had been widely and sensationally reported all over Connecticut. Yet I never thought a judge would have the intestinal fortitude to do what Judge Mulvey did.

Ericka was released immediately. Catherine Roraback led her into the corridor where she was engulfed by the several hundred people who had surged into the courthouse when they heard the news. She looked dazed, and when she got outside she blinked, looking around her with a sense of wonder.

"Look at the sun."

"What will you do now?"

"Live."

Bobby was still under Judge Hoffman's contempt sentence from the Chicago trial, and it took four long, agonizing days to get bail for him from the federal appeals court. The minute the bail order was signed, Bobby was driven directly to Kennedy Airport, and a few hours later he was meeting in Oakland with Huey for the first time in three years.

Warren Kimbro, after serving several years, was released, went to Harvard, and is now a dean at a college in Connecticut. George Sams was sentenced to life imprisonment but was released after four or five years and has been in and out of prison continually since then.

8.

Rape

A delegation from Miami came to my office late in 1973, asking my help to free Juan Garcia who was serving a three-year term in Soledad Prison for bombing a Los Angeles airline office. As they said they were Anti-Castro Freedom Fighters, I wondered why they had come to me—it was known that I both admired and supported Castro. Though they knew about my political beliefs they said they had heard I was honest and conscientious, that they felt if I took the case I would do a good job.

After reviewing what had already been done for Garcia in the California and federal appeals courts, I told the group there was nothing more I could do, that they would only be wasting their money.

Then, in the spring of 1974, Raoul Garcia and his wife, Boobie, came to see me. Raoul Garcia was the brother of Juan Garcia and Boobie was the sister of Inez Garcia, who was Juan's wife. Two brothers had married two sisters. Inez Garcia, they told me, had been raped. She had killed one of her assailants and was now being held in Monterey County Jail on a charge of first-degree murder. Bail had been set at $100,000. She was being represented by a public defender in whom they had little confidence.

On the surface it sounded a straightforward matter, and I was interested in the problems faced by rape victims in court. As the Garcia family was prosperous in Miami, I quoted a fee of $15,000 plus costs and took the case.

From my conversation with the Garcias I had formed the impression that Inez Garcia had killed twenty-year-old Miguel Jimenez either during or right after the rape. This would allow us to plead self-defense. However, it turned out that there had been a lapse of twenty minutes between the rape and the shooting and the shooting had occurred some distance from the scene of the rape. This complicated matters, for the prosecution could claim that Garcia had formed the specific intent to kill Jimenez during the twenty-minute interval, thus making it premeditated murder. Further, shortly after the incident, Inez had taped and signed an interview with the Soledad police chief in which she freely admitted to shooting Jimenez; she also said in the interview that she had tried to shoot seventeen-year-old Luis Castillo, who had actually raped her, but that he had run off too quickly.

Garcia had shot the 300-pound Miguel ("Mike") Jimenez six times with her .22 caliber hunting rifle, one bullet hitting him squarely in the eye and passing through his brain, killing him instantly. She also told the police that during the rape he had brandished a knife and that she had seen him draw the knife as she came upon him and Castillo right before the shooting.

At the time, Garcia was twenty-nine and weighed about a hundred pounds. She had been living in Soledad, a dusty, dreary little Salinas Valley town, to be near her husband who was still in prison.

She was charged with murder. Neither the police nor the district attorney would concede that she had been raped. They maintained before and during the trial that the rape was something she had invented later on to use in her defense. However, the transcript of her interview with the police chief of Soledad shows that she tried to tell him about the rape, but was unable to get through to him.

"They tried to rape me [she said in the transcript]. They tried to get fresh with me."

The chief made no attempt to find out what Jimenez and Castillo had done to her. When she mentioned the rape attempt again, he changed the subject. Later she described how Jimenez hit her and tore her blouse.

"Him and Luis, they got out of line, you know. I mean—I can't explain it."

Once more Chief Ben Jimenez (no relation to the deceased Miguel Jimenez) made no attempt to pursue the matter and showed no interest in it. Garcia tried a third time, to no avail. Chief Jimenez seemed totally uninterested in that part of her story.

The next day in the county jail she asked a matron if she could get a medical examination. The matron said she could tell it to the judge when she got to court. A day later she finally saw a doctor, who, without examining her, told her it was all in her head and would go away.

So there was no way for her to prove she had been raped. Castillo, a known heroin user and pusher, swore that he had never touched her. Therefore, she remained in the county jail on $100,000 bail while he went free. The district attorney confidently told the media he had an open-and-shut murder case.

Garcia had called her family in Miami immediately afterward and told them what had happened to her. Four days later she had talked to a priest in confession at the jail, but he refused to testify for her claiming it would violate the secrecy of the confessional.

Freddie Medrano, a twenty-five-year-old Vietnam veteran, was also charged with first-degree murder in the killing. The state charged that Jimenez and Castillo had beaten Medrano in his apartment and, as a result, he had decided to kill them. From the grand jury testimony we knew that one of the prosecution witnesses would say that Garcia had offered to kill the men for Medrano because, as her family had money, she would be bailed out.

Medrano had returned from Vietnam with a Bronze Star along with tuberculosis and hepatitis. After his medical discharge he had remained in Monterey County because he was undergoing treatment at the Army hospital in Fort Ord. He and Garcia had arranged to share his two-bedroom apartment, but they were not lovers. Medrano was engaged to a local girl and was due to return with her to his native Texas at the end of March. Because of the acute housing shortage in Soledad, Garcia had been living with another woman and the woman's four children in a farm-labor camp and was desperate to get out. She had made an agreement with Medrano to move in with him in the middle of the month and then take over the apartment when he left for Texas. At the time of the shooting, she had slept there only once and was still in the process of moving in.

The prosecution's theory that Garcia had killed Jimenez and tried to kill Castillo simply because they had beaten Medrano didn't make much sense. Medrano had been beaten and had suffered a concussion, but, directly after the fight, he was able to walk outside, drive his car across town, and get into another brawl with Castillo and Jimenez. There had to be another explanation.

Both Garcia and Medrano were considered outsiders in Soledad, which had a large, tightly knit Mexican-American community that placed great emphasis on the "hometown." Medrano was resented because he came from Texas and because his Army disability pension enabled him to drive a fancy car. Garcia was resented because she steadfastly refused to date the "hometown boys." That she was an exceedingly attractive, sensuous-looking woman only exacerbated the situation.

After studying the entire matter carefully, I advised Garcia that if she pleaded guilty to manslaughter she probably wouldn't have to serve any more time in jail. She rejected that option immediately and flatly; she wanted to take the case to trial, sure that she would be vindicated. She wasn't ashamed of what she had done, as she later told a group of women:

"I was afraid and I had to defend myself. I would like other women to know about my case. I think they can identify with me. If they had the same thing happen to them, they will know how I felt. Maybe it will stop more rapes."

The fear she spoke of came from a phone call from Jimenez moments after the rape. He threatened to kill her if she reported the incident and if she and Medrano did not leave town.

As she was certain that she wanted to go to trial, I began to prepare the case. We moved for a bail reduction, making the rape an issue for the first time. Bail was lowered to $50,000, then to $5,000, and, three months after her arrest, she was released, along with Medrano. I arranged for her to live at the home of my legal assistant, Pat Richartz, in Berkeley and for her to see a psychiatrist, Dr. Jane Oldden, of San Francisco. It was clear we would need the support of psychiatric testimony to explain her state of mind following the assault.

From the police interview I had learned that she had emotional problems and had been taking medication for them. It also struck me as odd that she could not read, write, or tell time, because she was obviously intelligent. Her father was a school administrator in New York. In order to present her to the jury, I needed to get to know her better, so I began talking with her, much as I had talked with Huey. We developed a good rapport and she spoke freely about many things, telling me that she had married at fifteen, had her only child, a son, at eighteen, had divorced Juan Garcia because he had fathered another woman's child, but had remarried him a few years later. She had spent several days in the mental ward of a Miami hospital in 1963 after threatening to kill her husband, her son, and herself; prior to that she had been hospitalized with emotional breakdowns. However, there were parts of her life that she would not discuss with me, saying that there were certain things she just could not tell a man. I asked Pat Richartz to take over for me.

Meanwhile, Dr. Oldden told me that in her opinion it was the rape trauma that had driven Inez to kill Jimenez and attempt to kill Castillo. Dr. Oldden reported that sex had always been a problem for Inez, and had been at the root of her marriage difficulties. This information strengthened my own belief that a psychiatric defense was in order, but besides that we would argue for self-defense, based upon Jimenez's threat to kill her. We would also rely on the unwritten law which often exonerates those who commit so-called crimes of passion, which allows—though it is covered in no formal law—that it is sometimes permissible for people to take matters into their own hands in order to protect their dignity and integrity.

As the question of rape would be central to our defense, we felt that it would be good for women's organizations to know about Garcia. The case was typical of the difficulties women face in dealing with rape through law-enforcement agencies and the courts. The rapist, Luis Castillo, had not been charged at all; he was to be the prosecution's major witness against Inez.

Garcia's inability to get law-enforcement people to hear her story about the rape was not an isolated instance: women faced it all the time, one reason why only two in ten rapes are ever reported. We encouraged Garcia to speak to the women's groups we contacted and soon an Inez Garcia Defense Committee was formed in the Bay Area.

Defense committees can be invaluable, especially in political cases. They can create public interest, make it possible for the defendant's views to be aired in the media, raise money, hold rallies, bring supporters to court, find witnesses. In the beginning, the Inez Garcia Defense Committee helped us immeasurably, but radical feminists began to dominate the committee. They encouraged Garcia to say things on the witness stand that created discord among her supporters and ultimately hurt her. They took the position that not only had she done no wrong in killing Jimenez, but also that she had every right to kill him. They were her ardent supporters, making of her a heroine, a woman who had broken through centuries of male oppression. They idolized her, catered to her every whim, and she ended up living in their rented house in Monterey like a reigning queen.

Aside from the fact that I disagreed with the radical feminist position, there was simply no legal way for Garcia to maintain that she had a right to kill Jimenez and be acquitted. Furthermore, she did not really believe that herself. According to Dr. Oldden, she felt guilty about killing Jimenez and thought she ought to be punished. As a result, she was being pulled in two different directions most of the time.

On one side, Pat and I expected her to be the same warm, friendly, proud, but slightly shy person we had come to know. We expected that she might have some difficulty sitting through parts of the trial, but since she was determined to go through with it, we were confident her warmth and sincerity would come through and the jury would believe her—and not Castillo.

On the other side stood the majority of the defense comittee.

Although our defense trial team held almost daily consultations with the defense committee on such matters as which jurors to accept and which to reject and which expert witnesses to call regarding rape, there was a continual undercurrent of dissatisfaction among many of Inez's supporters. They felt that the psychiatric defense was demeaning, and objected to my telling the jury that Garcia could neither read nor write—points that I considered essential if the jury was to see the real Inez Garcia and to understand her motive for the killing.

Despite these background rumblings and Garcia's increasingly erratic behavior, there was nothing to do but plunge ahead and map out my trial strategy as I was not going to withdraw from a case to which I had committed myself. Furthermore, Garcia herself never raised any objections and seemed happy with what we were doing for her. Had she raised any objections, perhaps changes could have been made before the trial started. But as the radical feminists did not come into the picture until the trial was already under way, I could not change my trial strategy once it had been put into operation.

The trial began in August 1974, five months after the incident. On the bench was Judge Stanley Lawson who had gained a reputation for carrying a pistol under his robes—rumor had it he once had brandished the gun while trying a case involving Soledad Prison inmates. Other than that, his judicial record was undistinguished and from the outset he made it clear that he was annoyed at the amount of media coverage the case was receiving. He became impatient whenever he heard the word *rape*.

The prosecutor was Arthur ("Skip") Braudrick, a young assistant district attorney trying his first murder case. As a Berkeley undergraduate he had taken part in several peace demonstrations, which made him a flaming liberal by Monterey County standards. Still, he used the prosecutor's time-honored device of withholding important evidence from us before the trial.

Judge Lawson did allow us to question the jurors one at a time, out of the hearing of the others, combining the best features of the Connecticut and California systems. After three weeks, I felt we had a pretty good jury consisting of seven women, one of them a Mexican-American, and five men, two of whom were black. One of the white male jurors had recently testified for the defense at the Wounded Knee trial; his testimony had indicated that an FBI agent had lied on the witness stand.

During the voir-dire all the jurors finally chosen said that they considered rape a crime of violence and that they believed in the individual's right to self-defense.

THE TRIAL OPENS

In my opening statement I tried to portray Inez Garcia as I had come to know her—shy, diffident, extremely proud. I brought up her emotional problems as they would come out later on anyway. Then I discussed rape and how law-enforcement people treat rape victims. I told the jury that the police tend to disbelieve rape complaints and are reluctant to investigate rape charges, that as a result only twenty percent of rapes are reported. I was about to make the point that the alleged rapist had not been charged when Judge Lawson interrupted me.

"Counsel, I cannot permit this. We are trying a woman for murder. There is no man on trial for rape, and the attitude of the police for rape or murder, as far as I am concerned, has nothing to do with the guilt or innocence of this woman."

"But, you honor, that is the reason I killed this man," Inez said from the defense table.

"We are not trying a cause, we are trying a woman, Mrs. Garcia, and a man, Mr. Medrano," replied the judge, "and I am not going to make this courtroom a forum for a cause."

Lawson was perturbed that the case had attracted so much media attention, that women were coming to the trial from all over. His dislike for us was obvious and his antipathy to the whole issue of rape was evident. He was to say many times, "This is a murder trial, not a rape trial."

In his opening statement, the prosecutor contended that the rape issue was a smokescreen to hide the real issues in the case, so the judge's remarks fit in perfectly with *his* theory.

Luis Castillo was to be the first witness for the prosecution. We already knew that he and Jimenez had been physically handling two women friends of Garcia's visiting at the apartment, Alicia Alcarez and Rosa Bracamonte. They left because they did not like their advances and shortly afterward Medrano and a friend, Chris Solis, who was to be another prosecution witness, showed up and went immediately to Medrano's room to smoke marijuana. When they came out, Castillo and Jimenez began taunting Medrano. From the grand jury transcript we expected Castillo to testify that the argument had been over whether or not Medrano was a "big man," whether the hometown boys could run him out of town.

However, after admitting that he and Jimenez had been drinking beer and wandering about town all day before arriving at Medrano's apartment early in the evening, Castillo testified that the argument with Medrano had centered around dealing heroin, that Medrano had bragged he was going to be the top dealer around town, but that Castillo and Jimenez had laughed at him, telling him since he wasn't a hometown boy this would be impossible.

He further testified that a fight broke out between himself and Medrano. They traded punches and started wrestling on the floor. Then Jimenez stepped in, punched Medrano, and hurled him against a couch. Jimenez then pulled out a knife, held it near Medrano's face, and told him to get out of town. Then they decided to leave. Inez, who had been yelling at them to stop fighting, walked them to the door where they had a brief conversation with her before leaving, after which they walked to the house of a friend, Joe Mendoza; Jimenez phoned Inez from there.

They left Mendoza's house and began walking toward the center of town when suddenly Medrano's car pulled up behind them, the passenger door flew open, and Garcia leaped out and began firing at them with a rifle.

On cross-examination Castillo admitted that Garcia had a good reputation around Soledad. He said she was friendly and helpful, that she was willing to help anybody who needed help. He admitted to several arrests for possession of heroin and said that he had knifed a man a few years before, that Joe Mendoza had a contract out on Medrano and wanted him dead or out of town. I challenged his statement that the fight with Medrano was over dealing heroin.

"Isn't it a fact that you began to change your story regarding narcotics to divert attention in this case from yourself because you had been accused by Inez Garcia of raping her? Isn't that right?"

"It's not right."

"Isn't it a fact, Mr. Castillo, that when you arrived at the house, you put your arms around Inez Garcia and said that she was your girl?"

"No, I didn't."

"And you did the same thing to Alicia Alcarez, did you not?"

"Did not."

"Isn't it a fact that you and Jimenez started browbeating and pushing Inez Garcia around in the back of the house?"

"No, I didn't," said Castillo with a smirk.

"Isn't it also a fact that you raped her?"

"No, I didn't," he replied, smiling broadly.

"Do you think it's something to laugh about?"

"No, it's not true."

"If it was true, you wouldn't admit it, would you, sir?"

Braudrick's objection saved Castillo from having to answer.

"It's also true, is it not, that Mr. Jimenez showed the knife to Inez?"

"Don't recall."

I read his grand jury testimony. "Did he [Mike] show it [the knife] to anybody that evening?" he had been asked. "Yes." Castillo had told the grand jury, "He showed it to Inez."

Again I questioned Castillo about the rape; again he denied it. Tom Worthington, a young Salinas Valley attorney with an excellent reputation, was representing Medrano. He got Castillo to admit that he and Jimenez had begun the argument with Medrano.

Inez became extremely upset while Castillo was on the stand. I could feel the hatred and animosity she felt toward him. She was barely able to contain herself. The proceedings had been difficult for her from the beginning; she was a chain-smoker and smoking in court was not allowed. I had obtained Lawson's permission for Richartz to sit at the defense table next to Inez throughout the trial. She supplied Garcia with chewing gum and candy mints.

Castillo was followed by Chris Solis.

At first it seemed that Solis's testimony would be damaging. He testified that Garcia had not left the apartment with Castillo and

Jimenez (she had been raped in an alley outside the building) and that Jimenez had not ripped her blouse or hit her in the face. He stated that he had seen Medrano and Garcia leave the apartment together, she with the .22 caliber rifle, he with a shotgun, and he had heard them get into Medrano's car. He also testified that Medrano originally wanted to kill Castillo and Jimenez himself but that Garcia had persuaded him to let her do it because her family could afford to bail her out. It was this testimony that was the basis for the murder indictment against Medrano—that he drove Garcia to the spot where she jumped from the car and killed Jimenez.

Solis's testimony crumbled under cross-examination when we showed that he was close friends with the entire Jimenez family, especially with 250-pound Frank Jimenez, Miguel's brother, of whom he was terrified. Solis lived at the farm-labor camp owned by the Jimenez family.

His entire testimony was so contradictory that at one time Judge Lawson asked him, "Why do you say one thing one time and one another?" Having told the grand jury that he did not notice anything about Garcia's clothing, he claimed at the trial that her blouse definitely had not been ripped. The following passage was typical of the cross-examination.

"And you lied to this jury in the last five minutes, haven't you?"
"Yes."

"And you lied to me also, didn't you, when you told me that there was not one word about drugs mentioned at any time in the conversation between Luis, Freddie, and Mike?"
"I did."

"And you think that's funny, don't you?"
"Yeah."

He had heard Inez take the phone call from Jimenez but claimed she had not mentioned the threats to him. He said that before the fight Jimenez, who practiced knife throwing, had put a kitchen knife in his pocket, that it wasn't until Medrano got the upper hand that Jimenez intervened, that Garcia had been trying to break up the fight but could not, and that he himself had not helped anyone, inciting Medrano to later call him a coward and an SOB. Though he insisted that Garcia did not leave the apartment, he slipped once when he said, "She was still outside." He told us Medrano was not badly hurt, but that Castillo and Jimenez had taunted him about having TB.

Braudrick then put Alicia Alcarez on the stand. She testified that Garcia had walked into Rosa Bracamonte's house that evening and announced that she had just shot Jimenez and might also have hit Castillo. When asked why she did it, she replied either that she had been raped or that they had tried to rape her. Alcarez was not sure which phrase Inez had used. Alicia said that she had told Inez she didn't look like she'd been raped but then said Garcia looked disheveled and her blouse was ripped when she arrived at the Bracamonte house. Alcarez was concerned that the police would not believe Garcia's story, so she ripped the blouse some more and instructed her nephew Juan Cabrajal to hit Garcia in the face a few times, which he did. In later testimony, Cabrajal said that Garcia looked badly beaten even before he hit her, and Rosa Bracamonte's testimony confirmed this.

The four of them—Garcia, Medrano, Alcarez, and Bracamonte—then drove to the Alcarez house and because Garcia was so agitated Medrano and Alcarez went out again to buy her cigarettes. They were pulled to the curb by police who arrested Medrano. Alcarez told them where to find Garcia, and within an hour she was being interviewed by Chief Jimenez.

There were two other witnesses, both high school students. David Ferrell and Dima Gallardo had been sitting on the Gallardo front porch about a hundred feet away when the shooting occurred. At about nine-thirty they had seen Castillo and Jimenez walk past and the men had greeted them in passing, continuing up the street past a camper parked in a driveway. A car pulled up behind them and stopped, but the camper blocked the teenager's view of the men. Both testified they saw a woman get out of the car and start firing, although they could not see what she was firing at. Seconds later they saw Castillo run across the street headed for a park nearby; the woman fired several times as he was fleeing. David Ferrell said he heard the woman say, "Give me the shotgun! I want to go after Luis!" but Dima Gallardo heard nothing like that. Both thought another person was driving the car but they could not see who it was because of the darkness nor could they identify the woman who had done the shooting. Ferrell said that after the police arrived he went to where Jimenez lay and saw a knife next to his body. Castillo arrived back upon the scene and began talking animatedly with police.

There was little to be done with their testimony on cross-examination. There were no contradictions. They had told substantially the same story to the police and the grand jury. They had no connections to the Jimenez family. They seemed to be telling the truth. However, we were able to make one important point. One had said that the shooting did not start until a minute or so after the car pulled up. This was significant as Inez told us that she had gone out on foot to seek her assailants and Castillo, Medrano, and Jimenez had been fighting when she came upon them. Also Jimenez had been preparing to throw a knife at her when she shot him.

As the court recessed for that day, Garcia stormed out of the courtroom. She was furious but I did not know why. I later learned from Hedy Sarney, a defense committee member who had been very helpful, that Garcia was upset because I had suggested that a large contribution from a women's group be used in part to pay off the sizable phone bill the committee had run up at Richartz's house. As Garcia raced out of the courtroom, Sarney followed her up a flight of stairs to the office of the district attorney.

"Put me in jail," she demanded of the startled prosecutor, advancing on him. "I want to go to jail."

Braudrick backed off in a near panic, for any reaction on his part could provide grounds for a mistrial. The prosecutor cannot have anything to do with the defendant once the trial begins, except on the witness stand, but of course Garcia did not know this.

"Get away from me," Braudrick kept saying as he backtracked around his office. "You have to understand my position."

Unhappy with his lack of cooperation, she then marched to the elevator, followed again by Sarney, and went down to the basement to the sheriff's office where she demanded to be locked up and was once more refused.

Outside, still in a huff, she ran into Leroy Aarons, reporter for the *Washington Post;* answering his questions calmed her down. Later that evening at the defense committee house she was in high spirits and laughingly recounted her adventures that afternoon with the sheriff and the "District Detergent" as she called Braudrick.

THE PSYCHIATRIC TESTIMONY

The heart of our defense lay in the concept of impaired consciousness. This condition describes a state of temporary loss of conscious control over one's behavior, usually produced by overwhelming stress and panic. It is different from diminished responsibility in that diminished responsibility is not a complete defense to murder, but can be used to show lack of premeditation or malice aforethought, thus reducing a possible murder conviction to second-degree murder or manslaughter. But impaired consciousness, a state that can last for minutes, hours, or days, is akin to unconsciousness in that the person suffering from it has no conscious volition, no control over his or her actions. And unconsciousness is a complete defense to murder. This was why the psychiatric evidence was imperative. Impaired consciousness was the legal handle we could give the jury with which to acquit Garcia if they were persuaded her actions were justified. If they believed that she acted while in a state of impaired consciousness, they could acquit her.

We would argue that if there was no rape the whole thing made no sense. Medrano was not that badly hurt and though Garcia, too, had been beaten, this was not sufficient cause to send her out to kill two young men. It had to be the emotional trauma of a rape that provided the impetus for the killing.

We would show that Jimenez and Mendoza, another local man, had threatened her and taunted her about the rape when they telephoned, boasting that they had shown her what the hometown boys were like.

The main problem was that we did not have an eyewitness. Medrano had been trying to gather himself together and stop his nosebleed; Solis denied seeing anything; Castillo denied the rape; and Jimenez, who had witnessed it, was dead. The proof that the rape had in fact occurred would have to come from the psychiatric testimony and from Inez herself.

Dr. Jane Oldden, our major defense witness, talked about Inez Garcia. She told of her background, growing up in Spanish Harlem, the daughter of Catholic Cuban and Puerto Rican parents, that she had been sent to a school for emotionally disturbed girls as a teenager but had been released after one year. She explained that Garcia had great difficulty dealing with sex, a major cause of the breakup of her marriage.

Dr. Oldden offered the opinion that the rape trauma had put Garcia into "a deeply dissociated state of altered or impaired consciousness," something akin to sleepwalking, and that she was in such a state immediately after the rape when she shot Jimenez and therefore had no conscious control over what she did.

The psychiatrist said that Garcia was not a homicidal personality, that it would take an extremely traumatic event to make her want to kill. She described Garcia's actions at the Miami hospital, where she had threatened to kill herself, her husband, and her son, as purely histrionics—a bid for sympathy and attention, to let those around her know how unhappy she was. She observed that Garcia was regularly given to such dramatic displays.

On cross-examination, Braudrick asked Dr. Oldden if she believed Garcia's story about the rape.

"I certainly do. Inez is not a sociopath [sociopaths can lie easily and feel no guilt or shame]. She felt extremely guilty about what happened." She said that the guilt feelings applied to the rape as well as to the shooting.

Braudrick asked why Garcia had kept quiet about the rape, and Oldden answered that it was because the experience had been so painful that it was something to avoid thinking about. She likened it to Garcia's inability to read and write. "By not learning to read," she said, "she was able to withdraw from a good part of the world around her.

"She has a very idealized image of herself, which she tries to live up to, and the rape was particularly disturbing to that image."

Garcia had had feelings of self-hatred since adolescence, Oldden said, but she tried to cover them up by seeming outwardly calm, paying much attention to her personal appearance, and being friendly and helpful. Then Oldden said that in her opinion Inez would never kill again, that she was the type of person who goes into histrionics and threatens to do violent things but almost never does them.

On redirect examination, I began by asking Oldden exactly how rape affects the victims mentally and emotionally. Braudrick objected, saying that Oldden was not an expert on rape victims because her experience was limited to a relatively small number of patients.

Rousing himself from his midafternoon reverie and, leaning forward, he said in the condescending tone he usually reserved for minority people and women,

"Madam, have you ever conducted any experiments on rape?"

The spectator section, filled with Garcia's supporters, broke out in derisive laughter.

When she recovered from her surprise at the question, Oldden said, no, she never had conducted any experiments on rape.

And on that basis Lawson refused to allow her to testify about the emotional trauma rape causes.

Garcia suddenly leaped from her seat at the defense table and rushed to the bench.

"Why don't you just find me guilty?" she shouted up at the judge, pounding her fists on the wood in front of her. "That's what you want! Just send me to jail!"

Then she started to return to her seat, but took only a step or two before she whirled around again and screamed at the judge: "I killed the fucking guy because he raped me! That's why I did it!"

The bailiff moved in on the judge's order to lead her from the courtroom, but she struggled with him, shouting, "Keep your hands off me, you pig!" as he pushed her through the door.

A shocked silence descended over the courtroom. This was not the shy, proud, warm, concerned person we had been portraying with such care to the jury. The jurors seemed stunned. I was as surprised by the outburst as anyone else.

Later she came up to me and apologized, saying it wouldn't happen again, and then she went to seek reassurance from Father Eugene Boyle who had come to testify as an expert on the teachings of the Catholic Church.

Father Boyle, who had been a character witness for Bobby Seale in New Haven, told the court that the Church taught that women were to resist rape with every means at their disposal, even to the point of losing their lives. He cited a long list of saints who had been canonized for just that. He pointed out that the Spanish church in particular was quite strong on this point.

Then we called Juan Garcia to the stand. He told the court that his wife was extremely shy about her own body and never appeared without her clothes, even in their own bedroom. He acknowledged that there had been sexual problems in their marriage, that she had been frigid, but he said that he loved her very much. His testimony was necessary to make Dr. Oldden's assertions about Inez Garcia's sexual attitudes more real to the jury.

There followed a number of character witnesses, people who had known Garcia in the two and one half years she had lived in Soledad. There were the manager of the motor lodge where she had lived, a policeman, a man who worked at the lodge, a Soledad policewoman —all testified to her reputation for honesty and chastity. The latter was brought in because Braudrick had implied that she was having a sexual relationship with Medrano, had probably had sexual relations with others before him, and though Dr. Oldden had testified that this would be extremely unlikely for someone like Inez, we wanted to support our theory that one of the reasons for the rape had been that she had repeatedly rejected the advances of the hometown boys.

The policewoman also testified that Garcia had seemed in a state of shock when she had seen her at the Soledad police station an hour after the shooting.

In another attempt to get expert testimony about rape before the jury, we called Cameron Smith of the University of California at Santa Cruz. Ms. Smith had conducted a number of studies on rape, interviewed hundreds of rape victims, worked with several police departments on the problem, and had taught a course on the subject.

Smith testified that only a small percentage of rapes are reported to the police, one reason being that the victim would like to forget the experience as quickly as possible, another being the demeaning treatment that the police mete out to rape victims. It was my intention to question Smith about how the trauma of rape affects women, mentally and emotionally, and how long such an upheaval lasts. We wanted the jury to understand that Inez's reaction had been not much different from that of other women under the same circumstances. However, Braudrick objected to questioning along this line and Lawson repeatedly sustained him so the jurors never got this vital information.

We then called Dr. Penney Ellis, a Carmel psychiatrist who had examined Freddie Medrano before the trial. Her conclusion was that Medrano, too, was in a state of impaired consciousness, partly from the concussion he had received in the fight and partially from the large quantity of Colombian marijuana he had smoked with Solis just prior to the fight.

THE DEFENDANTS TESTIFY

All through the trial Medrano had sat quietly next to his attorney, Tom Worthington. Still afflicted with the tuberculosis and hepatitis, he looked thin and drawn. His quiet demeanor seemed to refute Castillo's assertions that he was a braggart. Even if the jury did not believe Solis's contention that the original idea to kill Castillo and Jimenez had been Medrano's, he could still be convicted of first-degree murder if they believed that he drove Garcia to the spot where the shooting took place.

Worthington discussed Medrano's background, his five years in the

Army, three of them in Vietnam, and said he was an expert marksman.

Medrano said that after the fight he left the apartment alone, got into his car, and "went out to see if I had any friends." He was dismayed by Solis's lack of help during the fight. He drove to his girl-friend's house with a towel draped across his shoulders, using it to stop the flow of blood from his nose.

He told the court that many of his recollections of that evening were vague, because his head was very foggy. When he got to his girl-friend's, he realized that he had left Inez alone in his apartment, and that Castillo had a key to it. While driving back he saw Castillo and Jimenez walking toward his place. He jumped out of his car, berated the pair for what they had done to Garcia, and got into another fight with them.

He thought he saw Jimenez pull a knife. Then, moments after the fight began, he heard a shot. Castillo ran away. Medrano then saw Garcia and shouted at her to stop shooting. He did not see her shoot Jimenez, but he knew right away that he was dead.

"I served three years in Vietnam. I saw people shot before."

He then ran to his car; Garcia jumped in beside him. Together they drove to Rosa Bracamonte's house. He didn't recall Garcia saying anything about a shotgun or telling her to get in the car.

"I have heard a lot of things in this trial you know, but I am still spotty and a lot of things they say I could have done, I think I couldn't have done."

He denied he had ever intended to kill either Jimenez or Castillo, saying he told Garcia to stop shooting because he didn't want Castillo to be killed. He also pointed out that he easily could have killed both of them back at his apartment simply by going into Garcia's room and coming out with the .22 caliber rifle.

Medrano had not seen the rape, having been in the bathroom trying to stop his nose from bleeding, so he couldn't testify about it. He did say that Garcia was extremely angry and upset when she returned from outside.

Braudrick tried but could not shake Medrano's story, even though his statements to the police and the prosecutor's office didn't completely jibe. Medrano continued to maintain that his memory of the entire evening was quite fuzzy.

It was now Garcia's turn to take the witness stand. I had talked with her at length about her testimony, about how she was to act even if

Braudrick came at her with hostile questions. She had promised she would cooperate and not lose her temper on the witness stand. As we had no eyewitnesses to the rape her testimony was crucial. Furthermore, she had to convince the jury that she was the kind of person we said she was, not a psychopathic killer. The evening before she testified, I was confident we understood each other, that she would do a good job.

But almost from the moment she took the stand she was angry and defiant. She spun from side to side in the swivel chair, answering my questions with uncharacteristic hostility. She said she killed Jimenez because he had helped Castillo to rape her, and because he threatened to kill her and Medrano. She identified the spot where she had been raped on two photos. She said Jimenez and Castillo had been drinking heavily, that they were harassing her before Medrano arrived.

"How were they harassing you?"

"Harassing me, touching me, pulling me, all over and you know, being nasty. I can't put it into words."

She said she had taken out her gun soon after receiving the phone call.

"I got my gun to defend myself."

She said she went looking for her assailants on foot. (This was borne out by the pair of house slippers she had been arrested in. They clearly showed evidence of having been used to walk out-of-doors.)

"Do you know how far you walked?"

"I really don't know."

"We're you frightened when you were walking?"

"I don't know. I don't think so."

"Were you scared?"

"Well, I was scared when this was happening to me. That's why I gave in and let them rape me!"

"Why didn't you tell the police about the rape."

"Because you just don't—I was ashamed to talk about it, that's all." Now she was getting angrier.

"Why are you able to talk about it now?"

"Because I have spoken to other people that have been raped and I see that there's a lot of women that is raped, and they keep quiet just the same way I was doing. They don't come forward because of the same reasons I have, most of them, and I think it's about time somebody did something about it and came forward. And not only me. Even kids get raped and nobody does anything about it."

By now her hostility and anger were such that I felt she was doing herself more harm than good with the jury, so I curtailed my questioning without asking her to describe how Jimenez had come toward her with the kitchen knife just before she shot him.

Initially Braudrick's cross-examination was not as harsh as we expected, but it was meticulous and detailed, and I could see that Garcia resented having to answer his questions. She said Castillo and Jimenez had taunted her, saying she thought she was too good for the men in Soledad, that they were going to show her what a hometown boy was really like. Braudrick questioned her minutely about where she had lived, when she had bought the rifle, and what happened before the fight. She said she had tried to break up the scuffle by screaming at the three youths, but she hadn't tried to physically intervene for fear of being seriously hurt. After the fight, wanting to get Castillo and Jimenez out of the apartment, she walked them to the door and then stepped outside with them. It was then that they grabbed her and dragged her behind the building. At first she tried to resist but felt that she would be hurt if she continued to struggle.

"I don't know what would happen to me, so I decided to give in. Anything they did was all right, as long as I was still alive."

She said was too scared to scream. While they were pulling her behind the house, she tried to agree with whatever Castillo and Jimenez were saying, hoping to talk them out of raping her. When Braudrick asked if they hit her anywhere else besides her face, she replied,

"I don't know. I was too nervous, and I was scared. All I knew is that I didn't want to get beat up, and I didn't want to get killed."

Braudrick then began to go over the details of the rape.

"After you say Luis ripped your blouse, you then said you just took your clothes off yourself?"

"Yes, I did. I gave in. I took them off."

"What was the first thing you took off, do you remember?" She didn't remember exactly, it was either her blouse or her jeans.

"We're you wearing a brassiere?"

"No, I don't wear a brassiere."

"Did you take your panties off, too?"

"Yes, I did."

She was becoming more agitated with each question. Braudrick asked her where she put her clothes, where Jimenez and Castillo were standing.

"Then what happened after that?"

"You want me to tell you what happened after *that?*"

"Yes."

"He fucked me!" She screamed. "What else do you want me to tell you?"

"What was Miguel doing while Luis, you say, was having sexual intercourse with you?"

"He was watching me having sex with this creep, and he was enjoying watching the other creep have sex with me!"

Braudrick wanted to know if Jimenez had actually held her down. Garcia said he hadn't but his 300-pound physical presence had kept her there after he helped Luis drag her behind the building. She herself weighed about 100 pounds. The prosecutor asked why she didn't try to escape out the other end of the alley.

"Because when something like that is happening, you don't think of another alley or anything like that! After it's happened you think of all the things you probably could have done, but at that moment you don't find anything to do. Just to give in. That's all, as long as you stay alive."

"What did Luis do after he finished having sexual intercourse with you?"

"He said we were all alike, that he would call and make sure all his friends knew about it. He told me to get out of town."

He continued this minute examination, taking her step by step back to the apartment, to the threatening phone call, and her own call to Florida. Then he asked when Medrano had left the apartment.

"I don't know. I know when I left. I left by myself, and I walked. I killed a guy and I missed Luis, but I meant to kill him too!"

Braudrick asked her what she did after she called her family.

"I took my gun, I loaded it, and I went out after them. If I would have had to walk to Jimenez Camp I would have. Another thing I want to say, I am not sorry that I did it. The only thing I am sorry about is that I missed Luis."

I was angry and dismayed. I had warned her not to say anything like that because I suspected some of her supporters were encouraging her to be defiant; but the place for statements like that is in the street. In the courtroom you're in the clutches of the enemy.

Braudrick persisted in asking her how she got the gun from her bedroom. Suddenly she stood up and said defiantly,

"I don't have anything to say to you no more. I shot him and killed him and if I had to do it again, I would do it again! That's all."

With that she stepped from the witness stand and started toward the door.

"You haven't been excused," Judge Lawson said querulously.

"I'm sorry, I don't have any more to answer."

"Mr. Bailiff, place the young lady back on the witness stand."

"I am not going to get back on the stand! Don't lay your hands on me!" she screamed at the bailiff, sweeping past him and out the courtroom door. Fortunately, Braudrick asked for a recess

Out in the hall, she apologized to me. "I'm sorry Charlie. I blew it."

"Oh, it'll be okay," I tried to reassure her, but I had a strong feeling she was right: I had seen the jurors' faces as she stormed off the witness stand.

After the weekend recess, Braudrick called one rebuttal witness, Dr. Roy B. Clausen, a court-appointed psychiatrist who examined both defendants. To the surprise of many trial observers, Dr. Clausen's diagnoses agreed substantially with those of Drs. Oldden and Ellis, that after the rape Inez had experienced deep feelings of anger, shame, and fright, feelings so intense that she would go ahead and shoot Jimenez even though she knew she would be apprehended; after the shooting, according to Dr. Clausen, she showed signs of deep anxiety, even regression, and she had experienced serious religious concern. He concluded that she nevertheless had the capacity to form the intent to kill, the only point on which he disagreed with Dr. Oldden.

Clausen also agreed with Dr. Ellis's evaluation of Medrano, saying that his consciousness was sufficiently impaired on the night of the killing that he could not form the intent to kill. That seemed to knock Medrano right out of the case.

CONCLUSION

In his final argument, Braudrick derided the idea that Garcia had been raped, asking why Castillo and Jimenez would drag her outside where they might be seen when they could have raped her in the apartment.

"They didn't rape Inez Garcia. That didn't happen."

He asked the jury not to be swayed by sympathies and emotions, saying that the American judicial system couldn't survive if jurors made decisions based on emotion when a woman said she was raped.

I put everything I had into the final argument.

"This case cried self-defense. If a woman cannot defend herself under these circumstances, then self-defense doesn't mean anything at all. I personally don't like to see death. I have been in the Army and I know what death is, but if there ever was a case that had any justification for one human being, in order to protect herself and her integrity, to kill another human being, then this is it.

"Inez Garcia at eleven-thirty at night told the Soledad police chief that they tried to rape her, and that they got fresh with her. What would you have done if you were the police chief? Wouldn't you have asked her more questions about it? Wouldn't you have investigated to see what she's talking about? Wouldn't you have asked her, 'What do you mean by they tried to rape you?' Don't you think that was in order, or do women get raped so often in Soledad and elsewhere that the police don't consider it significant?

"The evidence from the psychiatrists is that she thought that not only her life was in danger, but the life of Freddie Medrano was in danger, too. I don't know what I can tell you except this: Inez Garcia is an exceptional person. Inez Garcia has brought the story of rape to our courts and for the first time someone has said that a woman has the right to defend her honor, and that women should not be violated, assaulted, or threatened in any way."

Then Worthington spoke. He reminded the jury that Medrano had not actually been involved in the shooting, had not himself had the intent to kill, and had not known Garcia would do so, and that both the defense and the prosecution psychiatrists had said his consciousness was impared to the point that he was unable to form the intent to kill.

The jury deliberated for almost three days. As I waited I attempted to figure out Garcia's behavior on the witness stand.

Several theories were put forth by people who had seen most of the trial. One thesis held that she made those damaging statements to please her adoring feminist supporters who felt the impaired consciousness defense was demeaning. Another that she might have planned it all along, that her performance was her way of expiating guilt. Several observers thought she wanted to go to jail; she had told Dr. Clausen that she expected to be punished for what she had done.

While we waited for the verdict, she played with her son, Johnny, and talked to reporters. Once again she said she wasn't ashamed or sorry. She confided to the people she was close to that she expected to be convicted.

She was right. The jury returned a verdict acquitting her of first-degree (premeditated) murder but convicting her of second-degree (unpremeditated) murder. They had been unable to reach a verdict on Freddie Medrano, but we learned later that they had been dead-locked with nine jurors favoring acquittal, three for conviction.

Reporters who interviewed jurors afterward found that nine initially favored a first-degree murder conviction for Garcia, including all seven women and Ted Hughett, the man who had testified at the Wounded Knee trial. One male juror discussed the rape-induced trauma, but most of the jury doubted a rape had occurred.

The seven women claimed they would not have reacted so violently had they been raped, that they certainly would have calmed down in the twenty-minute interval. The question of self-defense barely came up in their deliberations. I felt we had been unable to bring it out sufficiently while Garcia was on the stand.

Furthermore, she had frightened the jury. They thought she was capable of shooting someone again, despite Dr. Oldden's assertions to the contrary. Her statements that she wasn't sorry and would do it again hardened the jury against her. They just did not view her sympathetically after that.

They didn't believe the two main prosecution witnesses, Castillo and Solis, but they did believe Dima Gallardo and David Ferrell. Apparently most believed Medrano. One juror said they were convinced that his mind was so messed up after he had smoked the three or four joints of Colombian grass that he couldn't rationally have done anything.

However, they were unwilling to believe that a rape could unsettle the mind of someone like Garcia. When the question of rape came up, one juror remarked, "There's no proof of rape. She's not on trial for killing a man for raping her." Apparently they took Judge Lawson's oft-repeated but legally invalid statement, "This is a murder trial, not a rape trial," quite seriously. At the trial's end, Lawson did give a formal instruction on rape, but I'm sure the jurors paid more heed to his informal statements.

One male juror said that he found himself fighting the women jurors on the question of rape. They were the most skeptical about it. None of them had ever been raped.

I felt there was an element of racism in the verdict. Had Inez been Caucasian, I'm sure the verdict would have been different. The jury would have seen her actions in a different light.

After the verdict, she was held without bail and later sentenced to from five years to life under California's indeterminate sentencing law.

I announced our intention to appeal, denouncing the trial as a complete miscarriage of justice, and while we wrote the appeal we moved for a reconsideration of sentence. She had undergone a series of tests and interviews in prison and the Adult Authority had concluded that she ought to be released after only four months confinement. Their findings appeared to uphold the conclusions of Dr. Oldden. We therefore expected Inez to be out of jail early in 1975. Unfortunately, Judge Lawson had to approve the Adult Authority's finding, and he refused to do so. He insisted that she was dangerous and should remain in prison. So there was nothing left to do but file the appeal.

In our appeal brief we charged that Lawson's open hostility to Inez, to me, and to our theory of the case [that a rape occurred] prevented her from getting a fair trial and that Lawson's refusal to allow testimony on how rape psychologically affects its victims was prejudicial.

> A jury could properly evaluate the issues in this case only if it understood that rape is a violent physical attack with a serious emotional impact on the victim. The jury had to decide whether the rape was adequate provocation for Garcia to have acted from heat of passion.

The brief attacked many of the myths that surround rape and cited numerous studies. One showed that in two-thirds of reported rapes the male used his physical strength alone to subdue his victim. Another concluded that one-third of all rape victims are attacked by more than one man. A third study reported that the primary emotional response to rape was immense fear and fear of being killed, but that "a significant minority experienced anger as their primary response." We argued that such evidence would have proved that the attack is usually a heavy emotional trauma, one that could well have affected Inez Garcia in the manner described by Dr. Oldden.

The brief stated that the judge had not allowed us to bring in evidence that would have shown that both Jimenez and Castillo had a history of violent and abusive behavior. Finally we said that Judge Lawson had made a serious error in his instructions to the jury about "reasonable doubt." Lawson first read the proper instruction on this important point but added an explanation telling the jury before it left the courtroom that reasonable doubt meant that they had to be convinced of the defendant's guilt after weighing the evidence on a scale, one side against the other. This instruction removed the burden of proof from the prosecution, which must prove the defendants guilty "beyond a reasonable doubt."

While the appeal was being argued, Medrano accepted a deal from the district attorney. He pleaded guilty to a lesser charge, accessory before the fact, and was given a sentence that required no further jail time. Garcia was at the Women's Prison at Frontera, California, as Judge Lawson had refused to grant her bail.

On December 29, 1975, the district court of appeals in San Francisco handed down a unanimous decision reversing the second-degree murder conviction. The court ruled that Judge Lawson's additional explanation to the reasonable doubt instruction was erroneous and highly prejudicial, that it had breached a fundamental concept of criminal law: that the burden of proof clearly rests on the shoulders of the prosecution.

On this basis alone, the appeals court ordered a new trial, stating, "The instructional error of the trial court was not harmless, and the judgment must be reversed." The decision said the other problems were not likely to arise again, which I took to mean that since Judge Lawson had already retired, another judge was not likely to be so biased.

Inez was released on bail once more although the state decided to appeal the reversal to the California Supreme Court. However, both the California Supreme Court and the United States Supreme Court refused to hear the state's appeal, and Inez was tried again, this time for second-degree murder, early in 1977. This time Inez dressed more demurely, there were no outbursts, and Luis Castillo refused to testify against her, citing his own Fifth Amendment right against self-incrimination. A jury of ten men and only two women found her not guilty. Inez's new attorney chose not to use psychiatric testimony, but asserted that she shot Jimenez in self-defense as he came toward her with a knife.

9.

Who Killed
George Jackson?

In February 1970, George Lester Jackson, a field marshal in the Black Panther party, Fleeta Drumgo, and John Clutchette were charged with murdering a guard in Soledad Prison. The defense was granted a change of venue from Monterey County and, therefore, the three men who came to be known as the Soledad Brothers were transferred to San Quentin to await trial. They had been accused of murdering guard John Mills about a month after another guard had killed three black inmates when he had fired into a crowded prison exercise yard to break up a fight. A grand jury had ruled these inmate deaths as justifiable homicide.

On August 21, 1971, at about two in the afternoon, Stephen Bingham, a Berkeley attorney, called at San Quentin's maximum security section, known as the adjustment center, to see Jackson. After leaving his cell, Jackson was skin-searched, a mandatory procedure for maximum security prisoners in which even the prisoner's rectum is searched. Before being admitted to the visiting room, he again was searched. After the visit with Bingham, which lasted about twenty-five minutes, Jackson was searched for the third time, and then escort officer Frank DeLeon walked him across a small outdoor mall toward his cell. Minutes later, the twenty-seven maximum security prisoners took control of the adjustment center and in the ensuing melee six guards were tied up and had their throats slashed. For the next half-hour, in the words of one eyewitness, all hell broke loose.

Firing automatic weapons, prison personnel moved in to retake the center, and Panthers Johnny Spain and George Jackson ran out onto the mall. Both men knew there was a gun tower to their right, a gun tower behind them, and another in front of them. Spain dove into a clump of bushes about fifty feet from the door but Jackson, holding an automatic pistol, kept going. Two shots rang out. Jackson went down and crawled toward the wall. Though unable to walk, he was not seriously injured. A short time later he was dead.

One shot was fired by the guard in the east tower to Jackson's right, who later said he had fired at Jackson's legs but thought he had missed him. The other shot came from the south tower, directly behind Jackson. That guard also said he had fired at Jackson's legs but believed he had missed. According to official report, no other shots were fired in the area, but Jackson was killed by a bullet that had entered through the back and exited through the skull. It seemed highly unlikely that either shot by the tower guards, coming from more than twenty-five feet above the ground, could have followed the trajectory of the bullet that killed Jackson.

Who then fired that bullet? Prison officials claimed that it was the guard in the tower behind him whose bullet crashed into the crouching figure moving toward the north wall. However, a bullet fired from that height would have had to turn more than ninety degrees inside Jackson's body before moving up through his head. That, to me, is clearly preposterous.

The first bullet, which downed Jackson but injured him only superficially, exited on the right side of his left instep. Thus, it could not have been fired by the tower guard to Jackson's right. The probability is that the bullet was a ricochet fired by the guard in the tower behind Jackson, that it bounced off the concrete mall and then went into Jackson's foot. And since that guard fired only once he could not also have shot Jackson through the back as prison officials claimed.

In all likelihood George Jackson was murdered. That is the opinion of the twenty-six other adjustment center inmates who signed a petition to that effect a few days later and it is the opinion of many others who have examined the facts behind his death.

Of the six guards whose throats were slashed, three survived, but two of the dead guards were found to have died from bullets fired from a nine-millimeter automatic pistol. Two inmates also died of slashed throats, and one other prisoner was shot—Allen Mancino, a white inmate who was shot in the leg as he lay nude on the ground with the others after the adjustment center had been retaken. According to inmates, Mancino was shot because he had asked the badly beaten black inmate next to him if he was all right. The others heard the guards, whom they could not see, call him a nigger lover after he had been shot.

The aftermath was pure hell for the prisoners, who were forced to lie on the cold concrete until late that evening. They were beaten, threatened with death, some forcibly shaved. For over a week later no visitors were allowed, food was sometimes withheld, and the prisoners were confined to their cells twenty-four hours a day.

During this time San Quentin was completely locked down as were other California prisons. Jackson's influence within the prison system had been immense, and prison officials clearly feared the spread of similar outbreaks, or even a recurrence at San Quentin. Reporters were kept out and prison administrators denied that any inmates had been harmed by the guards. But in a news conference later, wardens Louis Nelson and James Park said that Jackson had killed the three guards and the two inmates in an escape attempt that went awry, that the nine-millimeter Astra automatic pistol had been smuggled in to Jackson by Bingham, who concealed it in a tape recorder he carried with him into the visiting room. Jackson was said then to have smuggled it into the prison in a wig. The next day two reporters tried to conceal a similar pistol under an Afro wig but were unable to do it. It fell out when they walked normally.

When the other two Soledad Brothers, Fleeta Drumgo and John Clutchette, appeared in court on September 24, they had obvious injuries, but the presiding judge said that such matters were out of his jurisdiction. At that court appearance Jackson had planned to announce that I was going to defend him in the upcoming trial.*

Jackson's death was ruled justifiable homicide by the grand jury, and less than a month later murder indictments were returned against six other prisoners of the adjustment center. They were: Johnny Spain, 21, Fleeta Drumgo, 26, Hugo Pinell, 26, David Johnson, 24, Luis Talamantez, 28, and Willie Tate, 27, who soon became known as the San Quentin Six. In addition to murder, they were charged with assault on the three surviving guards and with conspiring to help Jackson to escape. Indicted along with them was Stephen Bingham, on the grounds that he was part of the conspiracy that resulted in the deaths.†

The indictments were returned in the midst of heated controversy within the grand jury. Before the final vote three grand jurors had walked out in protest, complaining that the proceeding was con-

---

*They went on trial late in 1971; both were acquitted of murder.

†Bingham disappeared shortly after the San Quentin incident was made public.

trolled by the district attorney. One said it wasn't justice, it was vengeance.

I entered the case on behalf of Johnny Spain, a Panther and the youngest defendant. At twenty-one, Spain had already been in jail for nearly five years. And it would take four more years for the many, complicated pre-trial issues to be cleared away!

For one thing, choosing attorneys for the San Quentin Six was a complicated procedure eventually going all the way to the state supreme court, as the defendants at first refused their local court-appointed lawyers. Hugo Pinell finally was allowed to defend himself, with the help of a San Francisco lawyer he liked, and Deputy Public Defender Frank Cox was to represent Johnson, while Luis Talamantez, Fleeta Drumgo, and Willie Tate were to be represented by court-appointed lawyers Robert Carrow, Mike Dufficy, and John Hill respectively. The court refused to appoint me to defend Spain, so we had to raise the money for his defense—only court-appointed lawyers are paid by the court.

Then we challenged one judge successfully and challenged a second but lost that challenge on appeal, and we petitioned repeatedly to have our clients unchained and unshackled in court, but these motions were consistently denied. The indictment was thrown out when we challenged the grand jury composition (as I had been doing ever since the Huey Newton trial). Judge Vernon Stoll, a retired Nevada County judge who was visiting to help out with the Marin County case load, heard the motion. He carefully listened to the evidence and deliberated for several weeks before ruling that the indictments were invalid because the grand jury had too few minority group members on it. He let stand the indictment against Bingham, who was white. The state, which could either convene a new grand jury more properly balanced or appeal, chose to appeal and, after another year's proceedings the appeals court overturned Judge Stoll's ruling,* reinstated the indictments.

---

*Stoll's ruling did have some beneficial effects. Immediately afterward, several counties tried to select grand juries that were more representative of the population. In San Francisco, what the media termed a "people's grand jury" was impaneled. It was drawn from the voting lists, rather than from among the friends of superior court judges. Several other counties adapted this procedure as well and for the most part stuck with it, even after Stoll's decision was overturned.

Of all the judges who took part in the case, Judge Stoll was the only one who did not have any trouble with the defendants. This elderly white man from a rural and conservative area of California treated our clients like human beings. He listened to what they had to say and as a result there were no outbursts, no banishments. Most of the other judges refused to listen if the defendants spoke up in court, ordering them to talk through their attorneys—running the courtroom like a third-grade classroom, banishing a defendant to a holding cell if he spoke out more than twice. This naturally led to resentment and vociferous protest sometimes laced with obscenities. To expect men who have been cooped up all day in small cells to be brought into court in chains and forced to sit still for hours on end without saying a word is simply absurd.

BACKGROUND

Why were our clients in prison, and why were they in the living hell euphemistically known as the adjustment center?

JOHNNY SPAIN

Johnny Spain went to prison when he was seventeen for being involved in a robbery in which someone was killed. Though I never asked him, he implied to me that he took the murder rap for someone else because, as a juvenile, he could not get the death penalty. During his first years in prison he was considered a model prisoner, but in 1970 prison officials discovered by reading his mail that he was a Black Panther party member and friendly with George Jackson. They claimed to have found inflammatory literature in his cell, and he first was transferred to the adjustment center at Soledad Prison and then to San Quentin where he was given the cell next to Jackson.

Spain was born of a white mother in Jackson, Mississippi. Though his mother's white husband had made no attempt to divorce her when she had a black baby, and he tolerated the black child among his own white children, he called him "nigger baby" and abused him. Finally, when Spain was six years old, his mother, fearful for his life, sent him to a relative in Los Angeles who arranged for him to be adopted by a black family in Watts. He had no idea who his real father might be as his mother always refused to say.

WILLIE TATE AND DAVID JOHNSON

Tate also went to prison as a teenager, and while in prison was convicted of assaulting another prisoner. He was sentenced to an additional ten years. He had been removed to the adjustment center for throwing water on a guard who was making degrading racial and sexual remarks about the men as they showered. Tate is black.

David Johnson and Tate had together witnessed an incident at San Quentin in 1970 where guards threw a prisoner named Fred Billingslea into an airless cell, hurled in tear gas, and locked the door. When the cell was opened, Billingslea was dead. Both Tate and Johnson took an active role in getting signatures on a prisoners' petition demanding an investigation and in making the death public knowledge. Johnson also instituted a federal court suit over the Billingslea incident. Some time later, he was charged with having a weapon in his possession and he was put into the adjustment center.

Tate was never granted a parole. He served his entire ten-year sentence, which expired before the trial of the San Quentin Six began.

LUIS TALAMANTEZ

Convicted at the age of twenty-two of robbing two cab drivers of about forty dollars, Talamantez had been given a one-year-to-life sentence and had been in jail six years. The sentences were to run consecutively, causing Luis to tell a friend, "I don't know what they're talking about. I've only got one life. How can I serve one after the other?"

Talamantez had supposedly been placed in the adjustment center for his own protection, but we believe that the real reason was that he read a lot of revolutionary literature in connection with a Latin American history course he was taking through the University of California extension program. He was also active in settling disputes between black and Latin prisoners which the guards didn't like—one method of prisoner control was to set ethnic groups against each other.

HUGO PINELL

Another Latin, Pinell was serving life terms for murder, rape, and manslaughter in Soledad Prison's maximum security section. In early 1970 a Sgt. Maddix approached him and asked if he would like to talk to George Jackson. Unbeknownst to Pinell, Jackson was at the time in a strip cell—similar to the hole that Bob Wells had experienced: no bed, no toilet, very little light, and a bread and water diet. Pinell agreed to talk to Jackson; afterward he was taken to Sgt. Maddix's office and, as he testified in federal court, was offered parole in exchange for testifying that George Jackson had killed the guard that the Soledad Brothers (Jackson, Drumgo, and Clutchette) were accused of killing.

"If this is the only way I can get out of prison, I'll spend the rest of my life here," Pinell told Maddix and hurled a cup of hot coffee in his face. Within minutes Pinell found himself in the adjustment center at Soledad before being transferred to San Quentin.

FLEETA DRUMGO

Like the other five, Drumgo was involved in political activity. He had entered prison in 1967 on a second-degree burglary charge and by 1970 had become a friend of Jackson's, but he was not a Panther. He ended up with the others in San Quentin because he was accused of helping Jackson to kill guard John Mills at Soledad.

SECURITY, THE JUDGE, AND THE JURY

On March 23, 1975, when I walked into the Marin County Courthouse to begin the trial, security was so tight an unidentified mouse couldn't have got through. This was the same courthouse where Judge Harold Haley had lost his life in the escape attempt led by Jonathan Jackson. In order to get into the special high-security courtroom, everyone—newspeople, spectators, attorneys—had to pass through two metal detectors, sign a list, hand in identification, have a picture taken, empty out pockets, and be frisked. If one had to go to the toilet the same procedure applied. Counting lunch, some people were searched four or five times a day. Naturally, this discouraged all but the hardiest of the spectators and in my opinion seriously compromised our right to a public trial. Inside, reporters and spectators were separated from the participants in the trial by a panel of bullet-proof glass. A series of microphones imperfectly carried the proceedings to the other side.

We protested these stringent security precautions on the grounds that they were sure to give the jurors the impression that our clients were extremely dangerous men. In addition, all of the defendants except Willie Tate, who, having finished his sentence, was out on bail, were shackled to chairs bolted to the floor. The judge would make only one concession: he moved the two deputies stationed directly behind the defense table when we said we were deprived of confidentiality as they could see and hear everything.

We drew Judge Henry J. Broderick, who was bright, able, and charming, but his attitude toward the defendants was from the beginning that of an Army sergeant toward a group of raw recruits. The five defense attorneys were at odds with him from the outset.

We battled him through the four months it took to select a jury. There were times when he would not let us make motions, not let us ask the jurors certain questions, refused to hear arguments on important points of law, made prejudicial and derogatory comments about the attorneys and the defendants in front of prospective jurors, and generally harassed the defense team. He made arbitrary rulings and every defense lawyer except myself was fined for contempt of court during jury selection, generally for protesting these rulings.

We had tried to challenge Broderick, but the court of appeals ruled that even though there were six defendants we were entitled to only one preemptory challenge of a judge, so we filed a writ in superior court setting out our grievances. We asked the California Judicial Council and several other legal organizations to provide an observer at the trial to oversee and report on the conduct of the judge and the attorneys, but the request was denied. However, the matter had been brought to the attention of the proper legal authorities and, although there was to be no observer in the courtroom, we heard informally that they would keep an eye on the case. After that, Broderick eased up on us.

We did succeed in getting a fairly young jury—all in their twenties and thirties with the exception of one man who was fifty. Nevertheless we made the usual motion for a mistrial on the grounds that the jury did not represent a peer group of the defendants, four of whom were black and two Latin, while eleven jurors were white and only one black. The motion was denied.

THE PROSECUTION'S CASE

Jerry Herman, the prosecutor, told the jury that he could not prove that any of the defendants actually had killed anyone. As they were all charged with first-degree murder, this was a rather bizarre approach. What he said was that all had either been part of Jackson's escape conspiracy or had aided and abetted the murders and the assaults on the guards. Under California law, they could be convicted of murder if they could be proved to be a part of a conspiracy that resulted in the deaths.

The heart of the state's case was the testimony of the three surviving guards, Urbano Rubiaco, Kenneth McCray, and Charles Breckenridge, but especially that of Rubiaco, who had been transferred from Soledad Prison just a few months before the incident and who knew Jackson, Drumgo, Pinell, and Spain.

Rubiaco's testimony was riddled with contradictions between what he had told prison investigators in a statement made on August 21, 1971, and what he said on the witness stand at the trial.

At the trial he contended that he had noticed something odd about Jackson's hair when escort guard Frank DeLeon brought him back from the visit with Bingham, that he at first thought a pencil was stuck in Jackson's hair and then, upon touching it, discovered it was a metal object, that Jackson reached under what Rubiaco now perceived to be a wig, pulled out the Astra automatic, inserted a clip in it, and said, in quoting Ho Chi Minh, "The dragon has come." We questioned how Jackson could pull out the gun and load it so fast with the taller, heavier Rubiaco, who had had Karate training, standing right over him and the other guards, Krasnes and DeLeon, nearby, but he said it happened so fast the guards were unable to prevent it.

He had previously told prison investigators that he already had conducted the skin-search and that Jackson was totally nude when he noticed the object in his hair. But at the trial he changed this story, saying that Jackson had been clothed and had not yet been searched.

"Are you telling us now that Mr. Jackson was not in the nude when you first saw him. Is that correct?" Mike Dufficy asked Rubiaco.

"Correct," the burly guard replied.

"So again, the statement you gave a few hours after the incident on August 21 is erroneous, correct?"

"Correct."

Originally Rubiaco had said that Spain and another inmate named Gordon briefly stood behind him, but that he didn't know who tied him up or who slashed his throat. At the grand jury hearing, and at the trial, he said that Spain and Johnson tied him up and Pinell cut his throat. But on cross-examination, we brought out that in the ambulance on the way to the hospital Rubiaco had told another guard it was Kenny Divans—who was not charged in connection

with the incident—who had cut his throat. In spite of these contradictions, Rubiaco maintained on the witness stand that it was Pinell who
assaulted him.

At the trial Rubiaco testified that he had seen Drumgo kick guard
Paul Krasnes in the face shortly before Krasnes was killed, but the
autopsy surgeon said the bruises on Krasnes's face could not have
been caused by the kind of kick Rubiaco described. Further,
Drumgo's shoes were found in his cell, indicating that he probably
had been barefoot during the melee.

Rubiaco claimed that when Jackson pulled out the automatic he
shouted, "The dragon has come," loudly enough to be heard all the
way down the tier. McCray, however, testified that Jackson had
made the statement in a very low voice and that only those in the
immediate vicinity could hear it. The prosecution held that the statement had been a signal for a general uprising to begin.

Cross-examination also revealed that earlier in August Rubiaco had
told his girl-friend he knew something involving Jackson was going
to take place at the adjustment center. He also admitted that he
hated Drumgo and Jackson and that he had failed a college course
because he had refused to read Jackson's book, *Soledad Brother.*

Breckenridge testified that Pinell had cut his throat; McCray believed his throat was cut when Talamantez was in the cell where the
slashings occurred, but although he had heard two men speaking in
Spanish he couldn't say who said what, nor was he sure who his actual
assailant was. This was the only evidence presented against Talamantez.

Gerald Betts had been with the department of correction for fourteen years and was operating the inspectroscope that day; he had
passed both Vanita Anderson, a young black woman working as an
investigator on the Soledad Brothers case, and Bingham through. He
testified that he had opened her attaché case with a tape recorder
in it and inspected the tape recorder by removing the back plate and
looking under the batteries to where the speaker was. She was then
admitted to the visiting area.

This raised the question of how the gun had come into the adjustment center, if it hadn't—as the prosecution claimed—come in the
attaché case or the tape recorder. Betts further testified that virtually
anyone with a law-enforcement badge did not have to pass through
the inspectroscope, including the guards.

Daniel Scarborough, the guard who had been at the visiting room desk that day, knew both Bingham and Anderson well. He had processed Anderson nine times before, Bingham five. He testified that when Bingham first came in he did not have a tape recorder, nor did he ask to use one. It was Scarborough who asked if he wanted to use a tape recorder and when Bingham replied that he did not have one, Anderson volunteered hers. She then waited for Bingham to bring it back as she had not been able to obtain permission to see Jackson herself.

Another guard, a black man named Paul Fleming, who was in charge of the area just outside the visiting room, testified that he had seen escort guard DeLeon thoroughly search Jackson before leaving to return Jackson to his cell. He distinctly remembered seeing DeLeon run his fingers through Jackson's hair. This testimony lent credence to our own theory that the gun had been brought into the adjustment center by guard Paul Krasnes.

In addition to the testimony of the guards, the prosecution presented a wig that had been found in the toilet of Pinell's cell and some bullets that were found concealed in a piece of cheese in Spain's cell. The wig was a key part of the prosecution's case. The interesting thing about it was that when it was discovered it had been covered with human excrement, indicating to us that it had been in the toilet for some time before the incident because Pinell had come out of his cell when the uprising started and the entire adjustment center had been cleared and searched once prison officials had regained control.

THE DEFENSE THEORY

Our first witness was a prisoner named Charles Johnson. Johnson was known as a snitch, for having testified against fellow inmates, and he was no friend of any of the defendants. He testified that he had seen Krasnes walk into San Quentin on the morning of August 21 with an automatic pistol partially concealed under his jacket. He identified the pistol as a .45 caliber automatic, which is similar in appearance to the Astra that was used in the uprising.

We called Council McCoy, a former guard, now warden at the city prison in Gary, Indiana. In 1971 McCoy had been assigned to the visiting room area. He testified that he had seen Jackson on that day with a visitor and that Jackson had been wearing a Navy-style blue knit watch cap, which many prisoners wore habitually. On cross-examination the prosecutor asked McCoy why he had not stated this in his written report. McCoy replied that he had told the fact to three different supervisors on the day of the incident, and he furnished their names. He had been the last person to see Jackson leave the visiting area.

Our next witness was Louis Tackwood, an undercover agent for the Los Angeles Police Department's Criminal Conspiracy Section. Early in August 1971, Tackwood and two others, Sgt. Robert Sharrett and Sgt. Dan Mahoney, smuggled a snub-nosed .38 caliber revolver into San Quentin in a paper bag. The gun in the bag was given to a guard with a distinctive scar on his face. In 1975 Tackwood returned to San Quentin with two reporters from the *San Francisco Chronicle* and identified the guard. We hoped the prosecution would call him as a witness so we could cross-examine him, but they did not.

Tackwood's testimony was important to us because although Johnson had identified the gun he saw Krasnes with, another guard, a weapons expert, had testified to seeing a *revolver* in Spain's hand and there is, as anyone familar with handguns knows, considerable difference between an automatic pistol and a revolver. The automatic uses a clip to hold its bullets while the revolver employs a spinning cylinder.

Tackwood said the revolver had been made inoperable, that the criminal conspiracy section had planned to kill Jackson on August 23, either as he was going to or coming from court. (The idea apparently was to have the gun passed to Jackson who could then be gunned down by guards firing in self-defense [justifiable homicide].) Tackwood testified that there was an air of jubilation at the police headquarters on August 22 when it was learned Jackson had been killed, although there was some annoyance also because the people up north had "fucked up," killing Jackson on the wrong date and using a live automatic instead of the inoperable revolver. He described the meeting on that August 22 in detail, naming fifteen people besides himself present, including Sgts. Sharrett and Mahoney, Lt. Robert Keel, commander of the CCS, two FBI agents, and two men from the Los Angeles district attorney's office. Later Tackwood had been shown the .38 and told that they had got the gun back.

"Now what was your last completed assignment in northern California?" I asked.

"To assassinate George Jackson," was the even reply.

"To do what?"

"To assassinate George Jackson."

What the Los Angeles Police Department was doing operating undercover agents in northern California he could not say.*

There was testimony from the defendants and from other prisoners that just before Jackson went out for his visit with Bingham they had had a sense of something not being right (prisoners develop this sixth sense, as do the handicapped, because survival depends on it). In fact, Pinell testified that Jackson had told him to keep his eyes open because things just didn't feel right. As a result of this admonition, Pinell watched through a mirror as the prisoners returned from the visiting room. He saw Krasnes pull out an automatic and hold it on Jackson. Jackson flipped the gun out of the guard's hand into his own and ordered Rubiaco to open the cells. But Pinell repeatedly denied he had cut any throats.

Another inmate, Bernard Duran, said that when the cells were opened Pinell had said to him, "No one is to get hurt, including the officers." Duran also stated that Pinell had cautioned him that, "They tried something with George Jackson. I think they are out to kill us all." Pinell suggested that they move toward the rear of the building, something that had already been borne out by testimony from the guards who said that when they retook the center all the inmates had been gathered in the corner farthest from the door, except for Spain who had run out with Jackson, but the evidence pointed not to an escape attempt but to Spain's trying to get out of the unbearably tense situation; one guard had heard him cry out, "Won't somebody let me out of here?"

Duran also painted a graphic picture of the violence unleashed upon the prisoners in the wake of the uprising. Every guard had denied that such brutality had taken place, but Duran described being slugged over the eye with a rifle butt, being clubbed down, ordered to get up, and clubbed down repeatedly. He said he was

*Much of what he said about other actions taken against the Black Panther party was corroborated by documents that were coming into our possession as a result of lawsuits we had filed and through the Freedom of Information Act. Furthermore, my good friend Don Freed (co-author with Mark Lane of *Executive Action,* and one of the country's leading experts on assassinations and conspiracies) had worked with Tackwood over a period of five years, and he assured me that almost every piece of information Tackwood had ever given him had checked out.

forced to crawl about on his hands and knees while guards kicked him in the face and hit him with clubs. Most of the prisoners received similar treatment.

In addition to our theory that Jackson had been killed in a conspiracy engineered by the state, which also resulted in the deaths of the three guards and two other inmates, we had to develop for the jury evidence to support our other theory that there had been no prisoner conspiracy to help George Jackson escape, but that the uprising had been a natural reaction of men brutally treated and existing under inhumane conditions.

Dr. Frank Rundell, a former Soledad prison psychiatrist, took the stand to testify. He said that the climate of the Soledad adjustment center—and he believed all the other adjustment centers in California prisons—was pervaded by fear: the staff feared the prisoners, the prisoners feared the guards. Inmates in these maximum security prisons had less access to sensory stimulation—they were deprived of reading material, television, physical activity, even the commissary. Kept locked in their cells twenty-three and a half hours a day, with communication between cells difficult (only by shouting), they soon developed symptoms of psychological isolation, which can result in permanent emotional damage, making it difficult if not impossible for the person so affected to enter into normal emotional relationships with others, building up a state of sustained anger and deep resentment which engenders a preoccupation with revenge and a liability to burst into uncontrolled rage. These conditions eventually impair the ability to assess what is real, which in turn leads to obsessive fantasies as a way of dealing with isolation and the loss of a sense of self-worth. Guards working inside the adjustment centers also suffer. They, too, lose perspective after a time and tend to treat the men as animals in cages, becoming themselves dehumanized. As a result, the centers were never free from a heavy sense of oppression.

Much of the defense revolved around revealing these conditions at the adjustment center, conditions we contended would drive people half-mad with bitterness, resentment, distrust, and hatred.

In 1974 the six defendants had filed a suit in federal court in an attempt to have the conditions improved. During that trial, Spain and Drumgo told of being confined nearly twenty-four hours a day in cells that measured less than six feet by eight feet, of having to hang candy and extra food from the ceiling to keep it from mice, of having to run water continuously—hot in the winter, cold in the summer—to make the temperature of the cells bearable, of not being allowed out for the regulation hour of exercise daily, of sometimes being deprived of the weekly shower.

The six also testified that their food was frequently inedible or contaminated, laced with pieces of wire or human feces, that the guards threatened them constantly with death, a favorite taunt being, "You'll never get out of here alive."

They also testified that every time they were taken out of their cells, whether for exercise or to visit their families, friends, lawyers, or doctors, they were forced to submit to a skin-search, and to put on white prison coveralls which were used over and over by different prisoners without being washed. Their hands and feet were shackled; chains were placed around their necks, waists, and groins. It was in this condition that they were led to see visitors.

Drumgo's mother testified that she had to pass through two metal detectors and wait as long as four hours before she could see her son.

"It's like they've got a shackle around my heart. I know he doesn't want me to see him like that." She added that her son was often trembling and had tears in his eyes when she saw him.

Luis Talamantez told his attorney of the anguish of not being able to touch his young son or see him without being in chains.

Pinell testified to repeated beatings and tear gassing in his cell; he suffered from headaches and memory loss.

A former black guard, Cedric Jackson, testified that he had seen Pinell being clubbed in the groin in 1973 and that all the men were subject to verbal and physical abuse from the guards.

Drumgo testified that a guard once held a knife to his throat, although the guards were not allowed to bring lethal weapons inside.

William Whitney, a former white guard, testified that he was not allowed to pass out hot food on Christmas Day 1972, that he watched an inmate go through an epileptic seizure because another prison worker withheld medication.

Whitney said that after he threw his wife through a screen door he realized that his whole personality had changed because of his work at the prison and he quit.

Several defendants described the noise level inside the adjustment center as maddening. Spain and Drumgo said they had to stuff cotton or pieces of cloth into their ears to be able to think. The cell walls were steel and the only means of communication was to shout back and forth.

Only one man was allowed into the exercise area at a time. Under these conditions the health of all deteriorated. Spain lost forty pounds, began to get tension headaches, lost several teeth because of poor dental care, and developed a hemorrhoid condition that made it difficult for him to sit for any length of time without pain. Tate's eyesight deteriorated because prisoners saw natural light only when walking across the mall to the visiting area. Talamantez contracted tuberculosis and had difficulty breathing. Johnson suffered from hypertension.

During the federal suit, Dr. Lee Coleman, a psychiatrist, testified that the six defendants all had strong feelings of injustice and a tremendous rage over their prolonged stay in the isolation cells. Dr. Coleman said he considered such emotions normal and not pathological.

"Each of these men is really in a struggle that is overwhelming to him," Coleman said. "Each is desperately striving to maintain some sense of self-worth and some hope for the future."

Alphonso Zirpoli, the federal judge who heard the suit, ordered several modifications at San Quentin: no longer were prisoners chained about the neck, waist, and groin; regular exercise and shower periods had to be provided. But the order was limited and many of the conditions—such as the state of the food and the constant abuse from the guards—were not dealt with and, even so, the state appealed it! Clearly the conditions in California prisons were not much different from what they had been thirty years ago, and that was what we tried to show the jury and the public in the San Quentin Six case.

Along about midway through the defense case, in the spring of 1976, the state supreme court ruled that prisoners could no longer be tried in shackles and chains unless the trial judge had first held a hearing and the need to fetter the prisoners was clearly demonstrated. Although the court had ruled on an appeal filed by other inmates, the ruling appeared to apply to our case as well, but Broderick still refused to remove the irons, though we had already protested many times.

The second psychiatrist to testify on the effects of a prison environment was Dr. Phillip Zimbardo from Stanford University who had conducted research for the Office of Naval Research in the early 1970s. Dr. Zimbardo had a small, jail-type environment built in the basement of a Stanford psychology building and from a group of students who volunteered for the study he picked "inmates" and "guards" at random. The mostly middle-class white students did not know beforehand which role they would be assigned and no effort was made to see which people might function better in which roles.

After only a couple of days in the simulated prison environment there were rebellions and the student-guards began taking increasingly repressive measures to control them. Physical violence was not allowed, but the student-guards resorted to public humiliation, taunts, isolation, and other psychological pressures to control the student-inmates. Within three days, one of the student prisoners was on the verge of an emotional breakdown having completely lost sight of the fact that he was participating in an experiment—what he underwent became very real to him—and he had to be released.

Both groups became completely involved in their roles, forgetting they were dealing with their classmates. To the guards, the inmates became a group who had to follow orders, whims, and dictates. Originally to run for two weeks, the experiment was terminated after six days because other student-inmates were suffering severe psychological damage.

Zimbardo himself became so immersed in his role as warden of the mock prison that he was totally preoccupied by it, so he told the jury. On one occasion, for example, he became furious when a rumor was circulated that the inmates were planning to escape and he became so agitated that he could hardly talk with a colleague who had stopped by his office, saying, "Can't you see that I've got a jailbreak on my hands?"

On cross-examination the prosecutor derided the experiment because it had been conducted with students, causing Zimbardo to talk about an episode that had taken place at the brand-new Napa County Jail in February 1976.

The facility was to be a model institution—floors were carpeted, each inmate had a private cell, and small groups of inmates were given a common living space. Men and women were to be housed on the same floor, eat together, take exercise periods together. The prison staff had all taken pay cuts to work at Napa, "because we want to make jail administration more humane," as one said. They did not wear badges, uniforms, or guns.

Before the jail was opened, 132 Napa county residents volunteered to try it for several days to help the guards adapt to the new environment and to let the community see what it was like to spend time behind bars. Among the volunteer inmates were two superior court judges, five Napa County supervisors, the county administrator, businessmen, students, nurses, housewives, social workers, and attorneys.

After a day in jail, one volunteer became so distraught and depressed that she developed a fever, had trouble conversing with the other volunteer inmates, and paced up and down, sobbing uncontrollably, until she was released. She later reported that she had felt completely overwhelmed, that she felt she was barely hanging on to life. A second woman grabbed a kitchen knife in the dining hall and took another woman hostage.

Over the four-day period there were several successful escapes and many complaints—about the food, the overhead mercury lights, the jangling sounds of the jailer's keys, and the continual din of piped-in music.

At the end of the experience an attorney volunteer said, "I was struck by the fact that despite the jail's newness and cleanliness and the staff's courtesy, it really is a miserable place to be." Others were irritated by the lack of privacy, especially open toilets, and said their minds grew foggy after a day or so, that they felt dehumanized and abandoned. Some reported wanting to withdraw, others felt like rebelling.

Dr. Jane Oldden, who had examined Spain before the trial, followed Dr. Zimbardo. After detailing the difficulties of diagnosing a patient who is shackled and chained and her efforts to have the constraints removed, she spoke of the trauma of Spain's expulsion from his Mississippi home and his natural mother's care at the age of six and the lack of a sense of identity that had resulted. Though an indifferent student, he had not caused trouble and he had been good at athletics. His real mother wrote to him regularly and sent him presents, but he had stopped communicating with her and he had blocked his memories of her; neither was he close to the black family who had adopted him. At the age of seventeen, he entered prison. The psychiatrist at the Southern Reception Guidance Center in Chino, California, had written:

> This highly emotional, unstable, generally confused young man displayed rather marked ambivalency in regards to his racial and masculine adequacy. His underlying feelings of rejection and his ambivalent sexual and racial identification tends to provoke much anxiety related to his over-

whelming self-doubt. He shows no sign of becoming a custodial or severe management problem.

He recommended that Johnny receive "intensive individual and group therapy."

The psychiatric recommendations were not implemented, and Spain just drifted along in prison until he met Jackson and became a member of the Black Panther party, which gave him an identity for the first time. He then began to write, expressing his feelings in poetry and in letters. Both Oldden and a San Quentin psychiatrist testified that Spain's personality pattern was to abide by the rules— he first tried hard to find out what they were and then he followed them.

It was Oldden's supposition that when the cell doors were opened Spain, recognizing that all the rules were suddenly suspended, feared that he might be in great danger. This fear produced a state of high tension and anxiety in him and he blacked out. He was unable to recall anything that happened in the next fifteen or twenty minutes, remembering only that he had run across the mall and, realizing that he could be shot at any moment, he became frantic and jumped into the bushes.

This temporary loss of consciousness was in line with earlier testimony by Dr. Rundell who had treated Spain for tension headaches at Soledad Prison between December 1970 and April 1971. Dr. Rundell believed the headaches were a result of the continual sense of fear in the prison and lack of exercise. On April 30, 1971, Spain had been taken to the prison hospital with a severe headache and in a state of paranoid anxiety. While there, he had blacked out and was afterward irrational and incoherent.

Such impaired consciousness, a state in which there is a temporary loss of conscious control over behavior, due to panic or stress, when events become too much to handle, is legally a complete defense to any charge.

Oldden also had questioned Spain about his knowledge of any escape plans for August 21 and he had said he knew nothing. He also denied having any knowledge of the bullets found in the cheese or what the prosecution had described as an escape map which was found in his cell and which did not have his fingerprints on it.

As Spain had suffered a memory blackout, there was no point to putting him on the stand.

Drumgo testified in his own behalf and denied that he had kicked the guard or that he ever came out of his cell, saying that he had been barefoot the entire time. He also testified that Spain had seemed "out of it."

Tate testified that he had been writing a letter to his mother and in it he had described most of the incident. His attorney introduced the letter into evidence.

Talamantez testified and denied the allegations against him, and all four co-defendants who testified said that none of their co-defendants had killed, assaulted, or tied up anyone. They said they knew who had done those things but refused to name names.

In addition, there was the issue of the clothes worn by the prisoners during the uprising, which had been carted off to the dump. Though some of the clothes were retrieved, most was not, and it could have revealed which prisoners had blood on their clothes and would therefore have been more likely to have participated in the killing of the guards. Our argument was that any of the twenty-seven men let out of the cells could have murdered the guards. The clothing might have revealed who these men were, but it had been deliberately destroyed. We believed the prosecution wished to suppress evidence which might have exonerated those on trial.

Although Judge Broderick stated that he would not let the trial turn into an inquest into the death of George Jackson, we spent many days questioning the guards who fired the shots, ballistics experts, and the autopsy surgeon, trying to prove that Jackson was murdered as he lay helpless from the wound in his leg. The state tried in return to prove that the fatal bullet had come from one of the gun towers. There was much testimony on bullet trajectories and ballistics which only served to convince us that our theory of an assassination was correct. Though this matter was tangential to the trial itself, it was vital to many people, especially the defendants.

One of the last defense witnesses was Mrs. Ann Pitts, the mother of Johnny Spain. She had been flown from her home in Jackson, Mississippi to testify in her son's behalf. She told the poignant story of having given birth to a black child, of her love for him despite her husband's fulminations against him and his persistent beating of her, of her fear for her son's safety as he grew, went to school, and moved out into the white neighborhood. Though his mother lavished love and affection on him, he met with hostility both at home from his mother's husband and in the outside world, and his mother finally decided that she had to send him away. Dr. Oldden had already told us that the separation had bewildered the little boy because he had been happy in Mississippi and had loved his mother—and he grew bitter over what he perceived as his mother's total rejection of him.

It took the prosecution five months to put on its case, the defense took six months. In addition to the lengthy testimony and many witnesses, one factor that added to the length of the trial was that Pinell had been allowed to serve as his own defense attorney, giving him the right to cross-examine all witnesses. As he was unskilled, he often gave the prosecution witnesses the opportunity to say things damaging to other defendants and so the defense attorneys would have to again go over every bit of testimony and pin it down a second time. It is my opinion that Judge Broderick allowed Pinell to defend himself because he knew it would hamper the defense efforts. Though Broderick changed his attitude after we petitioned for a legal observer in the courtroom, we still had many disagreements over the admissibility of evidence and rulings he made.

The prosecution made no attempt to rebut important testimony. Herman might have called in Vanita Anderson who was known to be living in Houston, Texas, but he did not. He could have called on any of the seventeen men Tackwood had named, most of whom were still on the Los Angeles police force, with the FBI, or the district attorney's office. Nobody refuted Charles Johnson's eyewitness account of the guard bringing the automatic into the prison. No prison psychiatrists were called to refute the testimony of Drs. Rundell, Zimbardo, and Oldden. Rundell had stated in unequivocal terms that he had known prison guards to lie frequently about inmate behavior, but—even though most of the prosecution witnesses were guards—there was no attempt to rebut that testimony either.

By the time the case was ready for final arguments, it had run for fifteen months, making it the longest and most expensive trial in California history. The cost to the state was estimated at over $2.1 million, most spent on the ridiculous, and, in our opinion, unconstitutional security measures—the bullet-proof glass, the metal detectors, and the large number of deputies used to search everyone and patrol the corridors and courtroom.

Final arguments took three weeks, with the district attorney using a week for his initial statement and a day for his rebuttal. The remainder of the time was used by Pinell, representing himself, and the five defense attorneys. Even as he addressed the jury, Pinell was shackled and chained. I took two days and most of a third to sum up the case.

"A famous writer once said that you can test the values of a nation by the type of prisons it has. Our prisons are hell holes. I wonder how many more San Quentins there are going to be, how many more Soledads, and how many more Atticas?

"How many of those are there going to be before we awaken to the fact that we cannot send human beings to warehouses? That we cannot take people we think we cannot deal with and cast them aside in the hell holes of the adjustment centers of California.

"These six men are on trial for their freedom, for their lives, because it's not any kind of life to spend your time in the prisons you have seen. Of course, you've seen it when the cells were empty.* The men are removed from the adjustment center when we go there to visit. You don't hear the noises, the turmoil, the groaning, and the pains of the human beings who are housed there. You don't hear that and you don't see that.

"You see five of the defendants sitting here in this courtroom shackled and chained. You've been told by the judge from the very beginning of the trial that you are not to consider the fact that they are chained, nor are you to draw any inferences from it. That is a great burden for you to undertake, and if you can handle it, you will receive a tremendous amount of credit.

"You are told that the plan was to escape. Escape to where, pray tell? Assuming you went through the adjustment center door, assuming that to be a fact, you'd be shot down, mowed down; there are gun rails all over the place. And then after you get there, how are you going to hurdle that wall? We've got to use our common sense. We've got to use our natural feelings about things.

"I say that this was an emotional upheaval. It was like a cesspool that opened up, and many different people there had pent-up emotions and hatred toward the guards, hatred toward the system, and bore hatred toward the harassment and degradation they had to live by day in and day out. Remember that when the bodies of the three dead guards were being carried out, the entire cell block—three or four hundred men—let out a spontaneous series of rousing cheers.

"They had an opportunity to get even and that is what happened. Whoever did it had no other object, and it was not planned. Any

*The jury had been taken on a tour of the adjustment center and visiting area late in the trial.

person there could have done it. But who did it? Where could they have gone? Where is the plan of escape? How could they get out of the prison?

"One of the questions that you are probably going to be asking time and time again—and you have probably asked yourself that question already—if these six didn't do it, who did?

"That's a good question, but it's not our responsibility to find the answer to that. That responsibility rests solely and completely with the prosecution. During jury selection we asked you if you would expect us, like Perry Mason, to produce the guilty person or persons at the end of the trial, and you all rightfully said, no, you would not place that burden upon us. The burden of proof rests solely on the prosecution."

I analyzed the evidence, noting that virtually none of our testimony had been rebutted, that the essential thrust of Tackwood's testimony about a state conspiracy to kill George Jackson had not been challenged seriously.

I concentrated on Urbano Rubiaco, the 230-pound karate-trained guard who claimed he had been unable to disarm the smaller, lighter Jackson.

I worked my way through the fifteen months of testimony and evidence, saving Johnny Spain for the end. After summarizing his background and probable state of mind on August 21, 1971, I concluded with a review of the testimony of Spain's natural mother and what I inferred from it.

"The story of Johnny Spain is the story of American racism. You heard Johnny's mother, his real biological mother, come here from Jackson, Mississippi, to testify. She said she had a loving, happy child, who at the age of four had learned to read and write. She said, 'I gave him all the love that any mother could give.'

"And here is a child who is called nigger baby by the man of the house. He doesn't even understand what the term means, but, in his mother's words, 'Johnny became a nervous wreck. He was nervous when he would come into the house. Every time he came into the house he would be upset for fear of what was going to happen.'

"There were problems with her taking Johnny into the community. In the community, Johnny was an exhibit, he was a different child in the group. Fingers were pointed and tongues were wagging. She even got calls from the Ku Klux Klan. 'You've got to remember that we're talking about Jackson, Mississippi, twenty years ago,'

Johnny's mother said. 'It hasn't changed much since then, but even twenty years ago it was different.'

"When I said the story of Johnny Spain is the story of racism in America, I don't think I'm exaggerating or being overly dramatic. Here's a loving child and a loving mother who has to send her child away at the age of six to a land he has never heard of before or belonged to. Is it any wonder that Johnny Spain thinks he is a freak? Is it any wonder that Johnny Spain feels that he is not wanted? Whose fault is it that when Johnny Spain entered prison at the age of seventeen, and was diagnosed as having serious mental problems, he did not receive any help? Johnny Spain's story ladies and gentlemen, is the story of racism in America."

Robert Carrow, defending Luis Talamantez, followed me; then Mike Dufficy, representing Fleeta Drumgo; Frank Cox, defending David Johnson; and John Hill, defending Willie Tate, followed him. The case went to the jury in the middle of July 1976. They deliberated for twenty-four days, excluding Sundays, the longest jury deliberation in California history.

During those four weeks, we had little notion of what was going through the minds of the jurors. Only rarely did they return to ask a question or to hear testimony re-read. At times, it seemed as if the deliberations would go on forever.

I had speaking engagements in New York and Boston on Friday, August 13 and Monday, August 16. Since the jury showed no sign of being close to a verdict, and since Judge Broderick had said he would not declare a mistrial, I took off from San Francisco early on the morning of August 12. Barney Dreyfus went to court for me that day. He was about to leave the courthouse when Broderick informed him that the jury had reached a verdict. I was somewhere over the Rocky Mountains. It took a while to assemble the defendants. Judge Broderick read the verdicts aloud to a packed courtroom.

Willie Tate, Fleeta Drumgo, and Luis Talamantez were acquitted of all charges. David Johnson was convicted of assault on guard Charles Breckenridge. Hugo Pinell was convicted of two counts of assault on a guard by a life-term prisoner, the jury evidently having concluded that Pinell had cut the throats of guards Charles Breckenridge and Urbano Rubiaco, although it was strictly the guards' word against Pinell's.

Finally, Johnny Spain was found guilty of the murder of guards Frank DeLeon and Jere Graham, both shot to death, and of conspiracy to murder them. The jury must have concluded that Spain had aided and abetted or conspired with Jackson on August 21, 1971, since there was no direct evidence that he did any killing, only testimony by several guards that he had a gun in his hand at one point, and that bullets were found in his cell.

The jurors later told reporters that they accepted neither the prosecution's theory of an escape attempt nor our theory of a state conspiracy to murder Jackson.

Their decision to convict Spain seemed to have come by taking little pieces of circumstantial evidence—the bullets hidden in the cheese, his membership in the Black Panther party, the map allegedly found in his cell, and the fact that he was the only person to run out of the adjustment center door with Jackson.

I was bitterly disappointed with the verdict, but I remain optimistic. I believe that the appeals courts will overturn the convictions of Johnny Spain, Hugo Pinell, and David Johnson on the grounds that they were shackled and chained throughout the trial. Furthermore, Judge Broderick made many judicial errors. I am confident that, just as Huey Newton was eventually freed, Johnny Spain will some day walk out of San Quentin and start to live.

Within a few days of the verdict, Fleeta Drumgo and Luis Talamantez both were released from prison. Drumgo had been inside nine years, originally sentenced for second-degree burglary, an offense that usually draws less than a one-year sentence. While in prison he was twice charged with murder and twice acquitted.

Talamantez served eleven years, first going to jail in 1965 for robbery. Both men were euphoric that they had been able to survive two of the worst prisons in America, but, like Willie Tate, who had been free on bond for a year and a half, they were deeply concerned for the lives of the three men who had to remain behind as well as all the others locked away in California's prisons and those of the other forty-nine states as well.

Final Argument

From the preceding accounts, it is evident that real justice is not easily obtainable in this country. Our courts have been set up to see that people don't run into each other, but that has little to do with justice.

Too many Americans get no legal representation at all, and if they are represented by a government-appointed lawyer, he will try to dispose of their case as quickly as he can, because he just does not have the time to deal with it properly.

On the other hand, the police and the district attorney have almost unlimited resources. They have access to FBI files and computer-operated information banks on a state and national level to dig up the evidence they need, while most defense attorneys are lucky if they have one full-time investigator.

That's why I believe there's really no such thing as a "fair trial." The term "fair trial" implies that both sides are equal in strengh, and have equal resources. Only very wealthy people can afford to match the resources of the state in a criminal trial and as you might have noticed, a surprisingly large proportion of them are acquitted. If everyone had the ability to summon adequate legal resources to his defense, there would be fewer innocent people in jail today.

Until we can find answers to the problems of poverty and racism, I don't think we can talk about justice. As Oliver Wendell Holmes noted, administering the law and playing the legal game have little to do with justice. I believe that we will only have real justice in this country when all Americans can eat without having to steal, and when there is decent housing and medical care for everyone. When we have an equitible distribution of the wealth, and when racism and discrimination are unknown, then maybe we can start to talk about "justice."

As David Bazelon, Chief Judge of the U.S. Court of Appeals in Washington, D.C., said in a 1975 lecture: "Those who see the law as a moral force insist that it should not convict unless it can also condemn."

In my view, American society doesn't have the right to condemn many people, because so many crimes are the result of society's failures to provide all its citizens with the basic human necessities. Too often it has visited deprivations and degradations upon people that cause them to break society's laws.